IMAGES
of America

HISTORIC LINWOOD CEMETERY

IMAGES
of America

HISTORIC LINWOOD CEMETERY

Linda J. Kennedy and Mary Jane Galer

ARCADIA
PUBLISHING

ISBN 978-0-7385-1630-1

Published by Arcadia Publishing
Charleston, South Carolina

Printed in the United States of America

Library of Congress Catalog Card Number: 2004100871

For all general information contact Arcadia Publishing at:
Telephone 843-853-2070
Fax 843-853-0044
E-mail sales@arcadiapublishing.com
For customer service and orders:
Toll-Free 1-888-313-2665

Visit us on the Internet at www.arcadiapublishing.com

Contents

ACKNOWLEDGMENTS

Mentioning each person who contributed to this book would be impossible. Without the help of those who provided photographs, added bits of knowledge to the lives portrayed, and suggested stories, this book would not have happened.

Special thanks goes to Mimi Childs, who gave her time and talents, provided history, and knew where to obtain photographs; Sally Walden for delivering, on the rainiest day ever, the gigantic portrait of Agnes Affleck Rankin in the back of her convertible; Lynn Willoughby for changing passive to active sentence structure; John Lupold, who knows his Columbus history; Thornton Jordan for sharing his knowledge of wrought and cast iron; the Columbus residents who shared photographs and family history; Reagan Grimsley for digging through the files of Columbus State University Archives and providing photographs; Dorothy Yoder and Joan Ott, who always came through when we requested our photographs to be developed "yesterday"; John Kennedy for his willingness to perform a multitude of tasks; and lastly, the Historic Linwood Foundation Board for sponsoring this project.

INTRODUCTION

On a hill outside the limits of Columbus on the banks of the Chattahoochee River in Muscogee County, Georgia, four acres of land were set aside, which would become the cemetery for the settlers of the new town that was being planned.

The city was surveyed by Edward Lloyd Thomas; his crew plodded through forests and swamps, dragging chains and measuring city blocks. During the spring of 1828, Thomas's son Truman, who was helping his father, became ill with a fever. Truman succumbed to the fever and Mr. Thomas carried his son's body up the hill and buried him. He surveyed the four acres and designated this area as the cemetery. Since that time the citizens of Columbus have continued the tradition of going "up on the hill" to bury their loved ones. Strolling now among the huge elaborate monuments, the old worn tablets, the crumbling brick walls, and the simple stones and slabs, one is able to read the history of the city carved in stone.

Columbus's history abounds in tales of Indian wars, steam boating, cotton growing, shipbuilding, plantation owners, and industrial pioneers. It was a frontier town in the 1830s and was home to such people as Mirabeau Lamar, the second governor of Texas; Henry L. Benning, a Confederate general; John Stith Pemberton, the inventor of Coca-Cola; and Nunnally Johnson, a noted screen writer. While many stories can be told of these well-known people, there are also many interesting stories of lesser-known people who added significantly to the development of Columbus.

This book will endeavor to chronicle Columbus's history by sharing with the reader the stories of people buried in Linwood, pictures of the beautifully carved monuments, and stories of the carvers. The beautiful wrought iron and cast iron fencing that still survives in the cemetery will also be pictured.

The Historic Linwood Foundation is fully dedicated to preserving this history through restoration and conservation efforts of the stones, fencing, and walls in the cemetery. Our before-and-after photographs show what can be done. It cannot be stressed enough that proper techniques need to be used in restoring a cemetery. Please seek professional guidance before a project is undertaken.

You are invited to ramble through Linwood Cemetery. But, if you cannot visit Columbus, then perhaps a ramble through the photographs in this book will suffice.

One

Cemetery History

In 1828, when the town of Columbus was first laid out, surveyors designated a spot on the hill to the northeast of town as the town cemetery. This was the highest point in the city, and standing in the cemetery one could see down into the town and across the Chattahoochee River to the Alabama hills. Although there are many unmarked graves and some with simple tablets giving only names and dates, there are hundreds of monuments across the expanse of the cemetery. Linwood is a virtual outdoor museum embodying the history and culture of the city of Columbus.

Since the city began, Linwood Cemetery has been the final resting place of Columbus citizens. Starting with the surveyor's son, Truman Thomas, those who played a part in developing this frontier town, and whose time on earth came to an end here, were buried in the small plot of land just inside the original town limits. Columbus citizens were buried exclusively in Linwood Cemetery until about 1880. Those early families who were given lots or purchased lots in Linwood are still burying their loved ones here today. The cemetery has survived time, vandalism, and neglect, and it has grown to include approximately 28 acres.

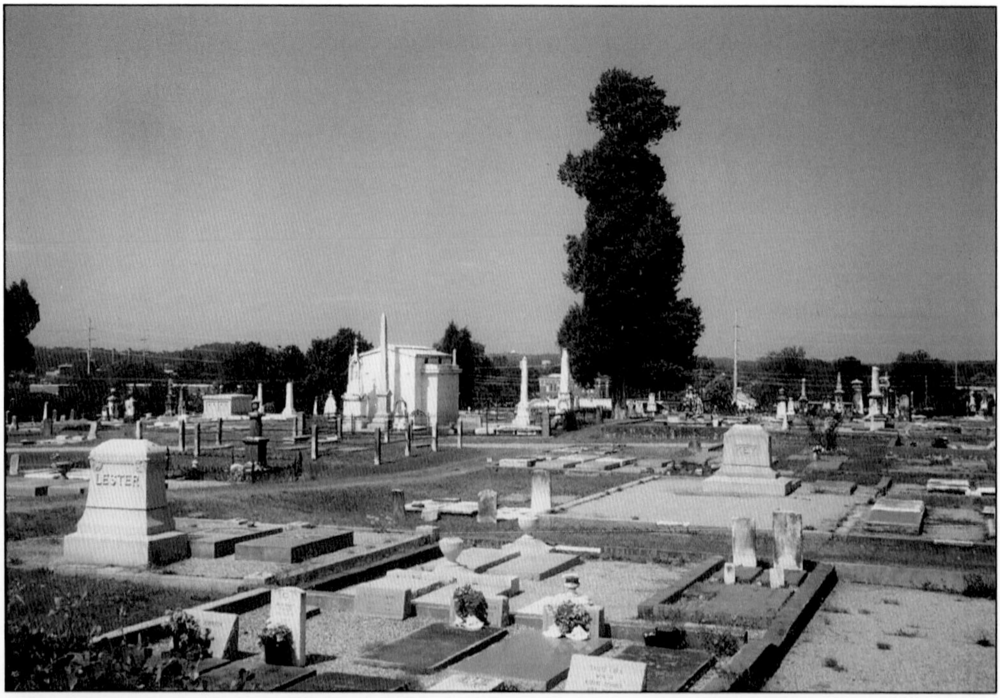

Many different styles of markers and monuments abound in Linwood. This is one survivor of the many cedar trees planted in the cemetery in the 1800s.

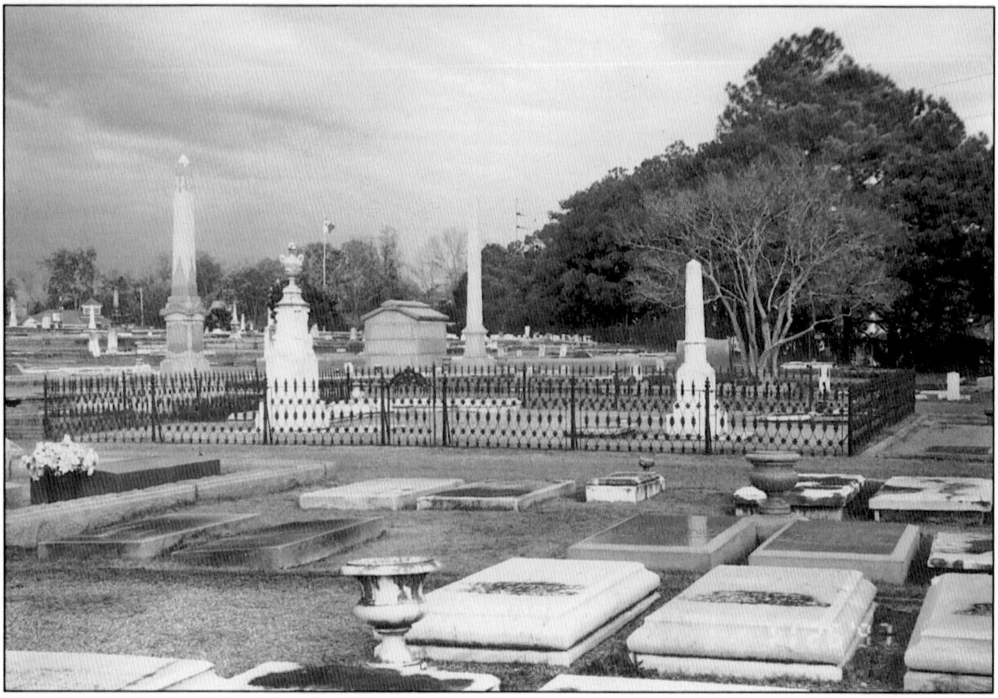

This wrought iron fenced lot is an example of the many cast iron and wrought iron fenced lots in the cemetery.

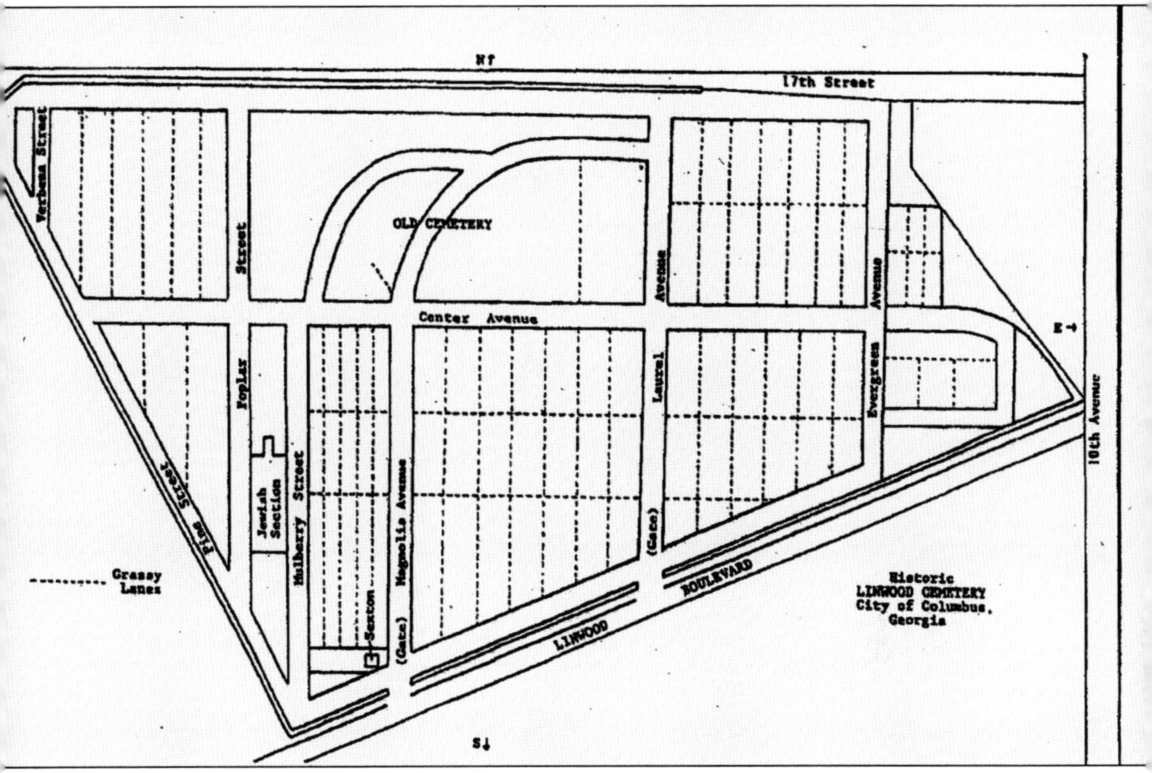

This map shows the current layout of the cemetery. The area designated the "old cemetery" was the original plot of land set aside as the City Cemetery. No lots were drawn; people were told to "go up on the hill and pick out your family lot." The city added more land until Linwood reached its present size in 1873. Land was set aside in the cemetery for the Jewish community and the first Jewish burial was in 1852. (Map drawn by Tracy Autry.)

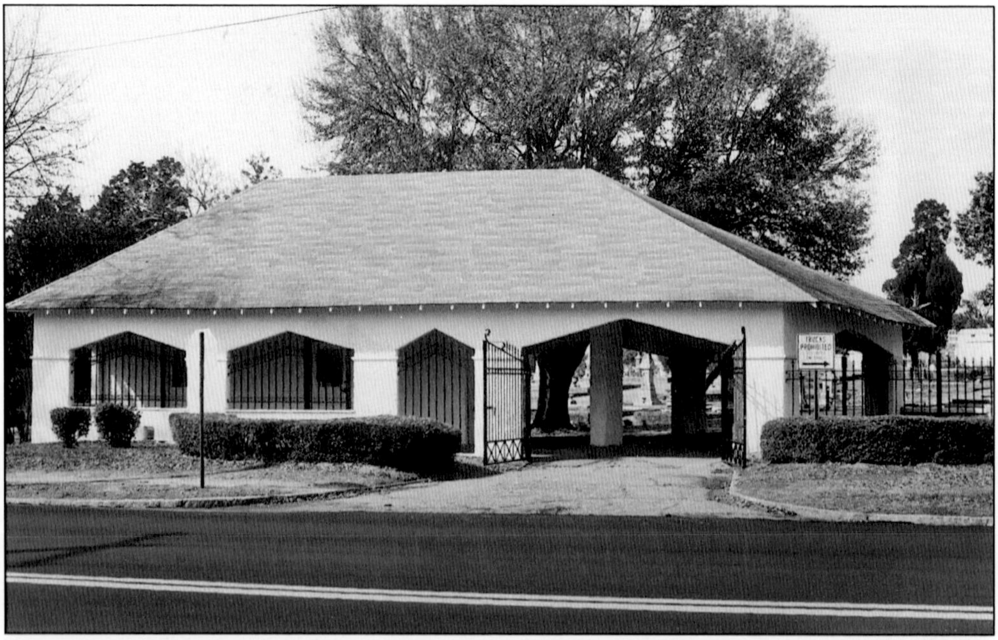

The City of Columbus built the cemetery gatehouse in 1885. Used as the sexton's office, it had "a desk for keeping records" and a place "suitable for reception of ladies in bad weather." According to early insurance maps, the building remained of wood construction until at least 1929 and was referred to as a chapel, then later as the "Rest Room."

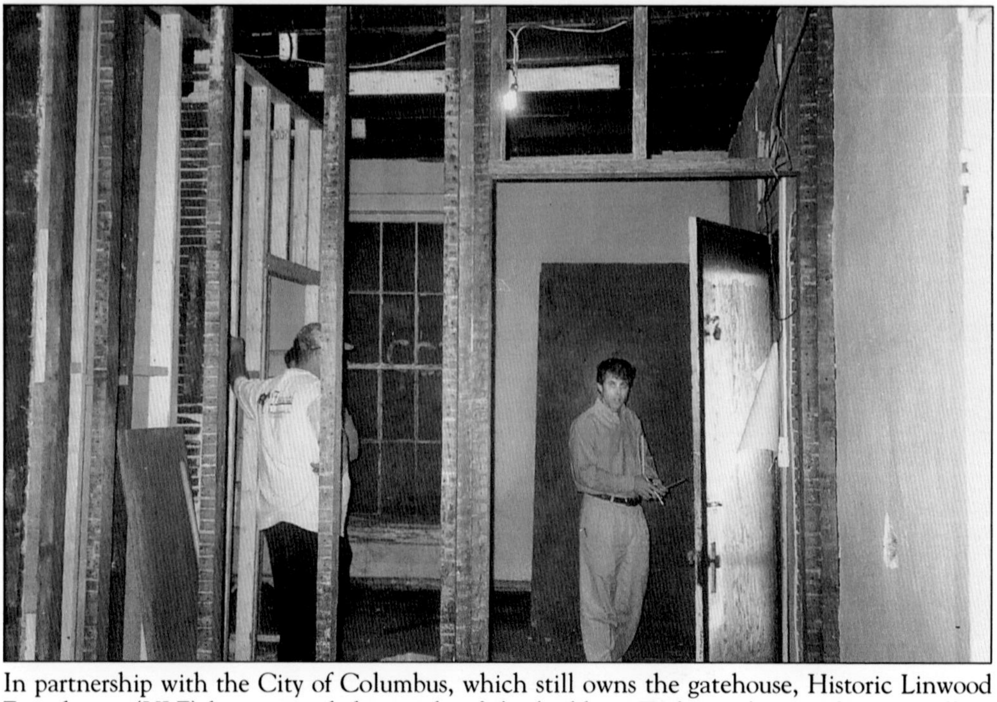

In partnership with the City of Columbus, which still owns the gatehouse, Historic Linwood Foundation (HLF) has restored the inside of the building. Today, it houses the HLF office, which oversees the restoration and preservation of the cemetery. The foundation's staff is present five days a week to help visitors find their loved ones' graves.

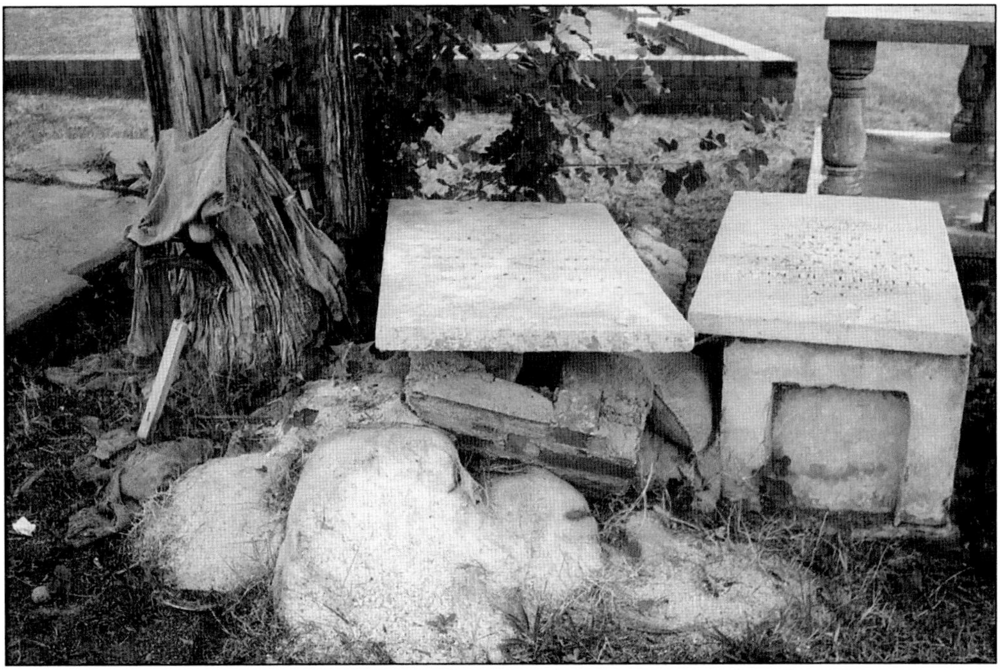

One of Historic Linwood Foundation's charges is the restoration of tombs. This stucco box tomb was completely demolished by the roots of a cedar tree.

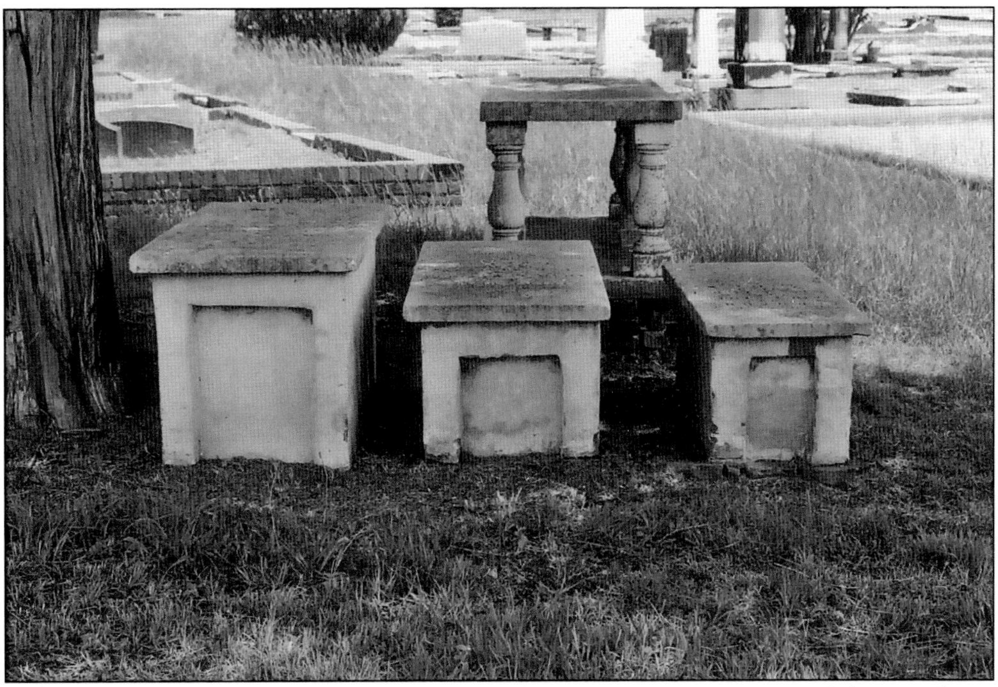

Using the services of a local craftsman, the tomb was returned to its original design. This is representative of the type of restoration the Foundation is undertaking.

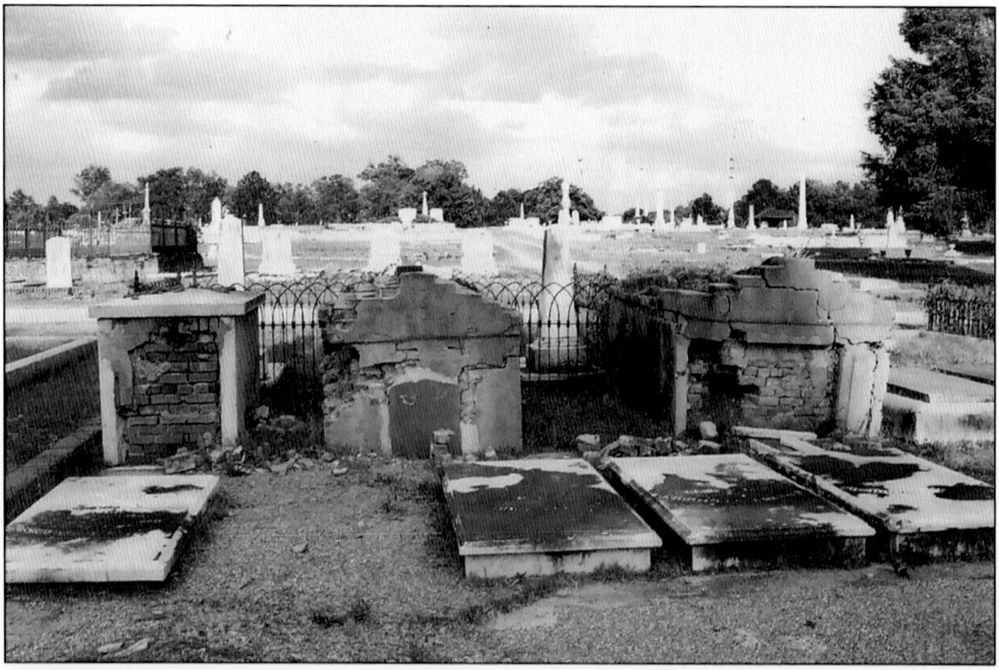

These tombs, similar to those found in New Orleans, had already deteriorated badly when vandals further damaged them.

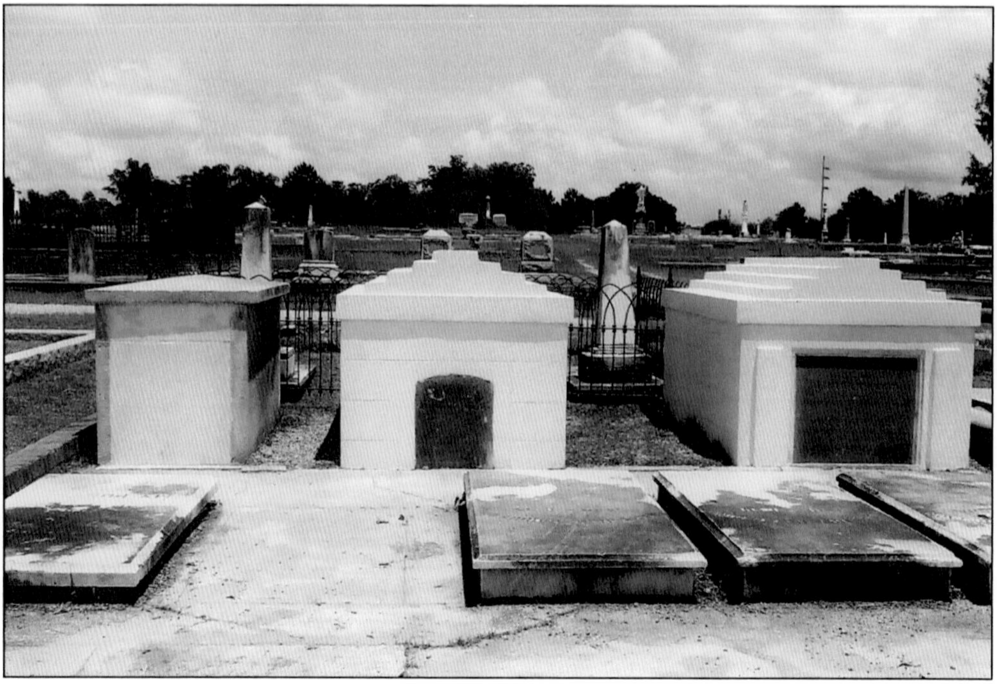

Using foundation funds, restoration brick masons reconstructed the tombs.

Two

Local 19th-Century Stone Carvers

Visitors to Linwood Cemetery can today admire an abundance of exquisitely crafted monuments. Those headstones dating from the mid-1800s to the early 1900s show an evolution in technique and style. Well-known carvers such as Henry McCauley, Patrick Adams, and Andrew M Elledge created beautiful memorials in stone to honor the deceased. Several early artisans immigrated from Ireland to this bustling town on the Chattahoochee; others were born here. No matter from where they hailed, their handicrafts have inspired and consoled many generations and set Linwood Cemetery apart as an architectural treasure.

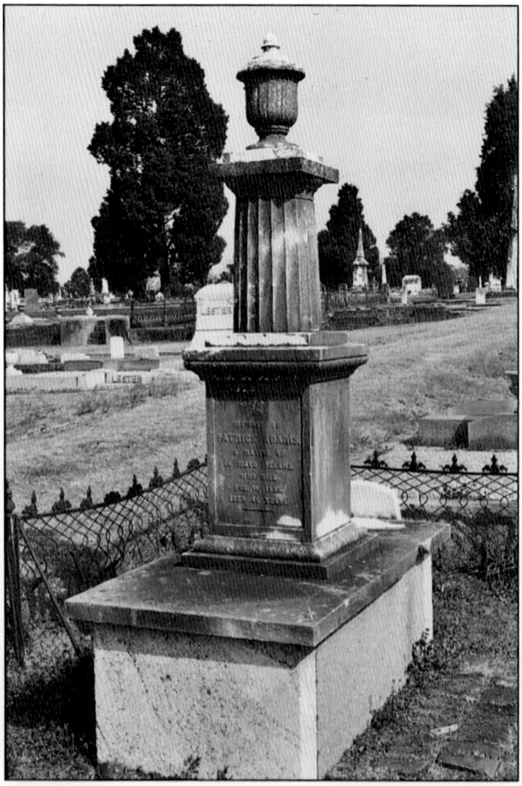

Patrick Adams supplied the first tablets to mark graves in Linwood. Adams was a brick mason and builder in Columbus from 1828 until his death in 1853 at the age of 46. He was also a respected stone carver. His monument is characteristic of the style he and his partner, John Madden, developed together.

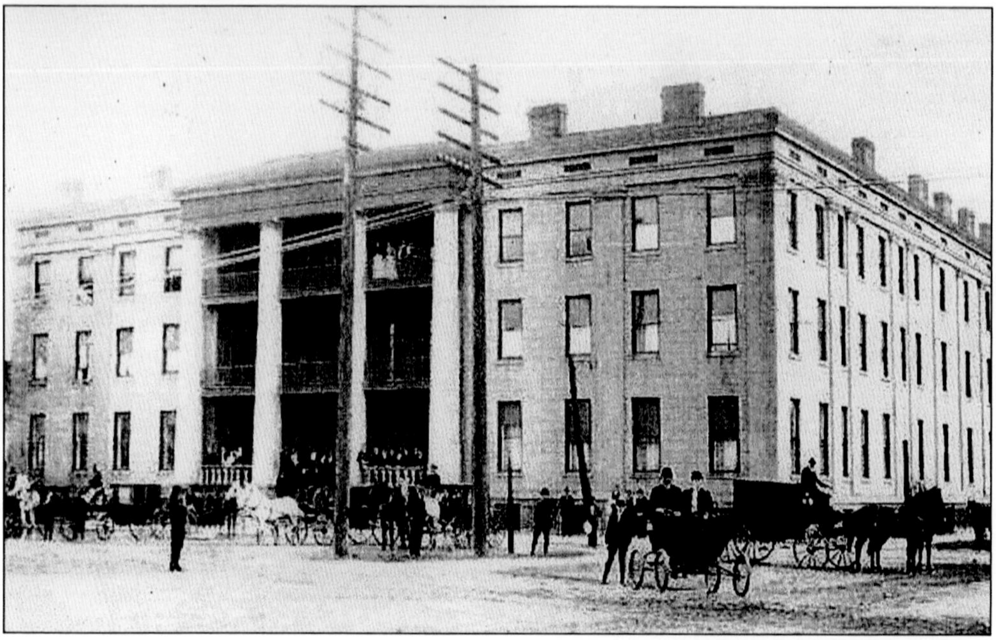

As a brickyard owner and a contractor, Patrick Adams fabricated everything from brick sewers to buildings in Columbus. Pictured is the Perry House, a hotel built by Adams in 1853. Later renamed the Racine Hotel, it was located on the northeast corner of Thirteenth Street and First Avenue. (Courtesy of Historic Columbus Foundation.)

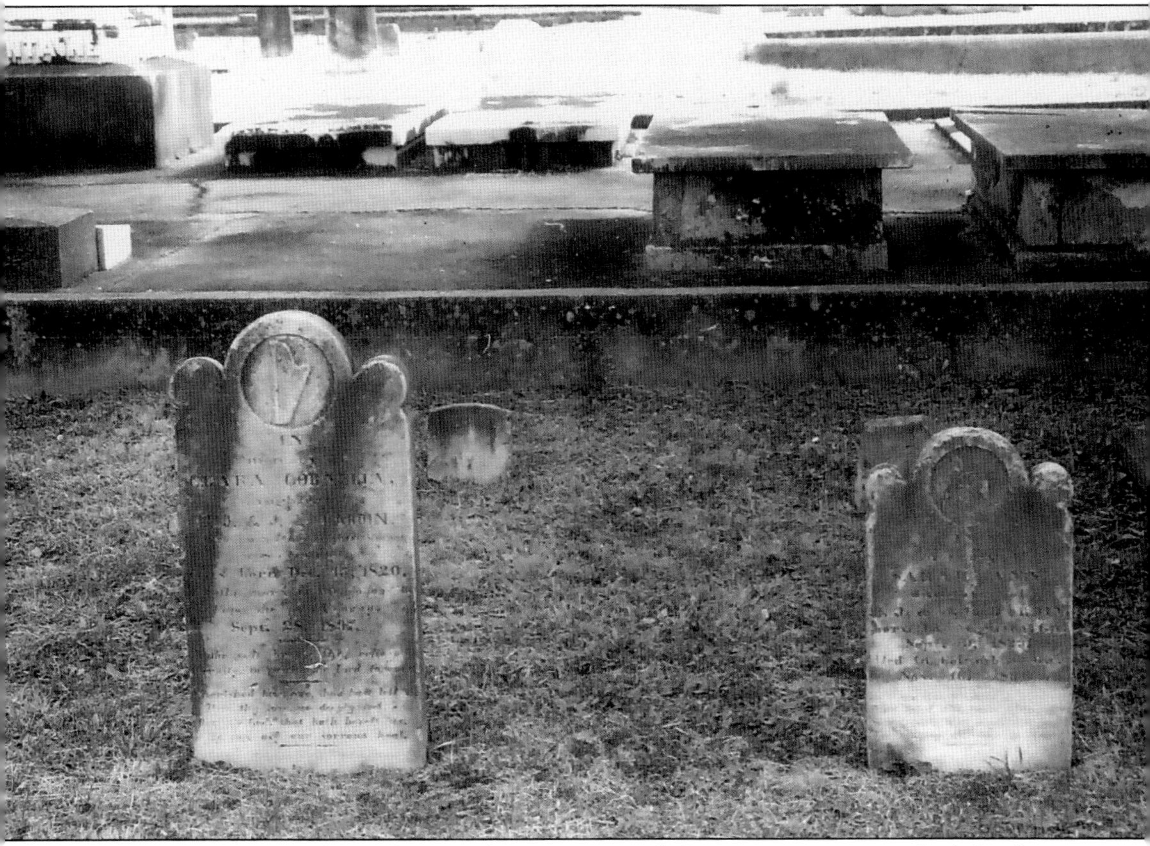

These tablets, some of the earliest markers in Linwood Cemetery, were typical of the first markers placed by Adams. The tablets mark the graves of Clara Hardin, who died in 1837, and her sister Sarah, who died in 1831.

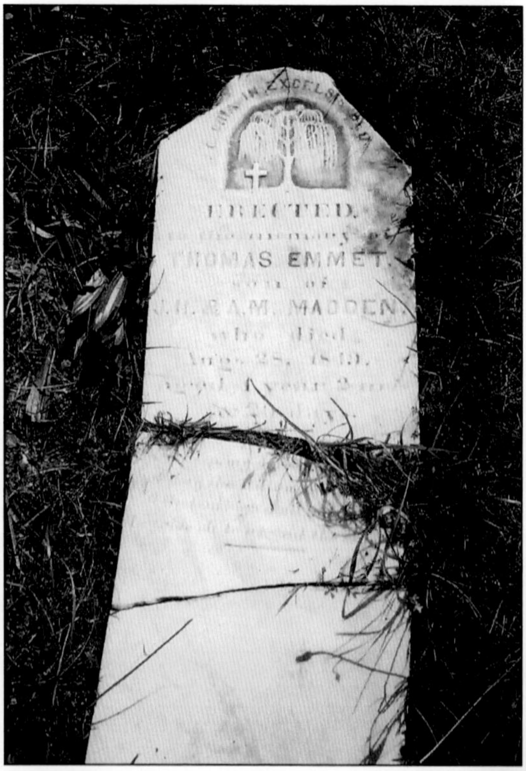

The grave of Irishman John Madden, who worked with Patrick Adams, is not marked, but this picture shows an example of his work. This motif is found on all three gravestones still in his lot. The stone pictured belongs to his son, Thomas Emmett. Patrick Tierney of Ballydessi, County Tipperary, Ireland, and John's brother Henry D. Madden are also in the lot.

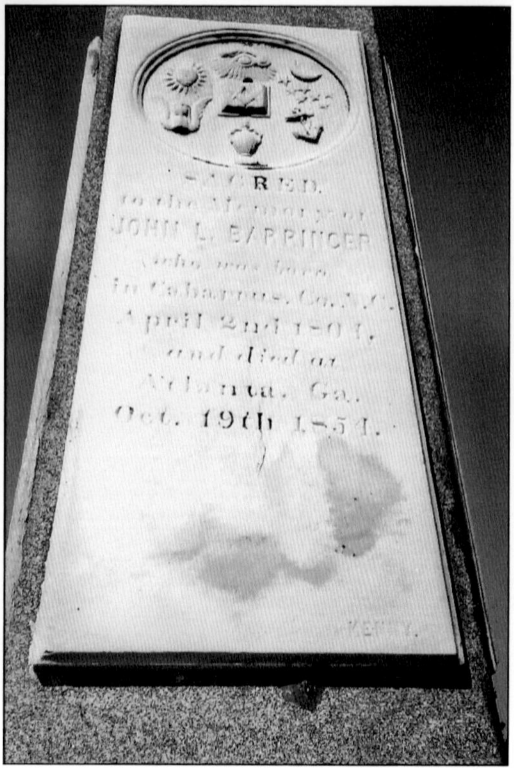

Thomas Kenny, also of Ireland, was another carver whose work is in Linwood Cemetery. This carving of Masonic symbols is an example of his work. Kenny died in 1865 but is not buried in Linwood.

This ad, published in the *Daily Sun* on August 5, 1856, shows that Madden and Kenny began a partnership for a "marble yard."

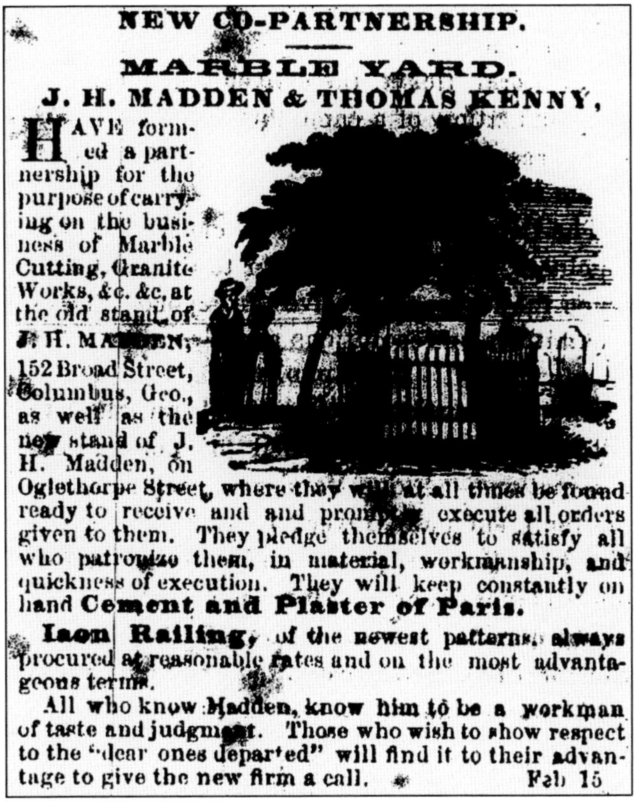

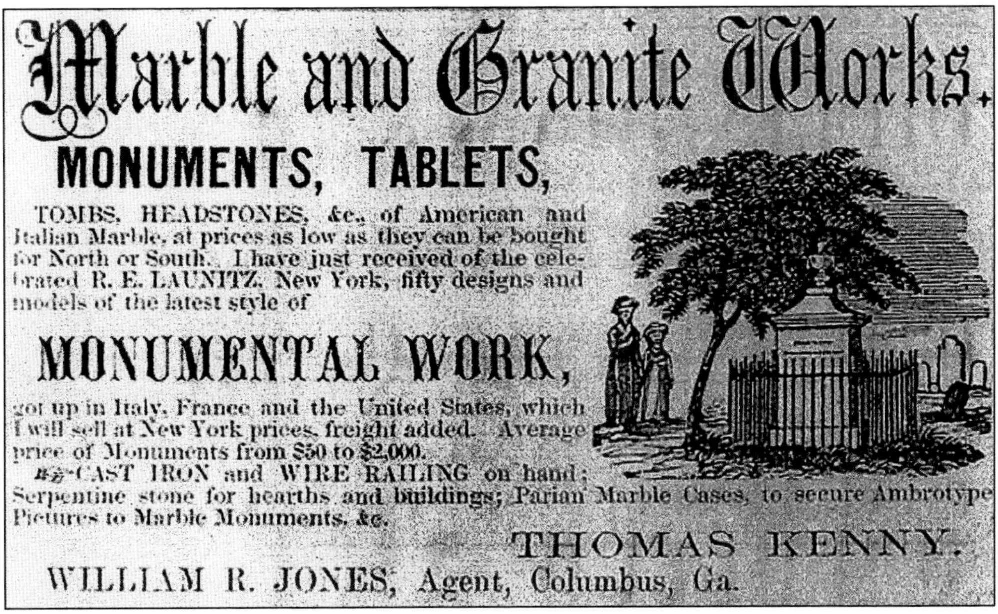

This later ad, published in the *1859-1860 Columbus City Directory*, tells us that Kenny is once again working alone.

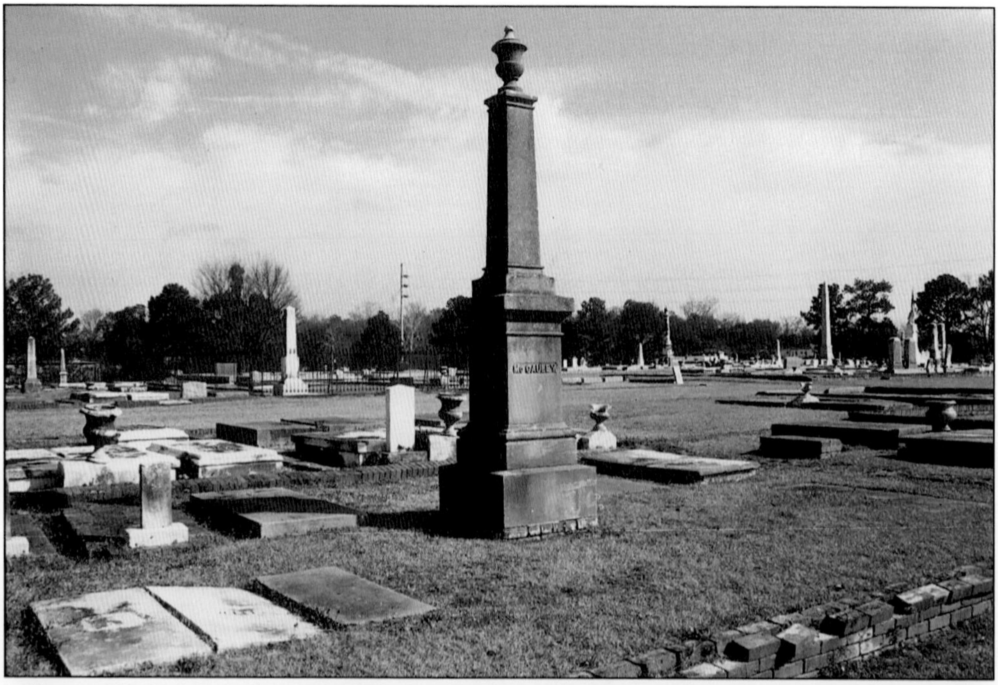

Irishman Henry McCauley was the most artistic and creative of the local stone carvers who crafted tombstones and grave monuments in the City Cemetery in the 19th century. McCauley operated a marble yard in Columbus from 1856 to 1879. In contrast to the ornate carvings he did for others, McCauley's family lot is marked by this plain brownstone monument.

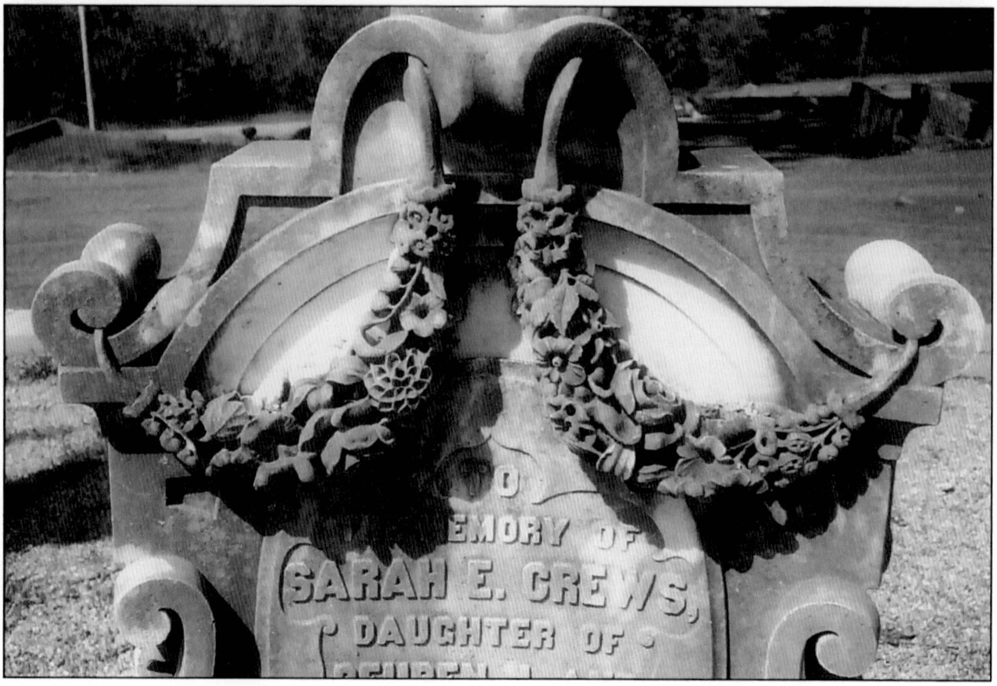

Much of Henry McCauley's stonework depicts finely detailed floral wreaths such as the one pictured here.

A Henry McCauley advertisement dated April 19, 1856, states, "He flatters himself that for workmanship he will give satisfaction to the most fastidious."

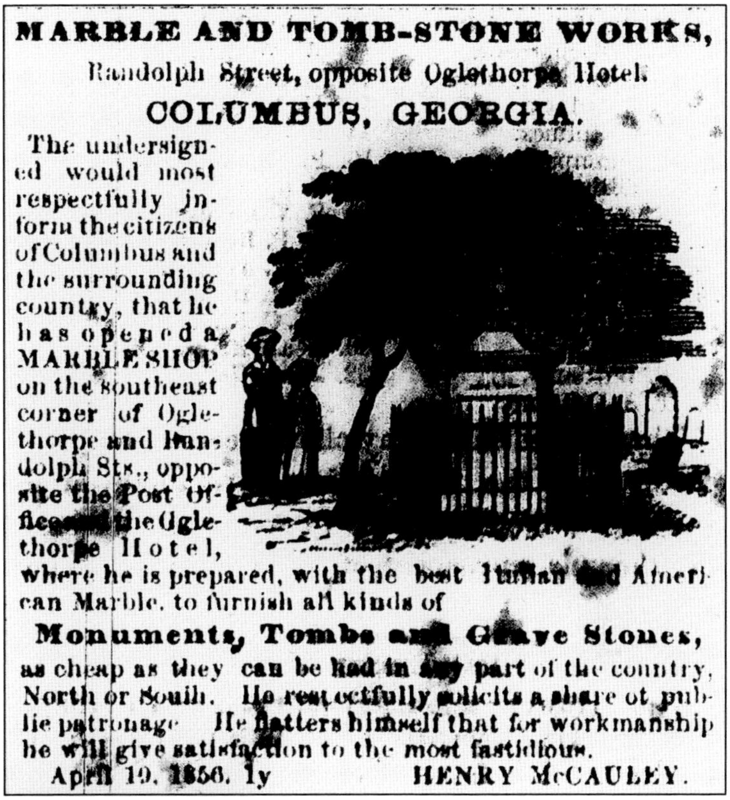

MARBLE AND TOMB-STONE WORKS,

Randolph Street, opposite Oglethorpe Hotel.

COLUMBUS, GEORGIA.

The undersigned would most respectfully inform the citizens of Columbus and the surrounding country, that he has opened a MARBLE SHOP on the southeast corner of Oglethorpe and Randolph Sts., opposite the Post Office and the Oglethorpe Hotel, where he is prepared, with the best Italian and American Marble, to furnish all kinds of

Monuments, Tombs and Grave Stones,

as cheap as they can be had in any part of the country, North or South. He respectfully solicits a share of public patronage. He flatters himself that for workmanship he will give satisfaction to the most fastidious.

April 19, 1856. 1y HENRY McCAULEY.

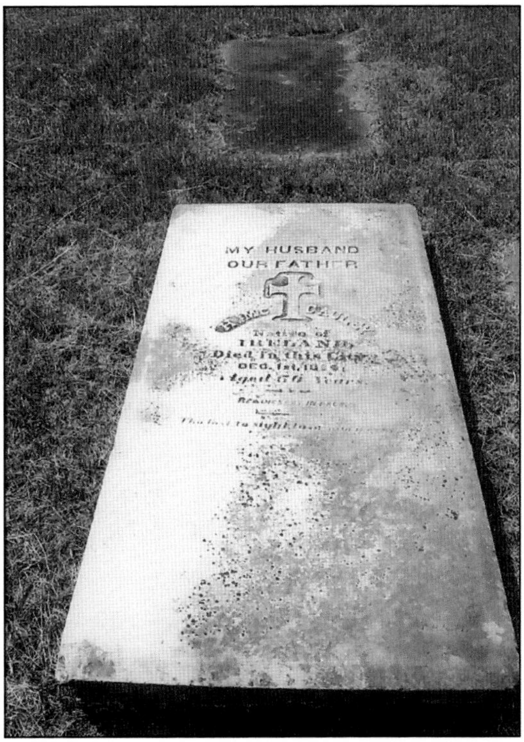

Henry McCauley's career as a stone carver was tragically cut short in 1879 when he was shot during an argument with a local citizen. Thomas Grier, one of his workmen, carved McCauley's stone.

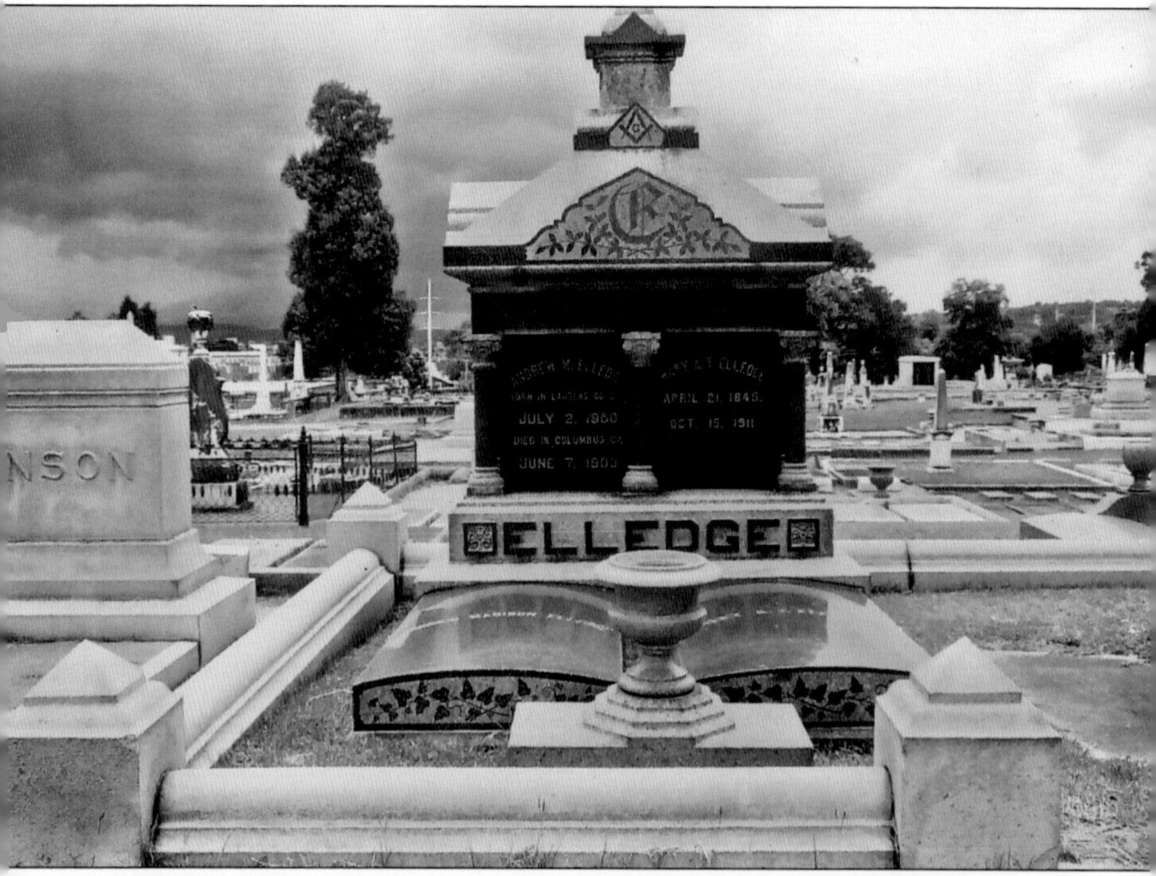

Andrew M. Elledge and John T. Norman, the second generation of Columbus stone carvers, operated the Marble and Granite Works at 907 Broad Street in Columbus from 1880 until 1903. They advertised themselves as "importers and manufacturers of marble and granite monuments, iron railings as a specialty, building stone of all kinds." After Elledge's death, Norman changed the name of the company to the Marble Company and remained in business at the same location until 1925. The heyday of the stone carver in Columbus ended at that point in 1925, and Norman's employees were then known merely as "stonecutters." They cut and sandblasted granite, creating a smooth, shiny surface for the lettering, which was done by template. Carved figures had to be imported from such places as New England.

20 ADVERTISEMENT.

MONUMENTAL

Marble Works!

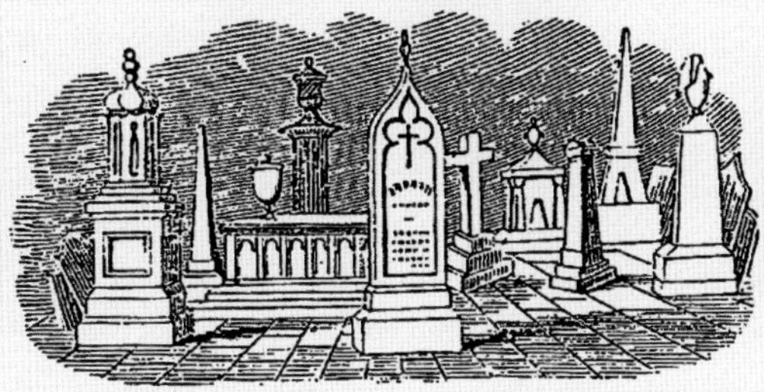

205 Broad Street.

Monuments of the Best Italian and American Marble on hand and made to order. I am also agent for a superior quality of

WROUGHT IRON RAILING!

For Fences and Cemetery Enclosures.

DIFFERENT STYLES and PATTERNS.

Information given and Estimates furnished on anything in my line.

A. M. ELLEDGE.

This ad, published in 1882, appeared in the *Catalogue of Columbus Public Library*.

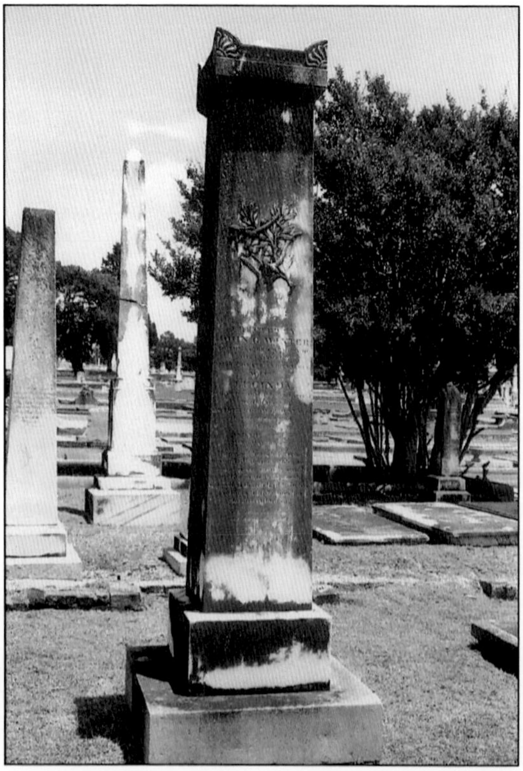

Several non-resident stone carvers provided monuments. One of them was E.C. Launitz, who fashioned the monument of John Gano Winter and his wife, Lucinda. Launitz, a New York artisan, set the standard for 19th-century stone carvers throughout the country. Thomas Kenny, a Columbus stone carver, advertised he had models and patterns from Launitz from which to choose. The John G. Winter monument is one of three known Launitz works in all of Georgia.

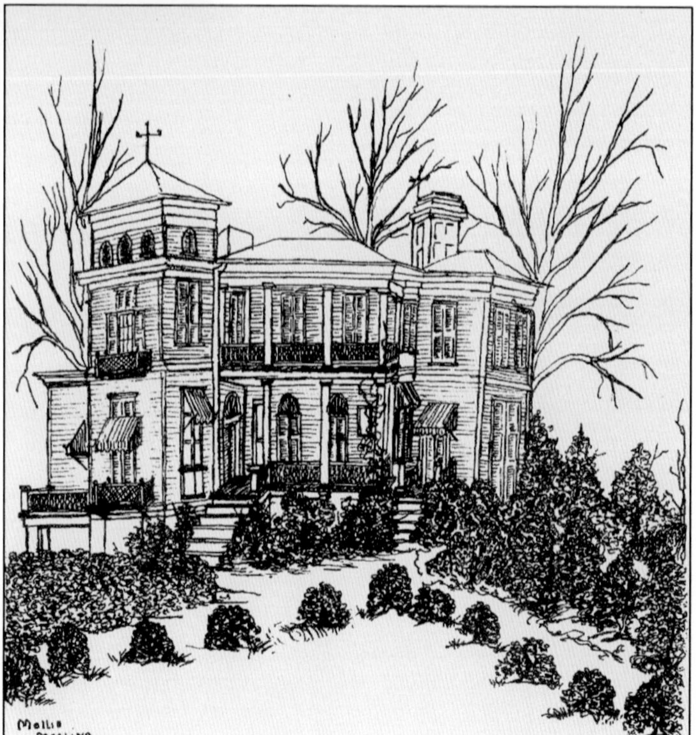

John Gano Winter's suburban estate, Bunker Hill, stood atop what is now called Benning Hills. A prominent businessman, Winter owned the St. Mary's Bank, Palace Grist Mill, and Rock Island Paper Mill. He was mayor of Columbus in the early 1840s and actually loaned money to the City during a financial crisis. A staunch Unionist, he sold his businesses in 1861 when the Civil War began, moved to New York City, and died there in 1865. Six years after that, his body was re-interred at Linwood to fulfill his dying wish. (Courtesy of Mollie Mealing.)

Three

GUARDIANS OF THE CEMETERY

Standing like silent sentinels over the cemetery, the beautifully carved figures of angels, women, and cherubs that now grace Linwood Cemetery remind visitors of a bygone era when steamboats plied the Chattahoochee River and ordinary men created beautiful symbols from cold slabs of marble. Many of these figures hold symbols that represent faith, hope, and heavenly reward. Whether erected in honor of a beloved husband, child, or uncle, graceful monuments such as these bring beauty and peace to Linwood Cemetery.

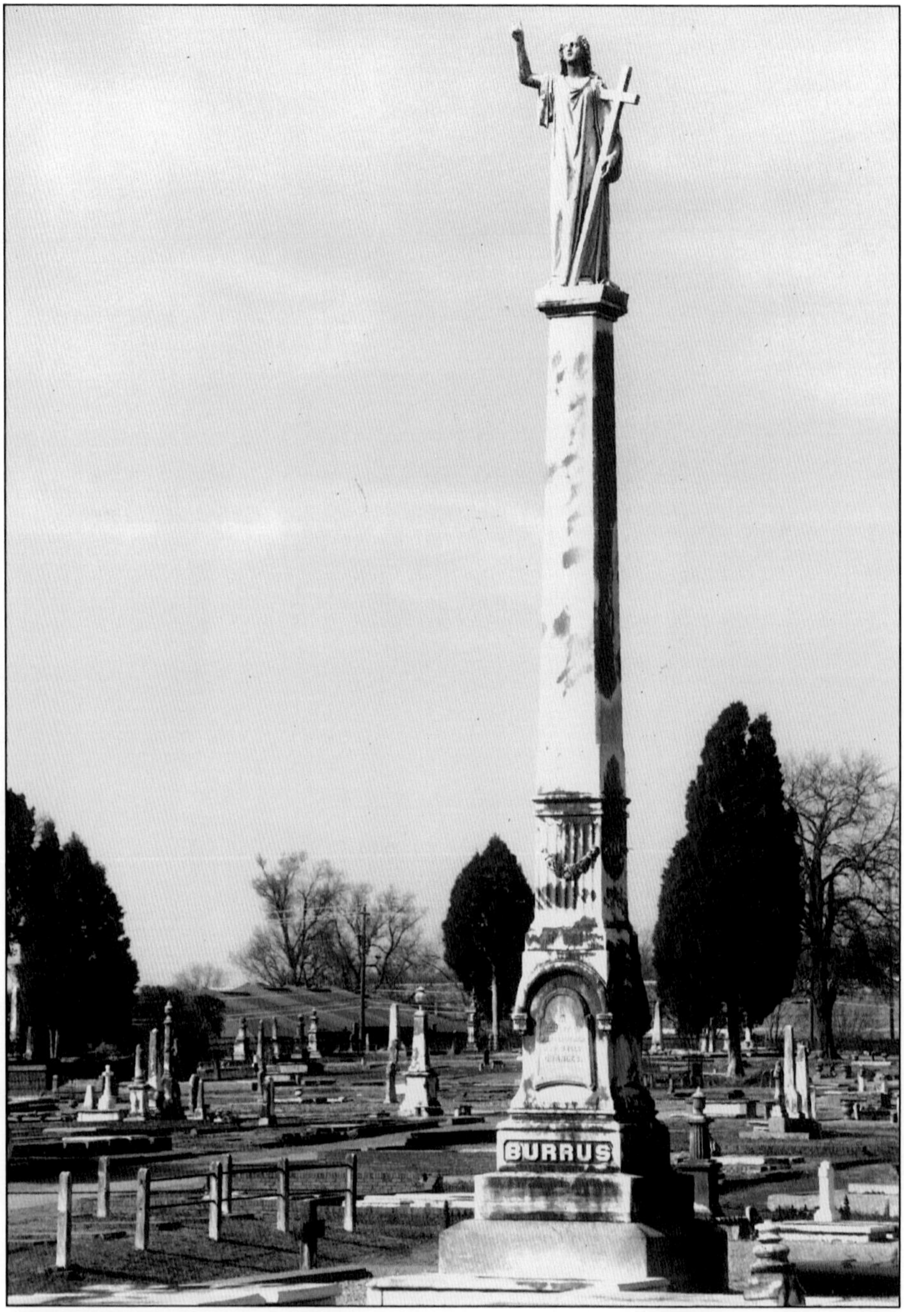

The tallest monument in the cemetery is topped by a woman's figure holding a cross, representing faith. With one hand raised, she points out the path to heaven. Buried in this lot is Catherine Francesca Brassel Burrus, the wife of George Joseph Burrus, a wine merchant who immigrated to Detroit, Michigan, from Marlenheim Province, France. They had 10 children. After George died in 1833, Catherine came to Columbus to be near other members of her family; the extended Burrus family was locally prominent in the grocery business and the manufacture of cotton. Catherine and her unmarried nephew Charles are the only two of the family buried in this lot. Charles left his money to his cousins, who erected this monument.

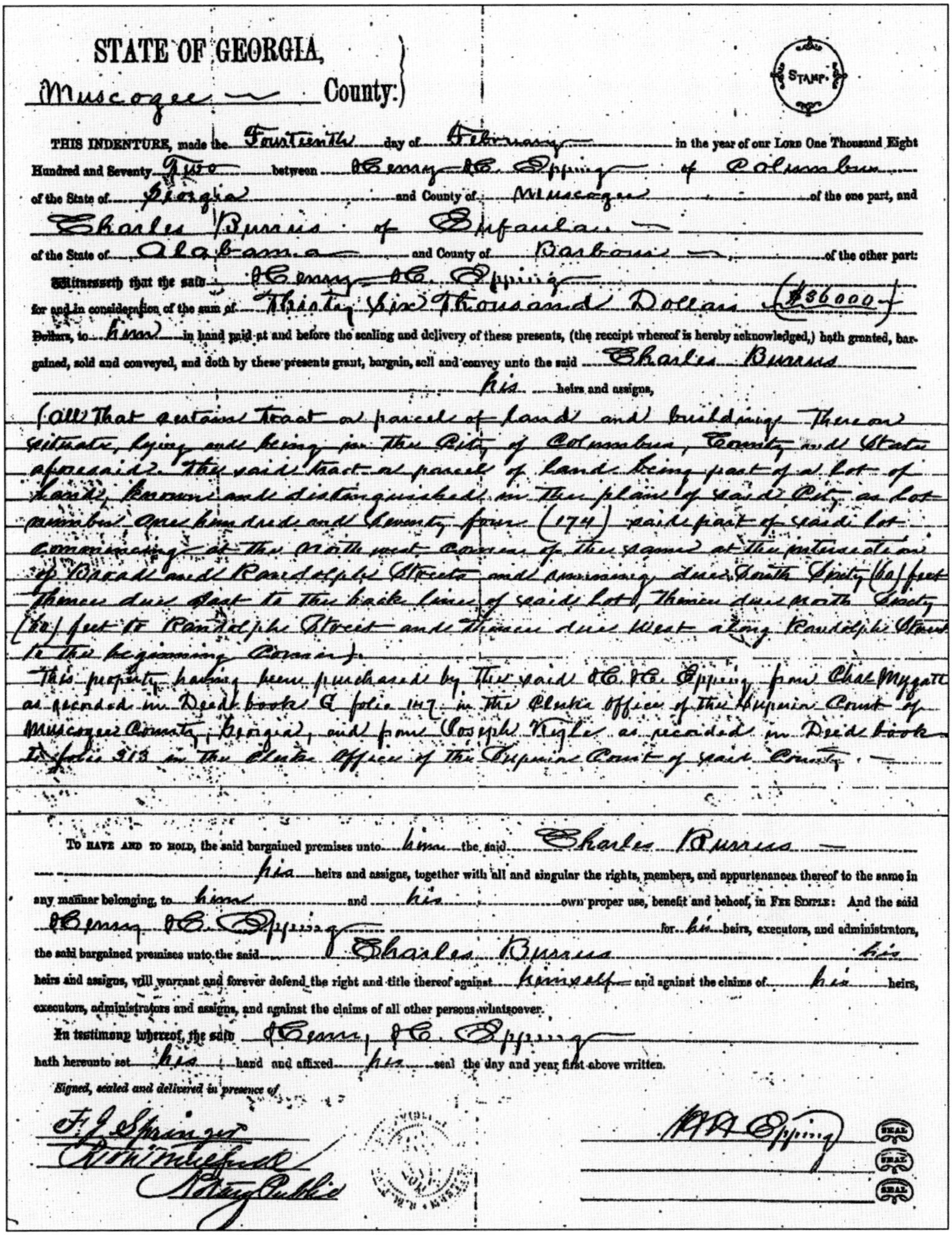

STATE OF GEORGIA,
Muscogee County:

STAMP

THIS INDENTURE, made the Fourteenth day of February in the year of our Lord One Thousand Eight Hundred and Seventy Two between Henry H. Epping of Columbus of the State of Georgia and County of Muscogee of the one part, and Charles Burrus of Eufaula of the State of Alabama and County of Barbour of the other part:

Witnesseth that the said Henry H. Epping for and in consideration of the sum of Thirty Six Thousand Dollars ($36000) Dollars, to him in hand paid at and before the sealing and delivery of these presents, (the receipt whereof is hereby acknowledged,) hath granted, bargained, sold and conveyed, and doth by these presents grant, bargain, sell and convey unto the said Charles Burrus his heirs and assigns,

All that certain tract or parcel of land and building thereon situate, lying and being in the City of Columbus, County and State aforesaid. The said tract or parcel of land being part of a lot of land, known and distinguished in the plan of said City as lot number One hundred and Seventy four (174) said part of said lot commencing at the North west corner of the same at the intersection of Broad and Randolph Streets and running due South Sixty (60) feet thence due East to the back line of said lot, thence due North Sixty (60) feet to Randolph Street and thence due West along Randolph Street to the beginning corner.

This property having been purchased by the said H. H. Epping from Chas Myzatt as recorded in Deed book E folio 147 in the Clerk's Office of the Superior Court of Muscogee County, Georgia, and from Joseph Kyle as recorded in Deed book I folio 313 in the Clerk's Office of the Superior Court of said County.

To have and to hold, the said bargained premises unto him the said Charles Burrus his heirs and assigns, together with all and singular the rights, members, and appurtenances thereof to the same in any manner belonging, to him and his own proper use, benefit and behoof, in Fee Simple: And the said Henry H. Epping for his heirs, executors, and administrators, the said bargained premises unto the said Charles Burrus his heirs and assigns, will warrant and forever defend the right and title thereof against himself and against the claims of his heirs, executors, administrators and assigns, and against the claims of all other persons whatsoever.

In testimony whereof, the said Henry H. Epping hath hereunto set his hand and affixed his seal the day and year first above written.

Signed, sealed and delivered in presence of

F. J. Springer
Robt. M. Mitchell
Notary Public

H H Epping (SEAL)
(SEAL)
(SEAL)

This is a deed for property Charles Burrus purchased in Columbus, which is now the site of the Columbus Bank and Trust Building. (Courtesy of Warren Foley.)

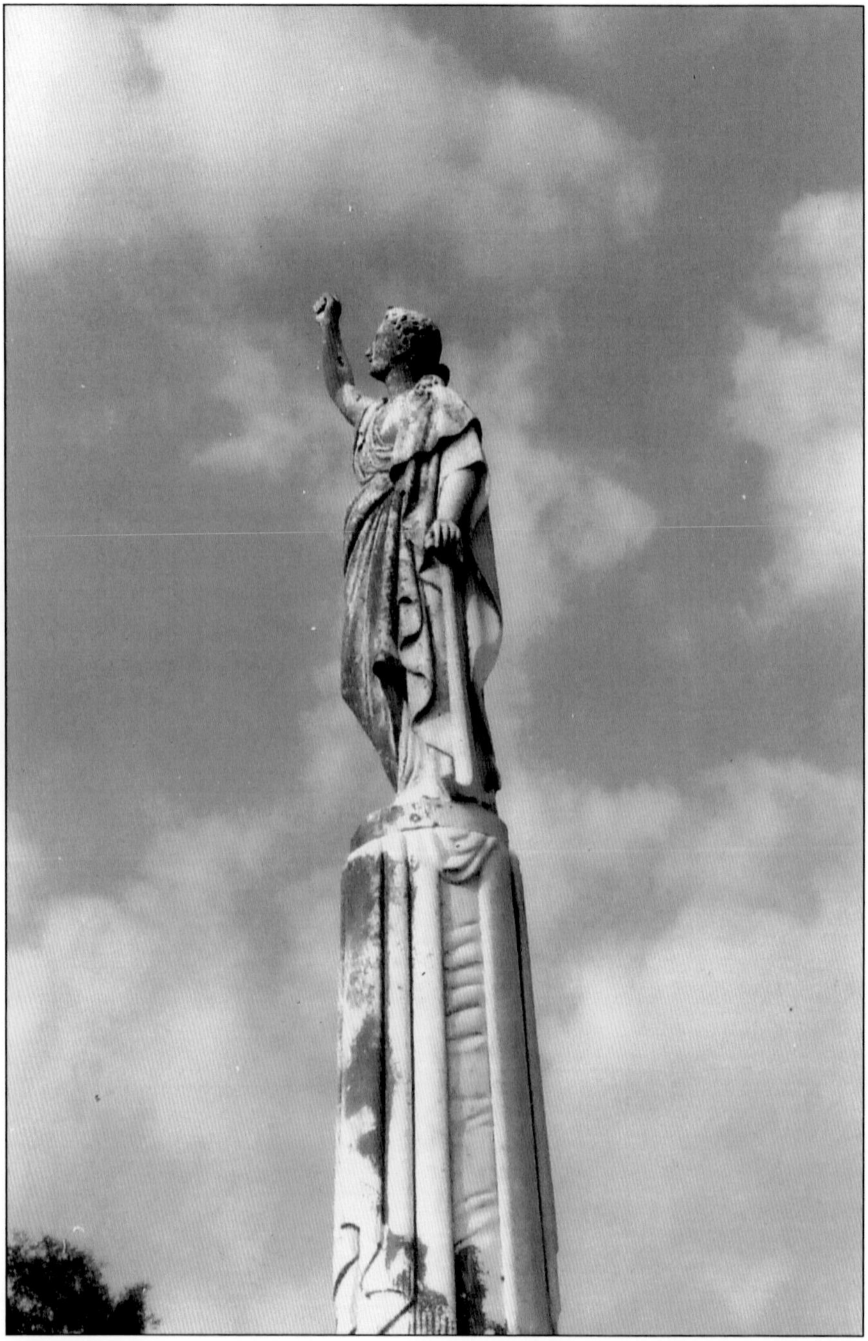

The woman's figure on top of this tall monument holds an anchor representing hope. John and Sarah Watkins Banks came to Columbus from Elbert County, Georgia, in 1836, when the town was very young; they were among the first settlers to build in the Wynnton area. John was a leading Columbus merchant, banker, and plantation owner. In 1848 he co-founded the Howard Manufacturing Company, later becoming its president. He served as a trustee of the Wynnton Male and Female Academies. The couple had nine boys and three girls, all of whom are buried in this lot. Four of the boys died during the Civil War.

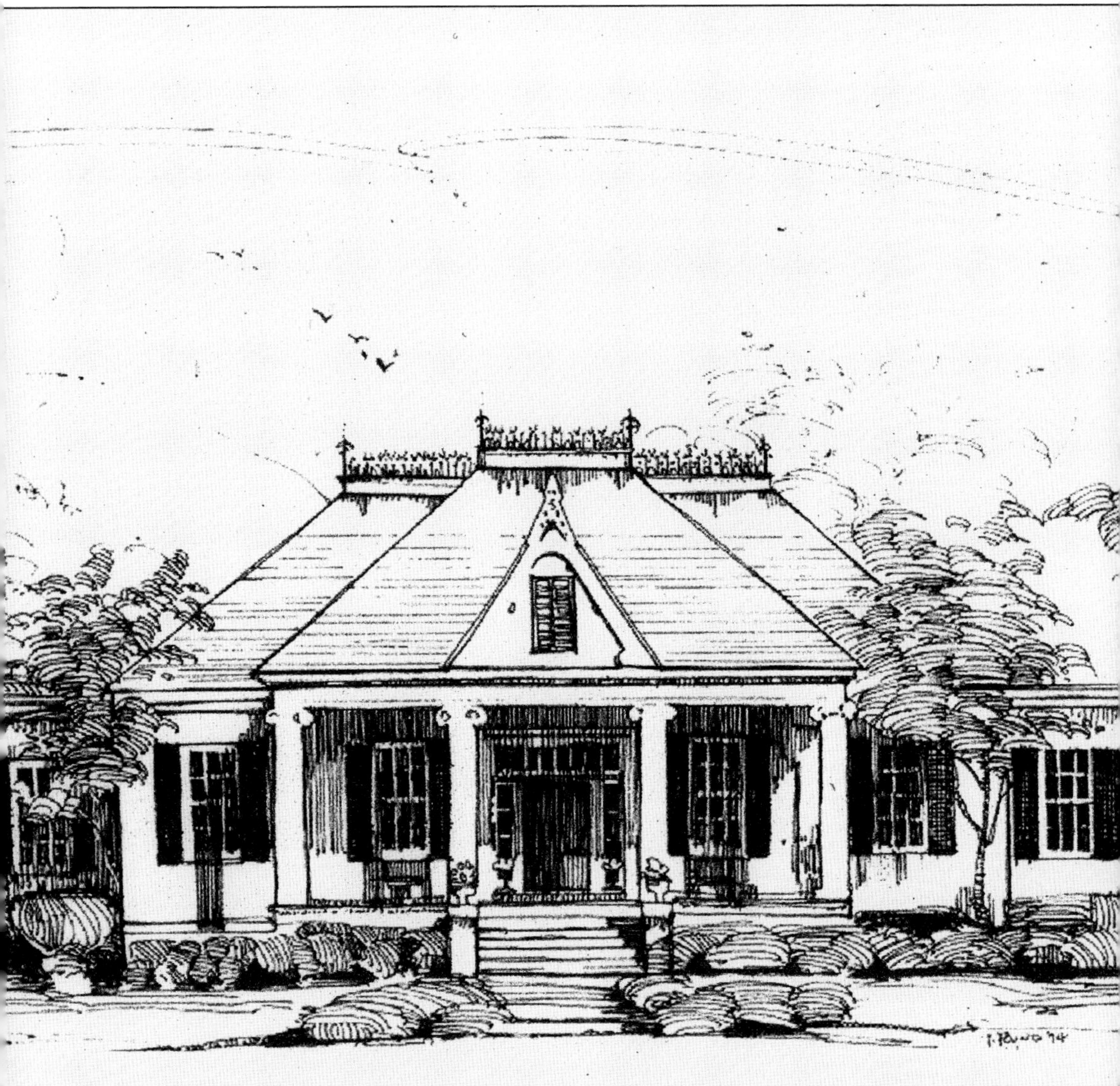

"The Cedars," built by John Banks in 1836, was the second house in the antebellum suburb of Wynnton. It has been continuously owned and occupied by direct descendants of Banks. (Courtesy of John Sheftall.)

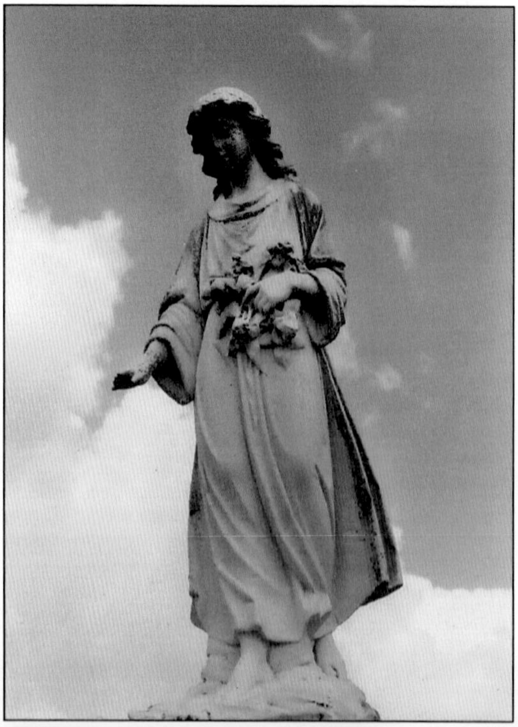

This child-figure overlooking the George Parker Swift family lot carries roses, symbolizing the completion of earthly existence; her outstretched hand indicates mortality. George Parker Swift was a textile manufacturer who arrived in Columbus from Upson County, Georgia, in the last days of the Civil War to take advantage of Columbus's larger cotton market, waterpower, and transportation network. In 1867 he organized the Muscogee Mills, later the Muscogee Manufacturing Company, one of the world's largest manufacturers of towels and ticking. His plant's electric current powered the first electric light bulb on Broad Street. Descendants continued in the textile business for four generations.

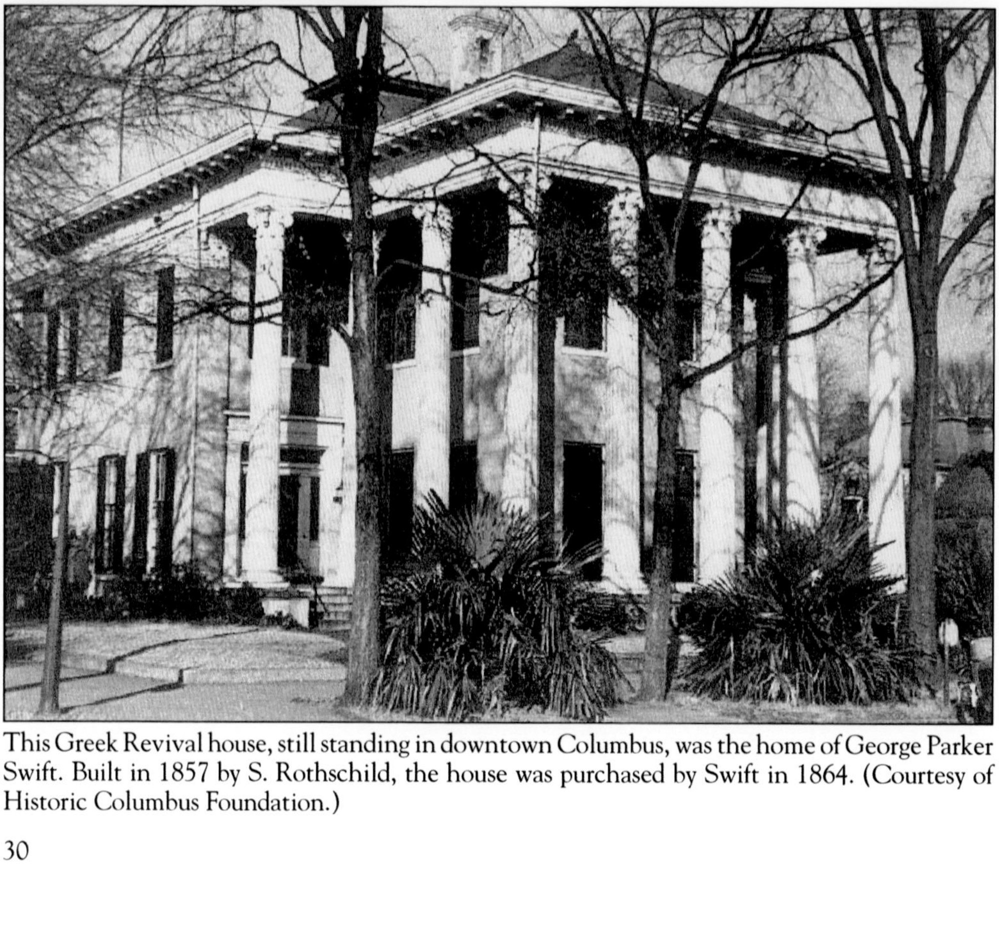

This Greek Revival house, still standing in downtown Columbus, was the home of George Parker Swift. Built in 1857 by S. Rothschild, the house was purchased by Swift in 1864. (Courtesy of Historic Columbus Foundation.)

The uplifted hand of the figure atop Willie L. Lewis's monument indicates heavenly reward. The scroll in her left hand expresses the deceased's life being recorded by angels. The inscription reads, "a devoted and affectionate wife, a fond and loving mother, a Christian." Willie was the daughter of Dr. Erastus C. Hood, a prominent physician and druggist of Harris and Muscogee Counties; she married James A. Lewis in 1879 and died five years later, leaving a daughter, Vernada.

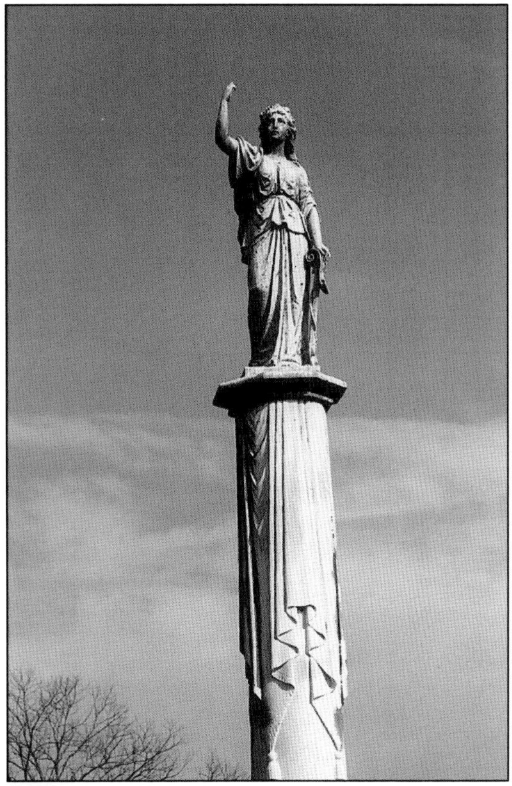

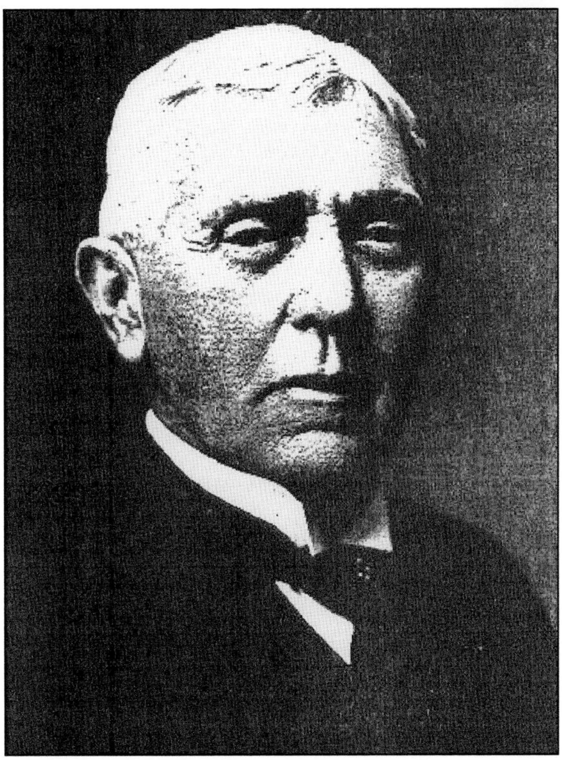

James Lewis, born in Fort Gaines, Georgia, was a director of both the Columbus Southern Railroad and the Third National Bank. (Courtesy of Lea Dowd.)

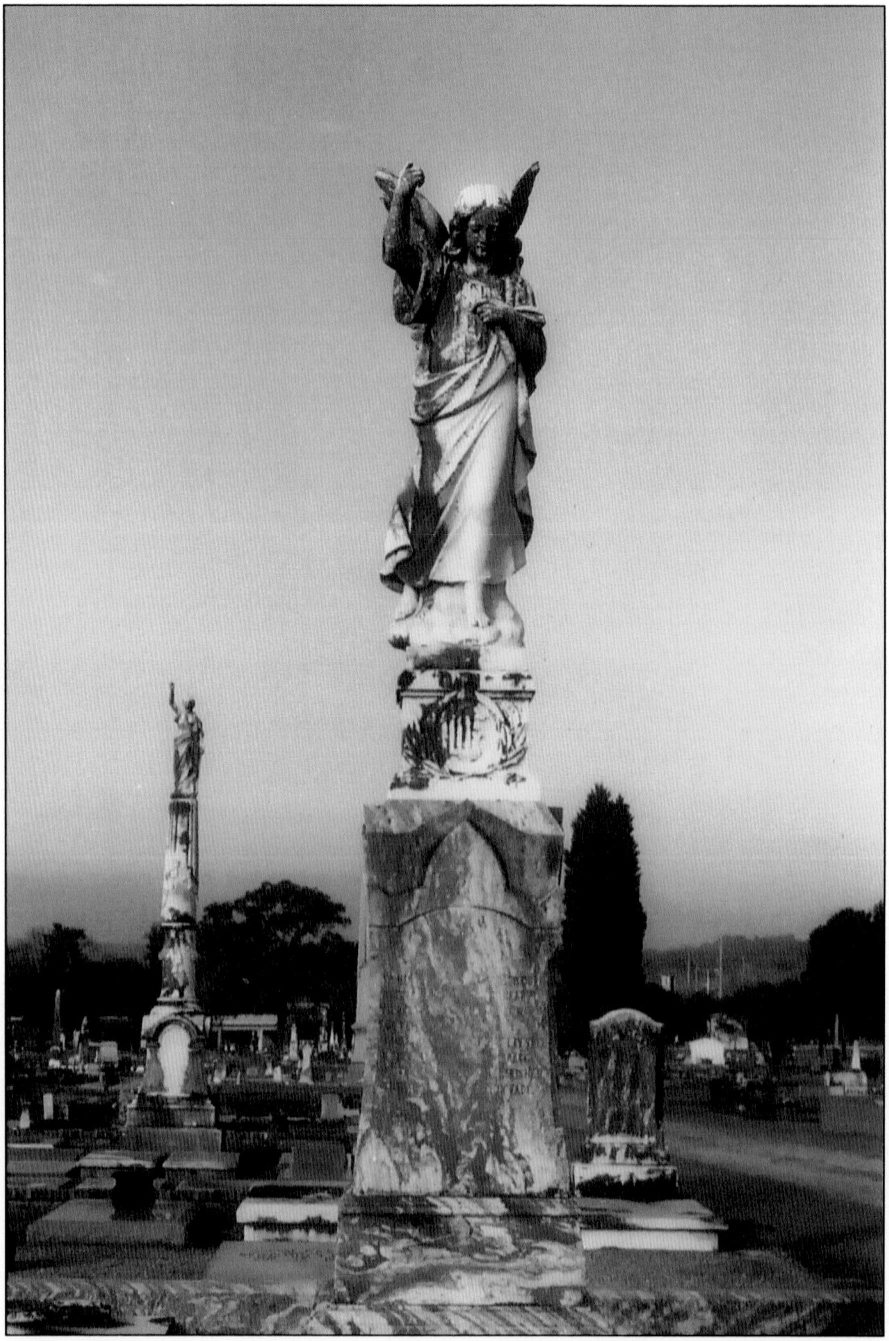

The Cosby family came to Columbus from nearby Geneva, Georgia. Two of the four siblings, Luther Tamoli Cosby and Alice Cosby Heath, are buried in Linwood. In 1901, Luther died of malaria in Brantley, Alabama, at the age of 42, leaving a wife and five children. Their brother, Forrest L. Cosby, a physician, served as Muscogee County health officer for 10 years and also served on the local draft board during World War I. Apparently he was the one who bought this lot and erected the beautiful monument, intending for other members of the Cosby family to be buried here.

Joseph Erickson Webster arrived in Columbus in 1835 when he was 14 years old. At an early date, he became involved in local politics; he was elected alderman, tax assessor, magistrate, and first wharfinger for the city in 1854, a post he held for more than 10 years. He and his wife, Caroline E. Ward, had eight children, all of whom are buried with them in this lot. Because the angel on this monument is so striking, it is used on Historic Linwood Foundation's information brochure. (Photograph by Greg Rodriguez.)

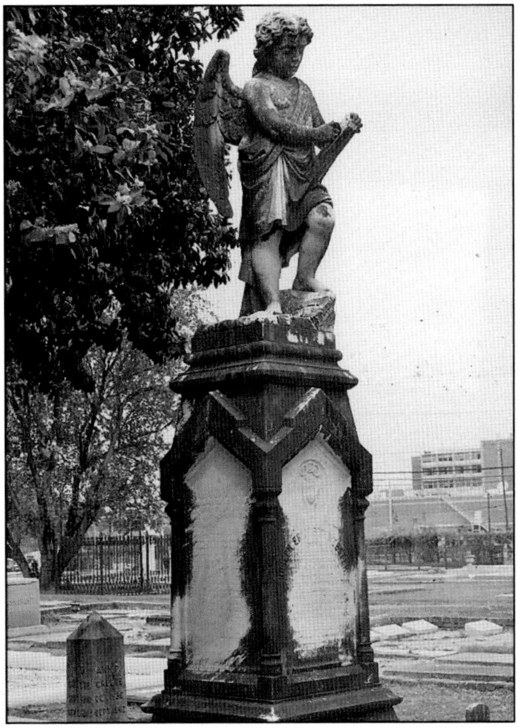

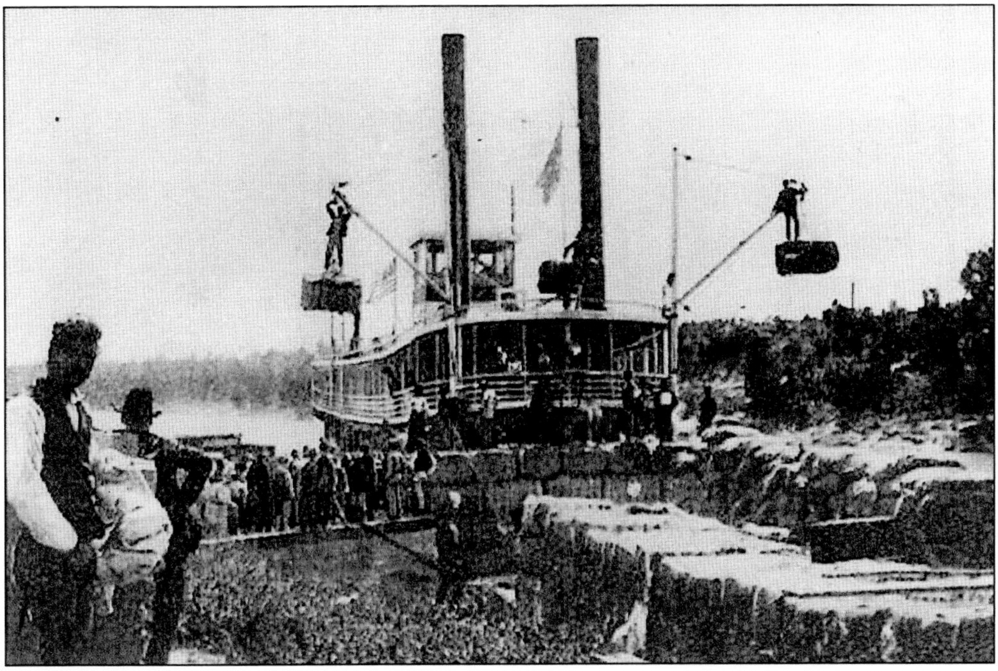

The City Wharf, in the charge of Mr. Webster, was a hub of activity. Steamboats traveled the Chattahoochee River from Columbus to Appalachicola and back with cotton, groceries, marble for tombstones, and other merchandise. Over 210 steamers plied the Chattahoochee between 1828 and 1939. The first was the *Fanny* and the last was the *George W. Miller*. (Courtesy of Historic Columbus Foundation)

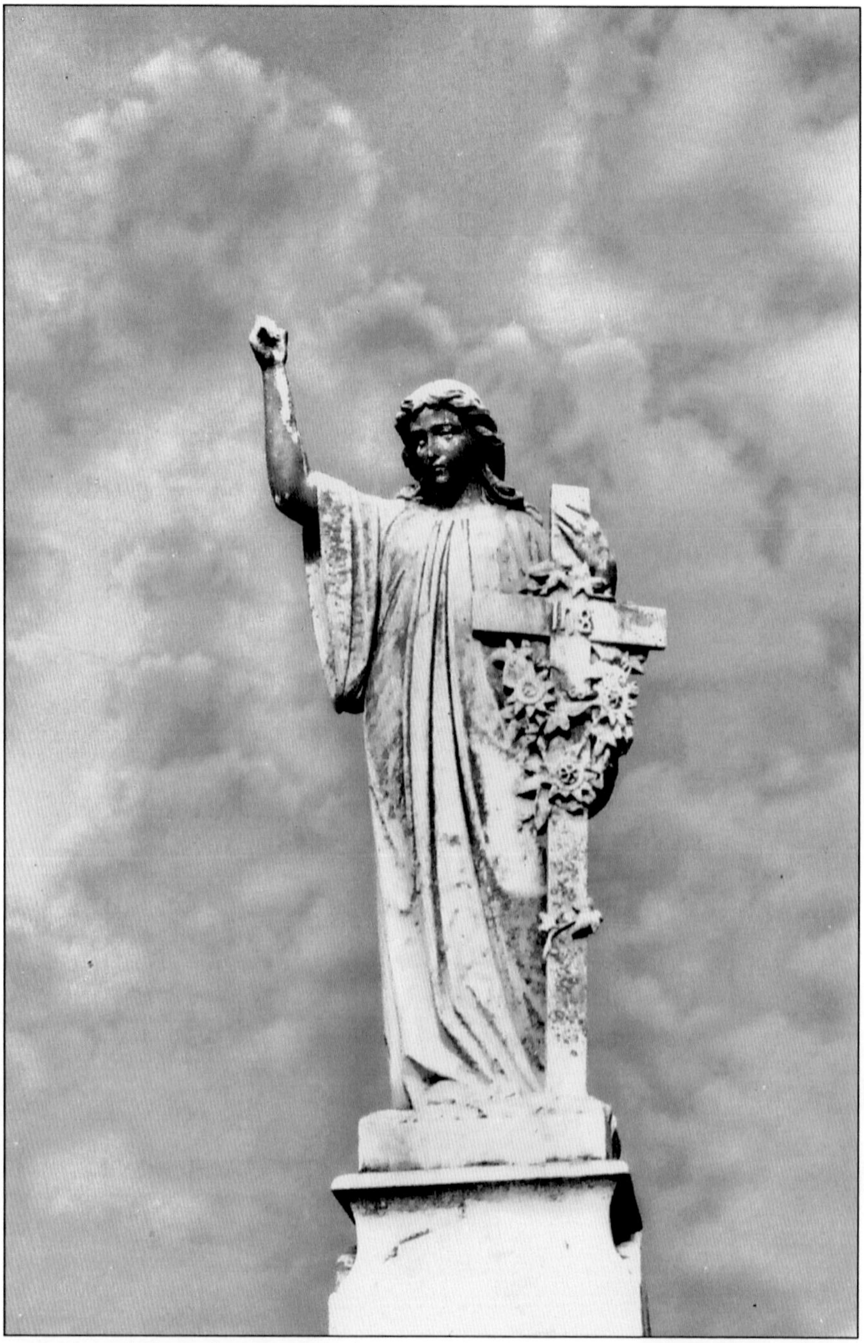

This monument, dedicated to "our uncle," was placed by nieces and nephews of Joseph W. Huff, a farmer who moved to Columbus from Taylor County, Georgia, after 1860. He resided in Wynnton when, in 1862, he joined the Muscogee Volunteers and was elected lieutenant. The troops left Columbus to be incorporated into new regiments for Confederate service. Huff died in 1901 at the age of 74, unmarried, and left his estate to cousins, nieces, and nephews. While not a wealthy family, they commissioned this magnificent monument for their uncle. He is the only one buried in this lot.

The female figure atop this monument appears to be dropping flowers down on the final resting place of Pleasant Jackson Philips, who died in 1876 and lies buried with his wife, who erected this monument.

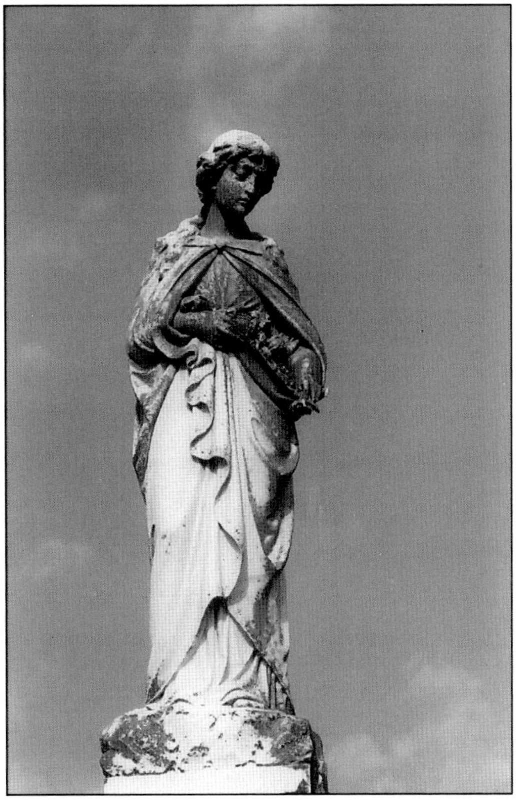

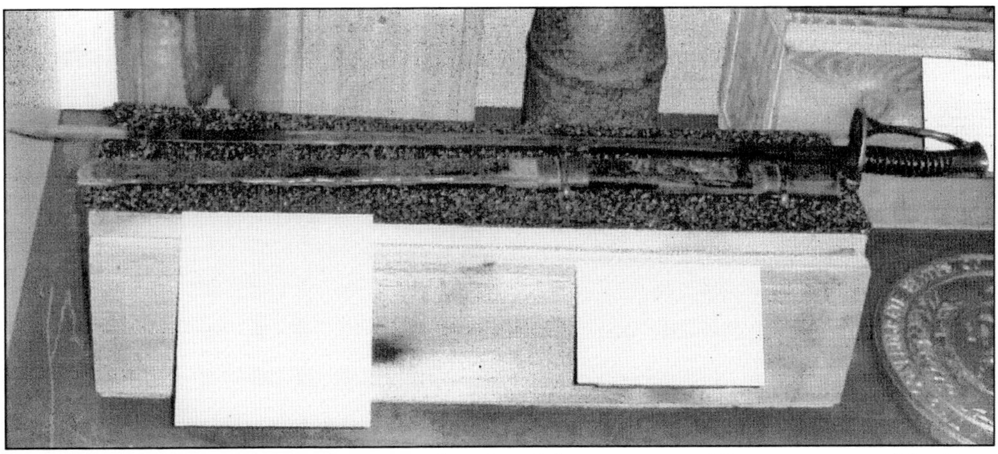

Pleasant J. Philips was a brigadier general in Confederate service. He was appointed by Gov. Joseph E. Brown to command the 2nd Brigade, 1st Division of the Georgia militia. His brigade was among those military units that unsuccessfully faced Gen. William T. Sherman on his "March to the Sea." Pictured here is the Columbus-made Haiman sword carried by Philips. (Courtesy of the Infantry Museum.)

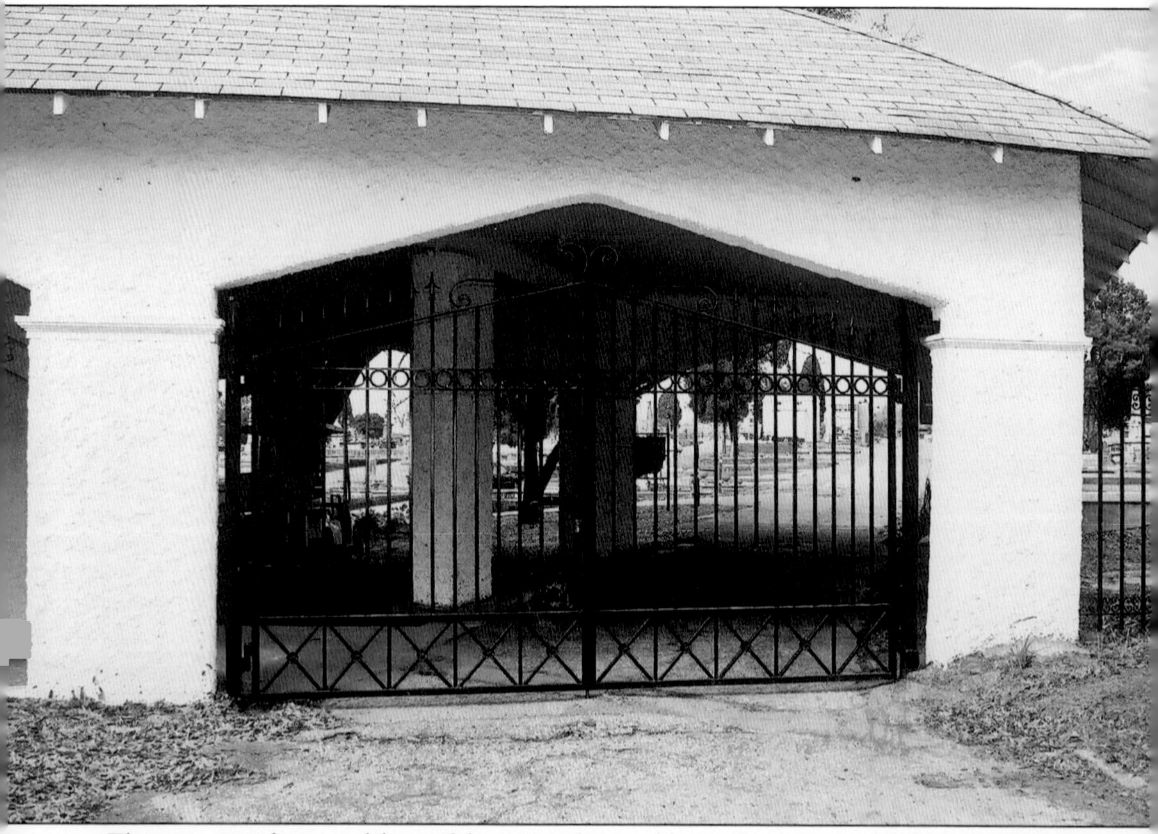

The new iron fence and beautiful gate made possible by the legacy of Evelyn Scarborough (Mrs. Hines Holt) are contemporary guardians of the cemetery. Her gift was the beginning of a campaign by Historic Linwood Foundation to replace a chain link fence with a decorative iron fence. The Holt family has played an important role in the history of Columbus; the first Hines Holt, a prominent attorney and U.S. congressman, was chosen to give the welcoming speech when Henry Clay visited the city during his presidential campaign.

Four

EARLY SETTLERS

In the hallowed earth of Linwood Cemetery lie soldiers, physicians, writers, and artisans. There are those who were well born and others who were well known. Although many are not represented by the grandest tombs and monuments, the early settlers of Columbus claim their rightful place as influential figures in the city's history. The grave of even the most humble among them represents the significant story of a life and times that are gone forever. While most of the details are now lost to history, here are a few of the more interesting stories of the people who rest in peace at Linwood.

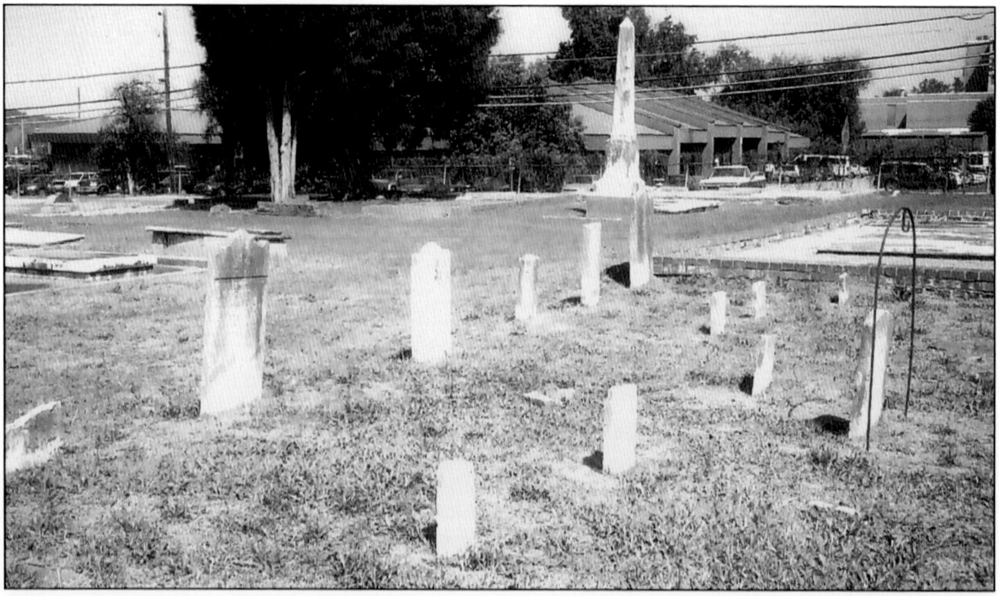

This is the family lot of Cassie Ann McGee, who was the first hospital keeper, or "Superintendent of the Hospital," appointed by the Columbus Council in 1838. She was paid $10 a month per patient and was required to furnish good and wholesome food and nourishment, fire, candles, and attendants. She also cared for the grounds. She kept a garden to raise vegetables on 10 acres surrounding the hospital. She died in poverty on May 9, 1849.

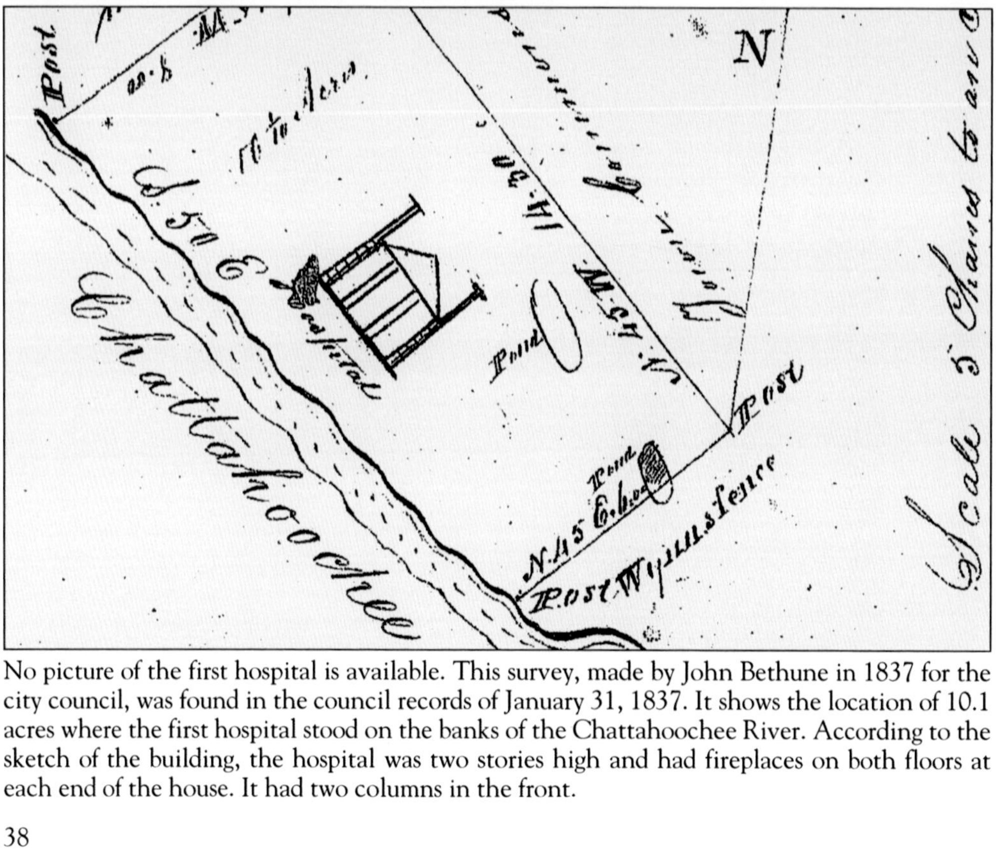

No picture of the first hospital is available. This survey, made by John Bethune in 1837 for the city council, was found in the council records of January 31, 1837. It shows the location of 10.1 acres where the first hospital stood on the banks of the Chattahoochee River. According to the sketch of the building, the hospital was two stories high and had fireplaces on both floors at each end of the house. It had two columns in the front.

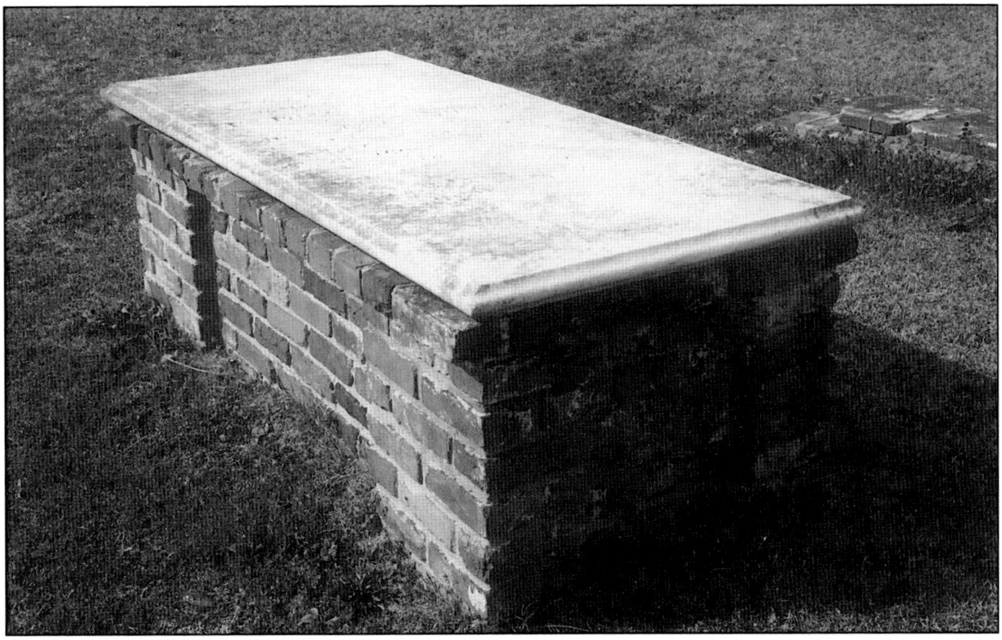

The tomb of Eliza McIntosh, who died in 1833, is one of the earliest marked graves in Linwood Cemetery. It was restored by Historic Linwood Foundation in 2000. Eliza, from New York, was the wife of Maj. James Simmons McIntosh, the commandant of Fort Mitchell, Alabama, on the edge of the Creek Nation. They moved there in 1825. Eliza is the only member of her family buried here. Eliza's husband, a great-nephew of Gen. Lachlan McIntosh, is buried in Colonial Park Cemetery in Savannah.

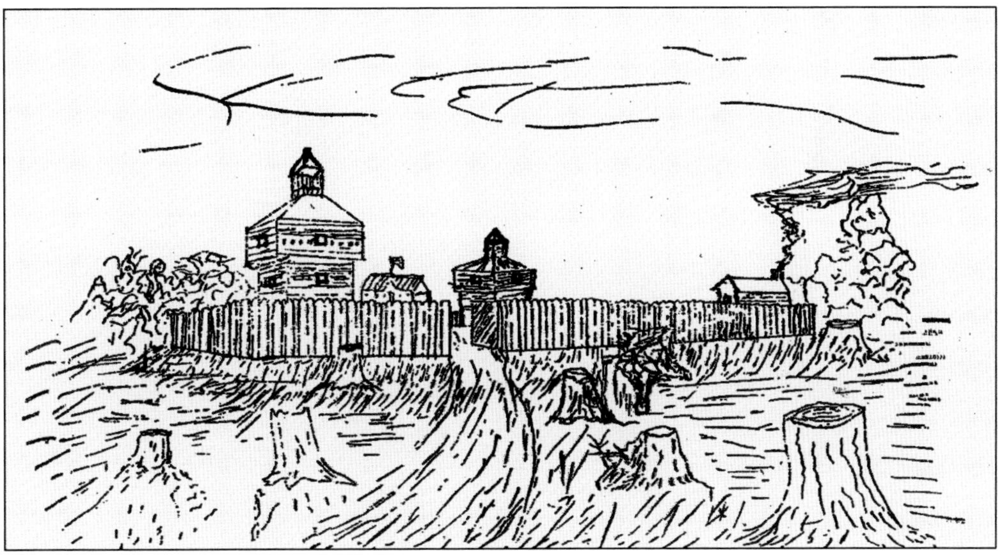

The small frontier fortification of Fort Mitchell, Alabama, was constructed in 1813. From 1821 to 1836, U.S. Indian Agent John Crowell headquartered there. By 1825, a second, larger fort housed U.S. artillery and infantry companies, garrisoned there to maintain peace with the Creek Nation. The fort was closed in 1837 after the army marched the remaining Creek Indians west of the Mississippi. Fort Mitchell was also known as the site of a number of duels. (Courtesy of T. Peddy.)

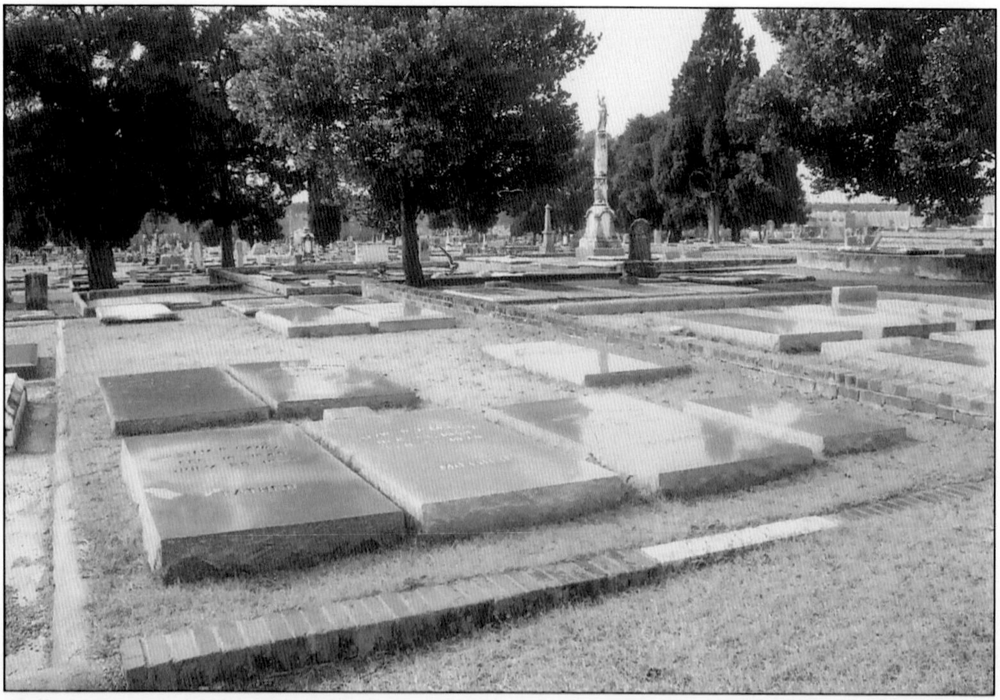

William Peters Langdon, his wife Lizzie Graves, and most of their nine children are buried here. William was born in the Broad Street home his grandparents Nathaniel and Diana Price Peters had built. After his marriage, William and his wife became the third generation to live in the house until their own family became too large for the dwelling. William Langdon spent his life as a shoe merchant.

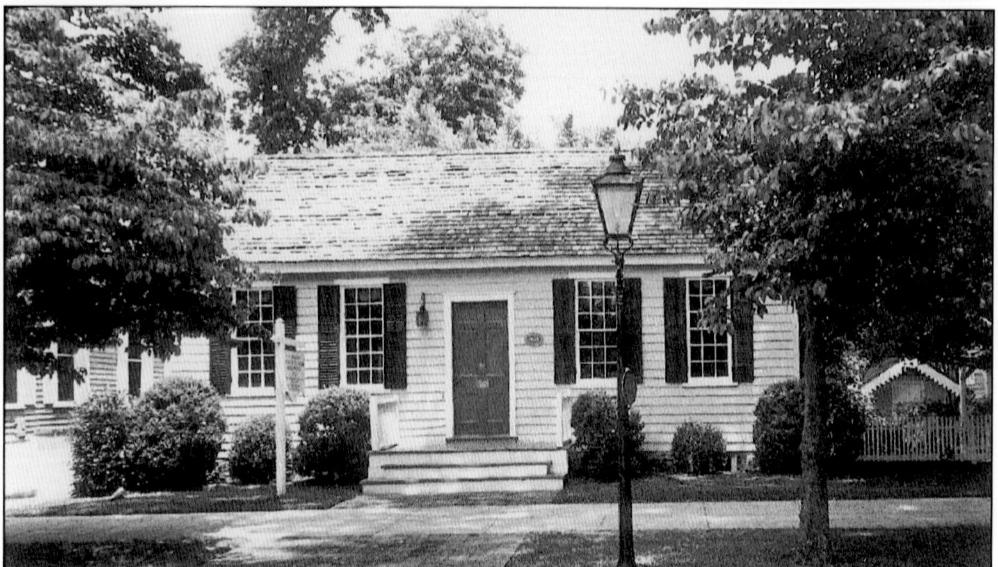

This is the Walker-Peters-Langdon House as it is today on Broadway. Family tradition states Nathaniel Peters built the house in 1828, the city's first year. Many of the original hand-blown windowpanes remain. The Walker-Peters-Langdon House is today the property of Historic Columbus Foundation. (Courtesy of Historic Columbus Foundation.)

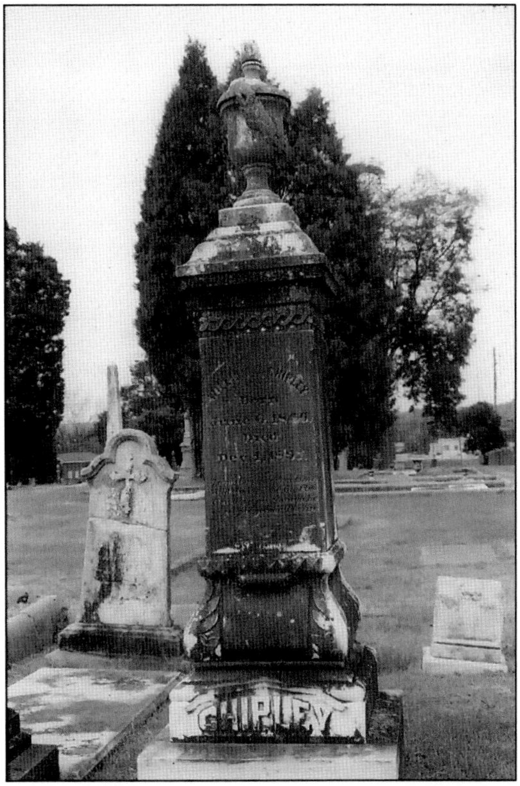

William Dudley Chipley was born in Columbus on June 6, 1840, and died while visiting Washington, D.C., on December 1, 1897. He was arrested as one of the "Columbus prisoners" charged with the 1868 murder of George Ashburn, a Republican scalawag. Chipley and the others were released after the Georgia legislature ratified the 14th Amendment to the U.S. Constitution and rejoined the Union. Later, he became a railroad promoter. Two railroad towns—Chipley, Florida, and Chipley, Georgia (now called Pine Mountain)—are named for him.

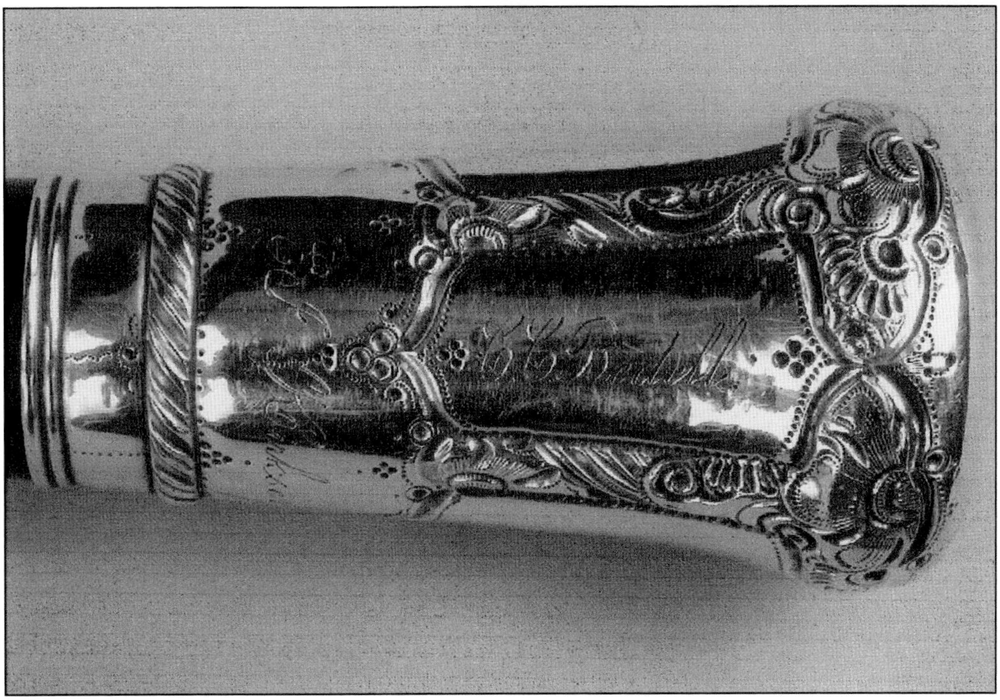

In appreciation for being acquitted, Chipley and the others charged presented this inscribed cane to Hon. James B. Beck. (Courtesy of Columbus Museum.)

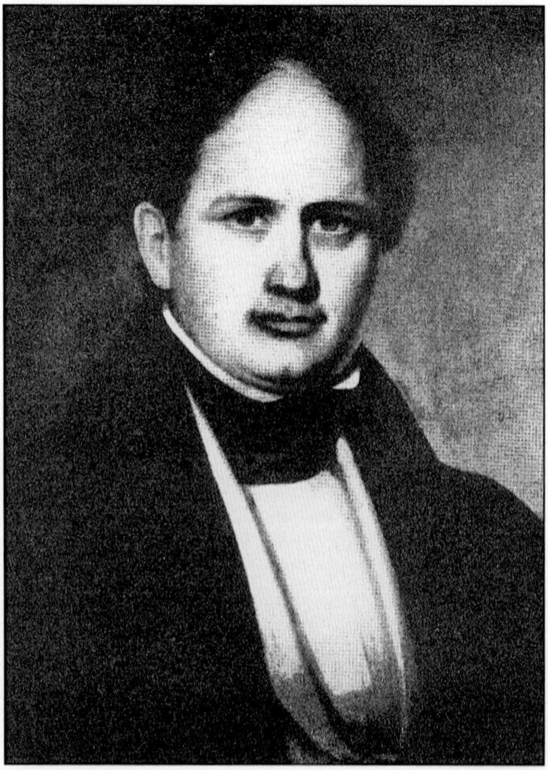

Daniel McDougald was one of Columbus's first citizens; he was one of the founders of Girard, Alabama, which became Phenix City. He was director of the Bank of Columbus in 1832, and in 1836, McDougald served as general of the Georgia militia forces that assembled in Columbus to protect the Georgia border from a Creek uprising. In 1838 he helped organize the Planters and Merchants Bank for the cotton trade, serving as its first president. (Courtesy of Columbus Office Supply.)

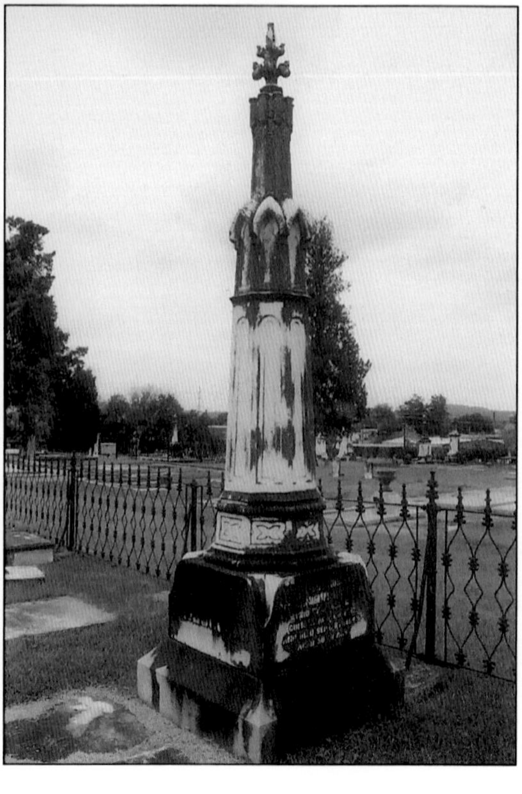

Gen. Daniel McDougald was born in North Carolina and died in 1849 in Columbus. He married Ann Elizabeth Alexander, who died in 1889 in Brooklyn, New York.

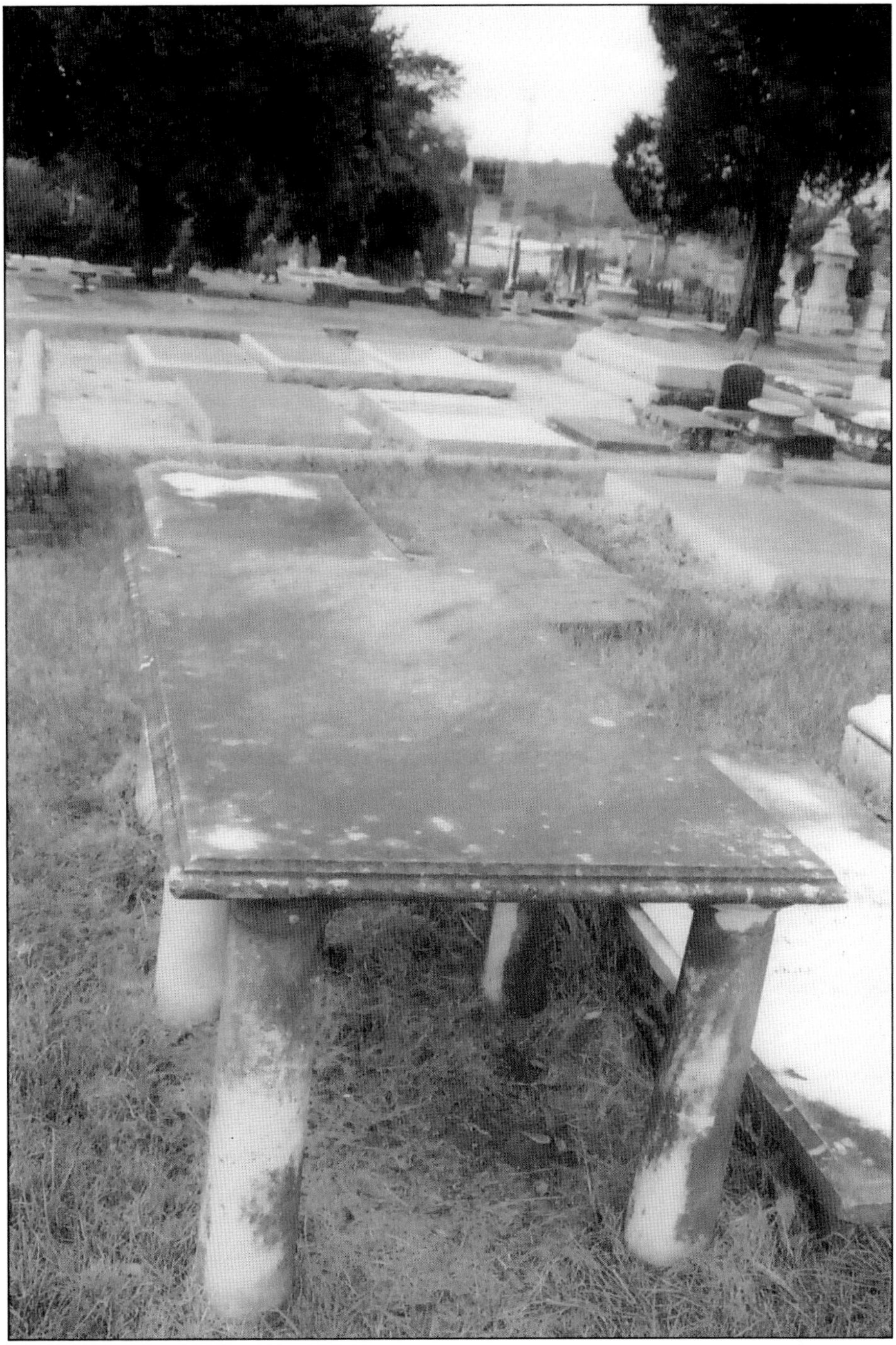

Samuel K. Hodges worked as a "warehouseman" in Columbus during the antebellum years, receiving cotton by steamboat. His ancillary businesses included auctioneering and running a "dray," a cart that moved merchandise for hire. Hodges was also a Methodist minister, being the presiding elder of the Columbus district of the Methodist Episcopal Church in 1838. He married prominent Columbusites Henry L. Benning and Mary Howard in 1839. Hodges's gravesite features a tabletop monument, one of many in the cemetery.

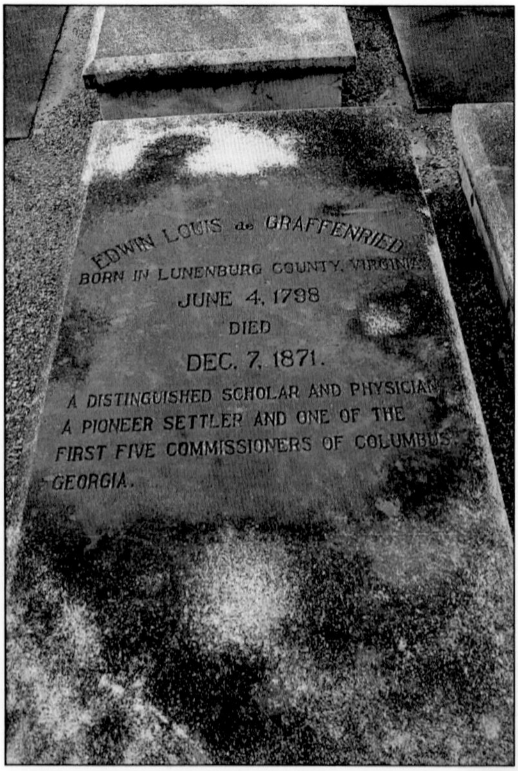

The marker for Edwin deGraffenried is similar to many marble box tombs in Linwood. Although discolored by pollution, it is still very legible after more than 125 years. This type of monument was constructed with a marble slab atop four six- or eight-inch high marble supports, making a box-like structure.

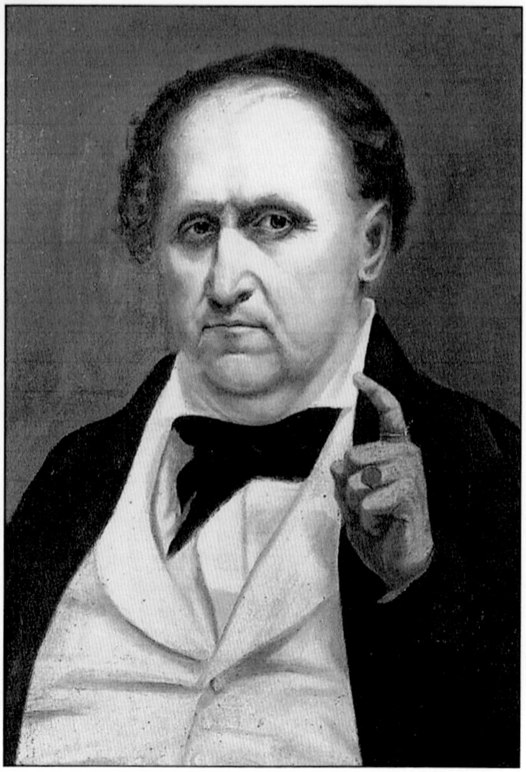

Edwin deGraffenried was one of five commissioners appointed by the governor of Georgia to survey the site at Coweta Falls on the Chattahoochee River for a new town to be called Columbus. It is believed he insisted on the downtown streets' wide expanses. He lived near the corner of Twelfth Street and First Avenue. One of the first doctors to settle here, he also established the Temperance Society and the first Episcopal church. (Courtesy of F. Clason Kyle.)

According to his headstone, Ulysses S. Lewis descended from Fielding Lewis, who married a sister of George Washington. Lewis was a lawyer in Columbus when the town was founded and the original lots were auctioned in July 1828. At the Fourth of July celebration that year, he read the Declaration of Independence. He was elected to serve as the first intendant, or mayor, of Columbus in January 1829, when the government was first organized.

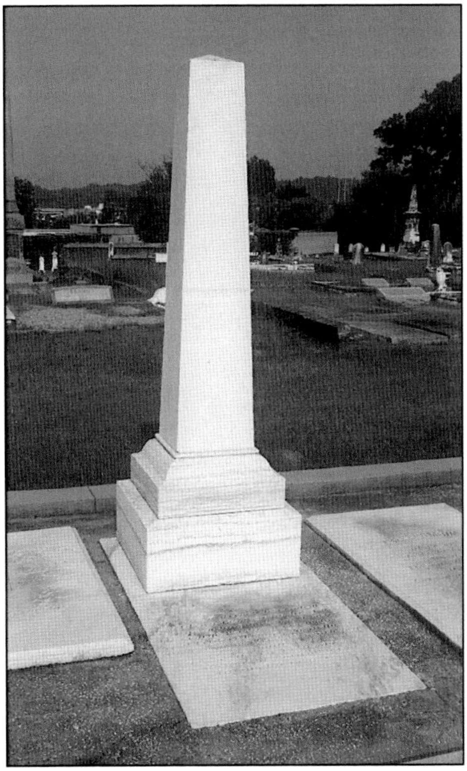

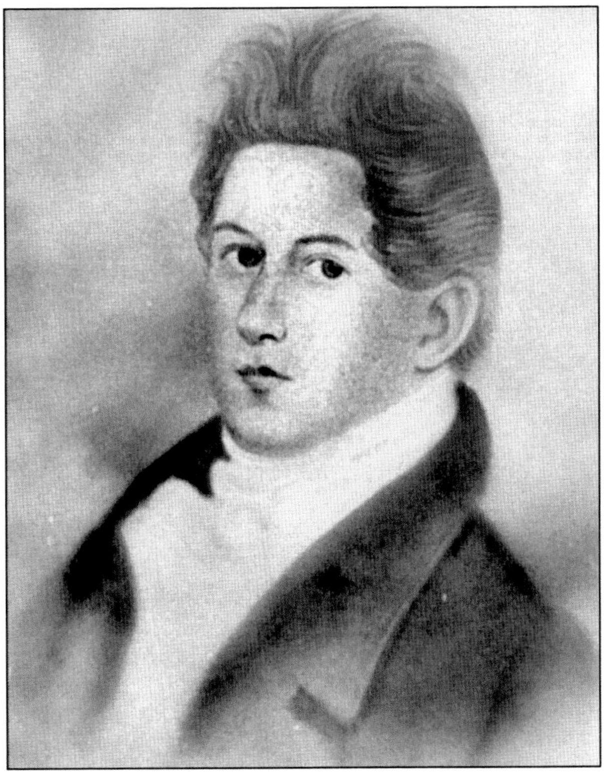

Ulysses Lewis was born in Jefferson County, Georgia, on February 5, 1799. and died in Russell County, Alabama, on August 8, 1856. He married Sara Abercrombie of Hancock County, Georgia. She died in 1876. (Courtesy of Columbus State University Archives.)

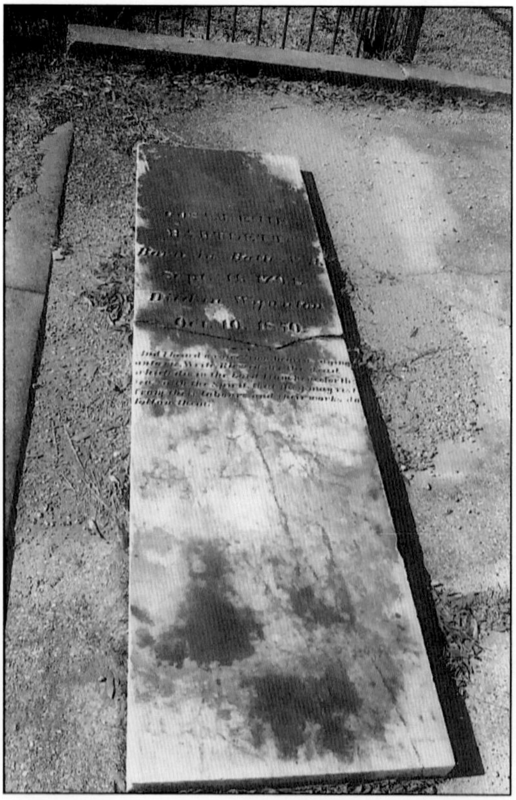

Cosam Emir Bartlett was the first editor of *The Democrat,* a weekly newspaper in Columbus. He was editor from 1830 to 1833, when he left Columbus to become the foremost editor of newspapers in territorial Florida. *The Democrat* flourished under other ownership until 1850, when it became *The Sun Sentinel.* Although he moved away for a time, Bartlett owned land in Wynnton, where he returned to live and died in 1850 at the age of 56.

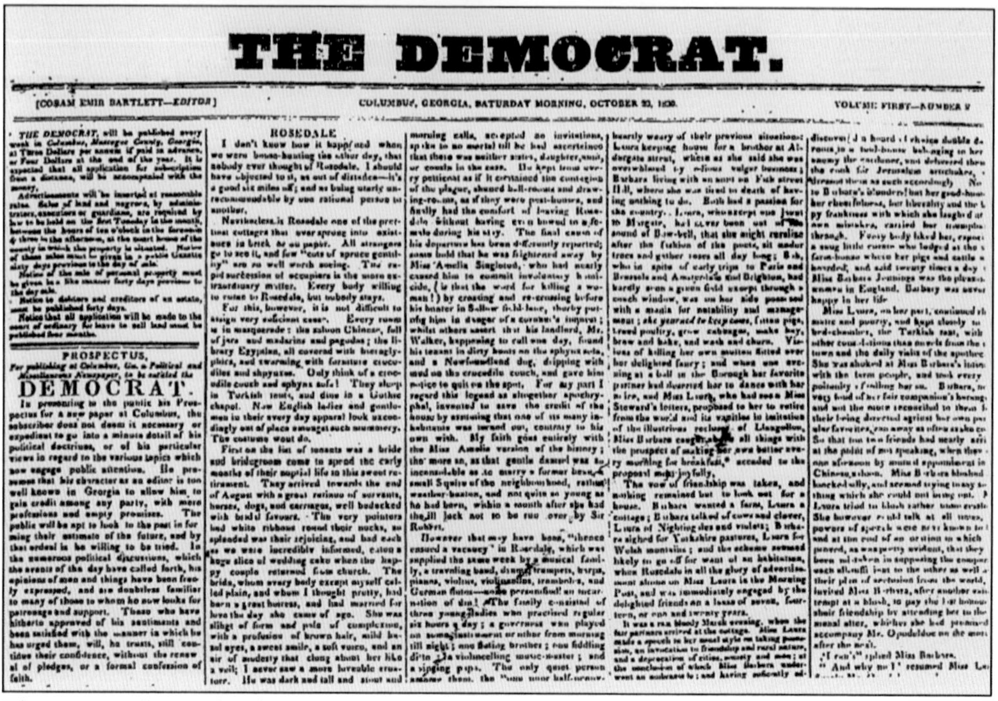

THE DEMOCRAT.

[COSAM EMIR BARTLETT—EDITOR] COLUMBUS, GEORGIA, SATURDAY MORNING, OCTOBER 23, 1830. VOLUME FIRST—NUMBER V

ROSEDALE.

PROSPECTUS,

DEMOCRAT.

This is an early masthead of the newspaper Bartlett edited.

Tabitha Jordan Lamar was the first wife of Mirabeau Lamar, who began the first newspaper published in Columbus. When Tabitha died in 1830, Lamar poured out his grief in poetry. Tabitha was first buried in a churchyard in Columbus but later was moved to Linwood, where this obelisk was erected on her grave.

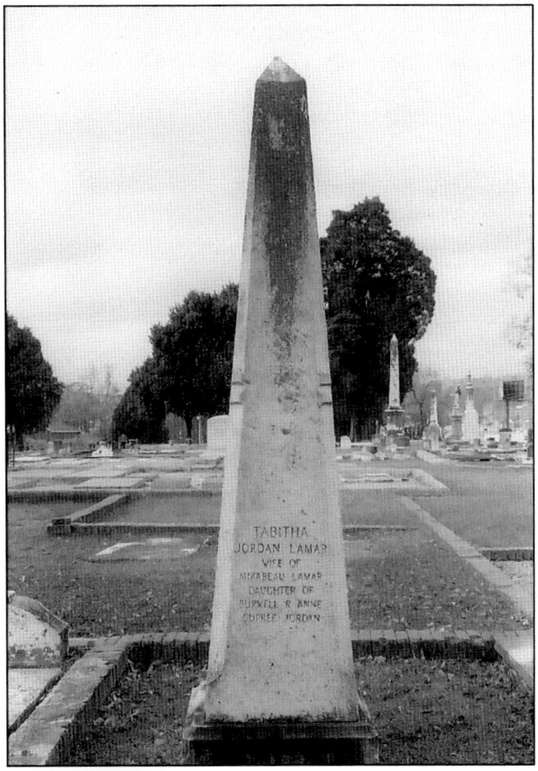

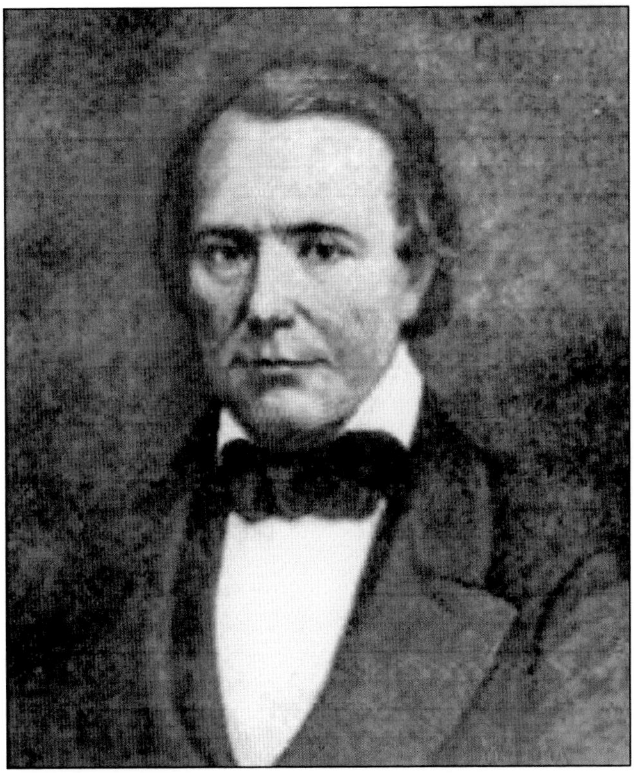

Soon after his wife's death, Mirabeau Lamar left Columbus and went west, where he became the second president of the Republic of Texas. (Courtesy of F. Clason Kyle.)

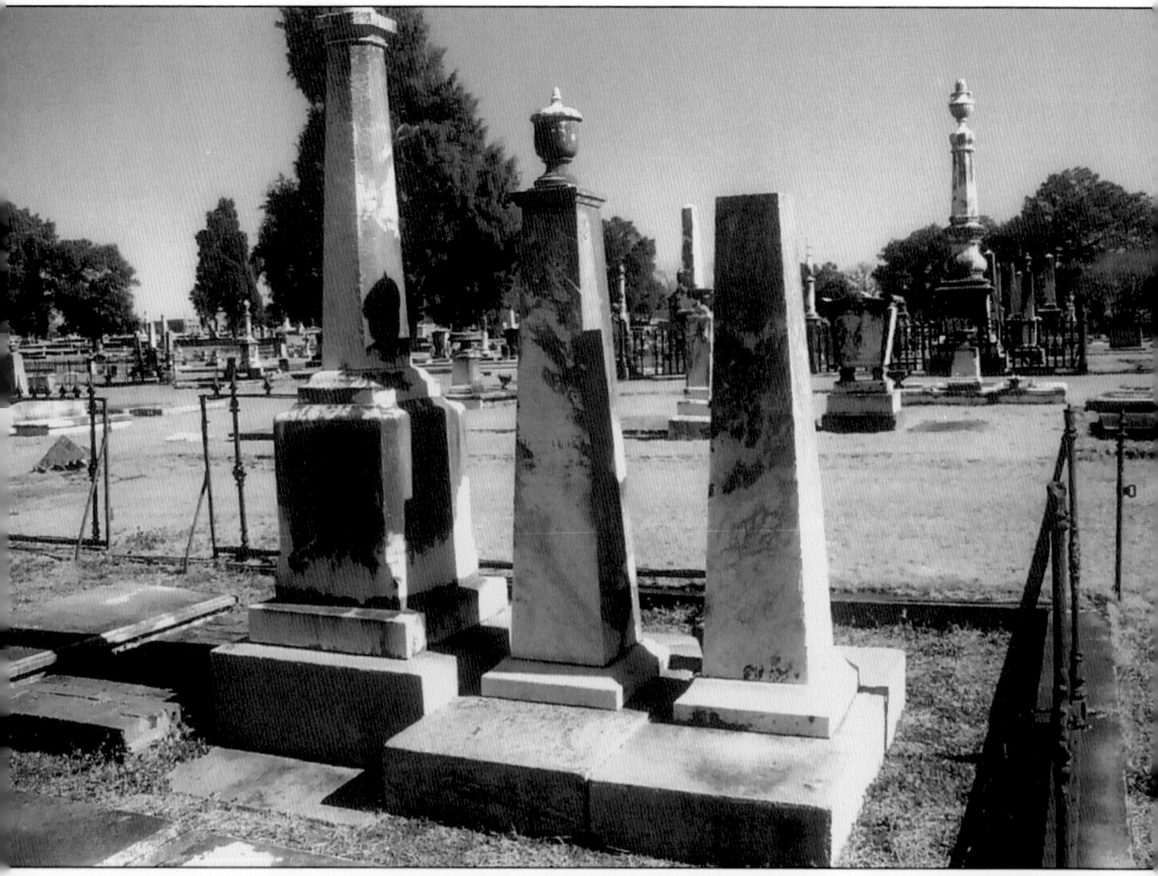

These two obelisks are a sampling of the many in the cemetery. At one time, both obelisks had urns. They mark the graves of Lock Weems and his wife Felixina. Weems was a planter and large landowner in Muscogee County, north of the city. He was known throughout the area for such civic contributions as serving as a trustee of the city asylum for the poor and of the Wynnton Male Academy. He was also associated with the Muscogee Railroad. Many of his descendants still live in Columbus.

Five

MILITARY STORIES

Although almost every American war is represented among the graves of Linwood, the majority of the soldiers fought with the Confederacy. Being far removed from the battlefronts, Columbus was able to develop its industry and agriculture to the point that it was second only to Richmond in supplying war materiel and foodstuffs. Columbus also became a hospital center, with wounded and ill soldiers sent here to convalesce. When a soldier died he was brought to the cemetery and buried in one of two sections that were set aside for the Confederate dead. Those two sections are a very important part of the history of the cemetery. There are many other graves in the cemetery that recognize Confederate service.

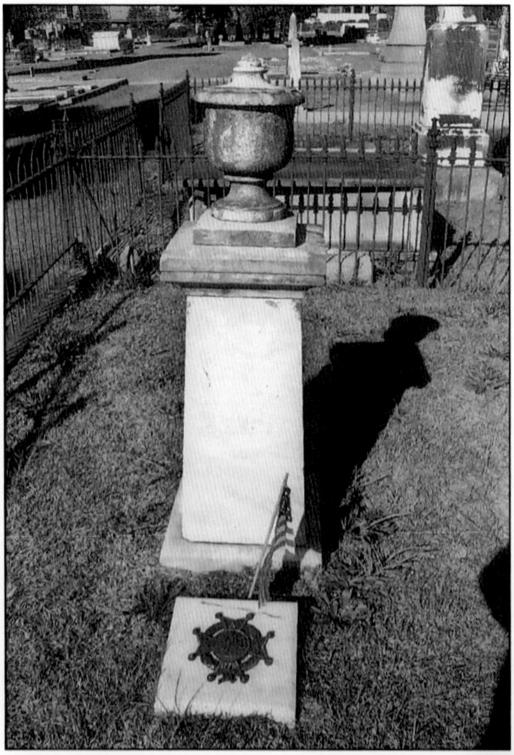

George Wells Foster served as a second lieutenant in Capt. John Morton's company of the Prince Edward County, Virginia militia, which fought against Gen. Charles Cornwallis during the Revolution. After the war Foster moved from Lunenburg County, Virginia, to Green County, Georgia. When his wife died in 1836, he moved to Columbus with his adult children. He was important enough at his death in 1847, at age 93, that the Muscogee County Superior Court adjourned for his funeral. They called him "our aged and worthy fellow citizen . . . few having lived so blameless a life and left so unblemished a reputation. . . ." Foster has many descendants living in Columbus today.

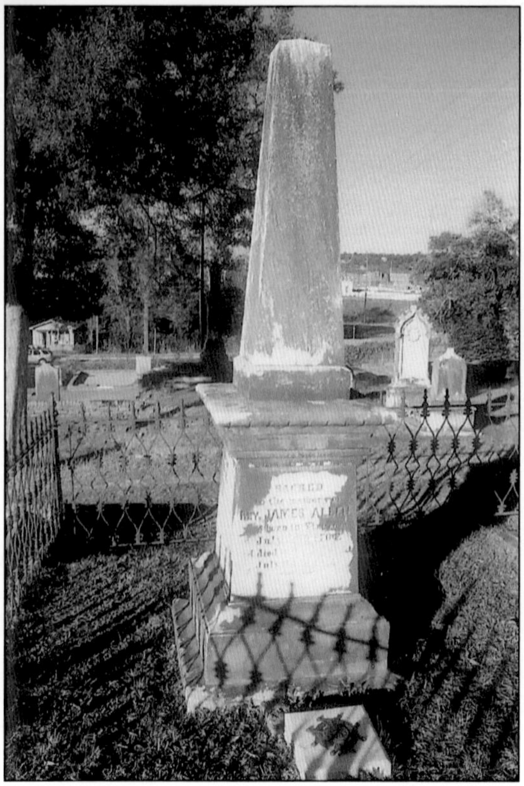

Rev. James Allen was born in Virginia. He took up arms at a very young age in the Continental service during the Revolution. Later, he lived in Wilkes, Warren, and Meriwether Counties in Georgia before settling in Russell County, Alabama. There he owned a large plantation with many slaves. He died at age 87. The last half of his life was devoted to the ministry and the practice of medicine without charge.

This house, called the Lion House, was purchased by James Allen's widow as her Columbus residence. The house was built in the 1840s and has recently been restored. (Courtesy of Columbus State University Archives.)

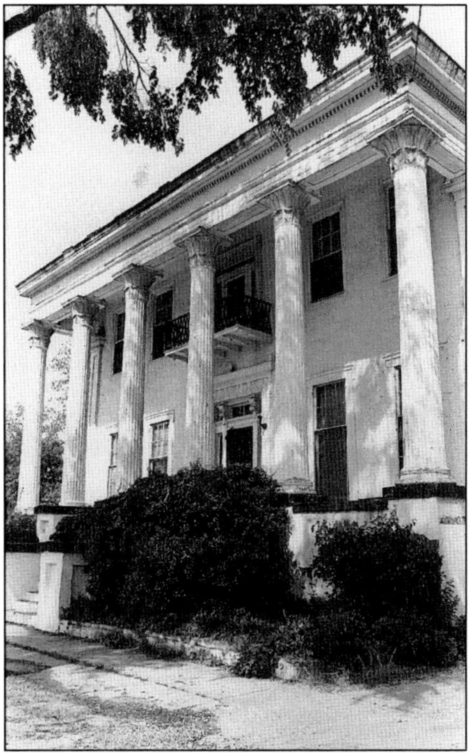

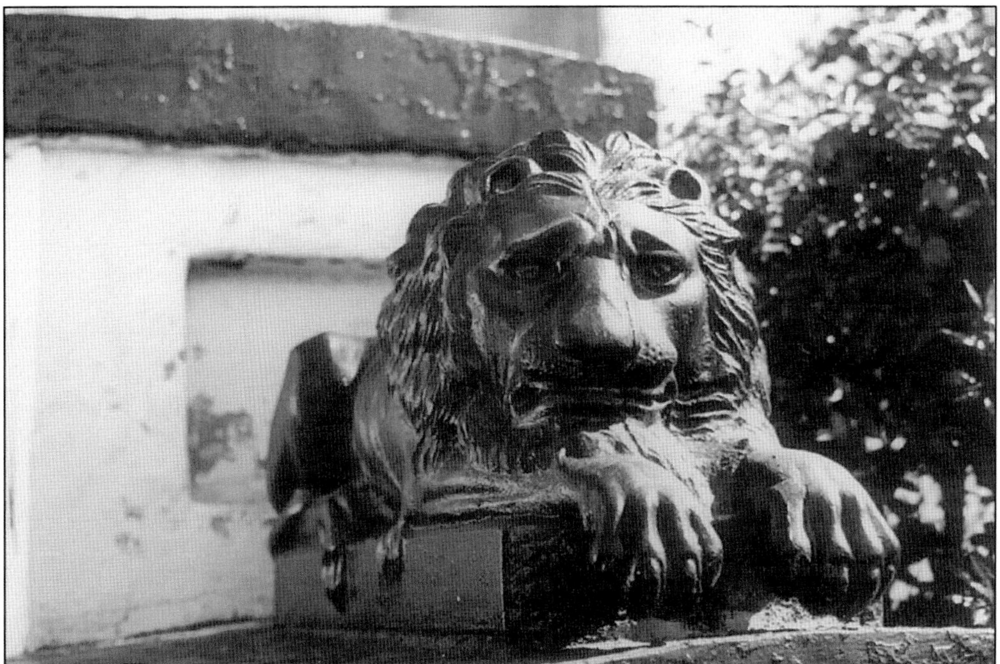

This lion statue is one of the two that give the house its name. The lions rest on either side of the steps leading to the front entrance of the house. (Courtesy of Columbus State University Archives.)

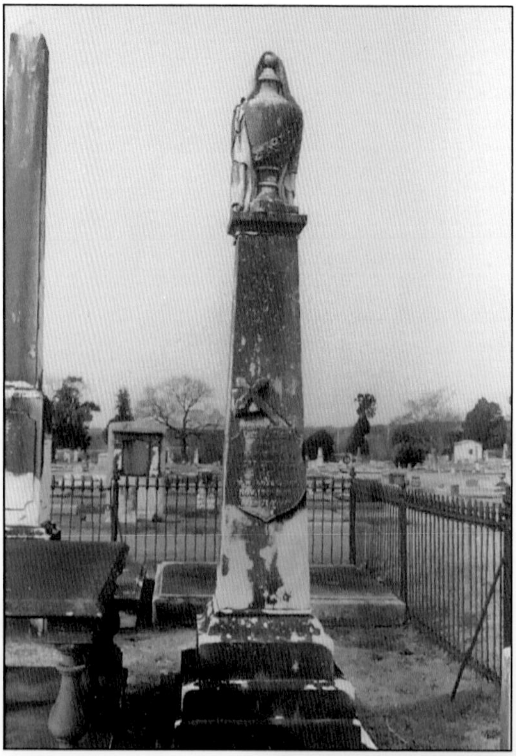

Maj. Thomas Manduit Nelson, grandson of Thomas Nelson, the governor of Virginia, served with the 10th, 18th, and 30th Infantry Regiments in the War of 1812. Because of wounds he received, he resigned his commission in 1815. He then became a representative in the 14th and 15th Congresses from 1816 to 1819. By 1838, he had moved to Columbus with his son and three daughters; they lived in Wynnton. Nelson was active in Trinity Episcopal Church for 20 years.

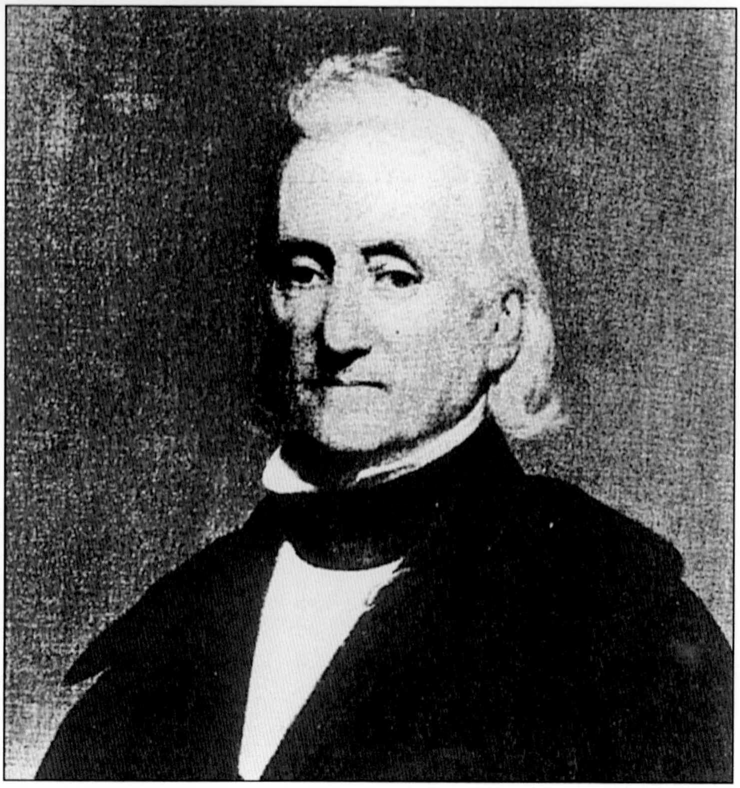

Major Nelson died in Wynnton in 1853 at 71 years of age. His descendants continue to live in Columbus today. (Courtesy of Eleanor Woolfolk Roberts.)

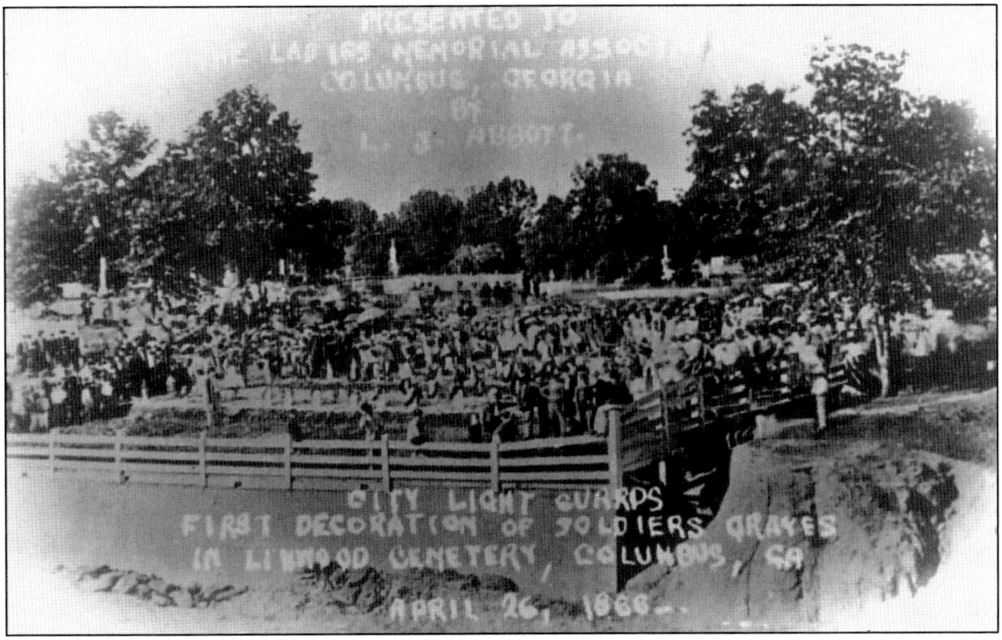

On April 26, 1866, Columbus held what may have been the very first Confederate Memorial Day services. This photo shows one of two sections that were set aside for the burial of Confederate soldiers who died in Columbus hospitals during the Civil War. (Courtesy of Columbus State University Archives.)

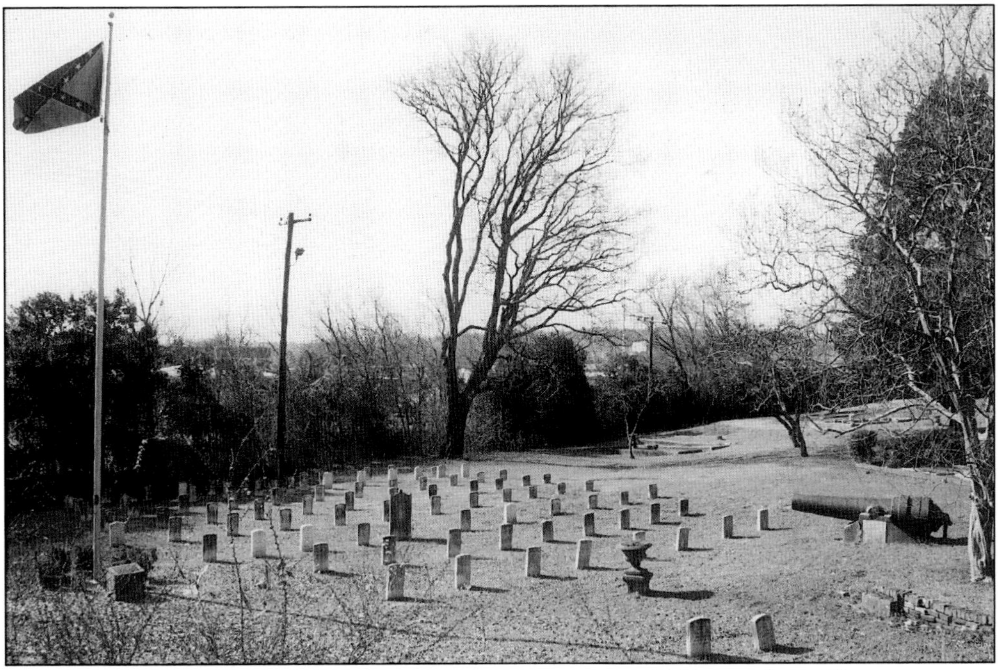

This photo shows the same Confederate section as it appeared 138 years later. The cannon was returned from the wreck of the ironclad vessel CSS *Jackson*, which the Confederates burned when Wilson's raiders came through Columbus on Easter Sunday 1865. The Ladies Memorial Association directed that it be placed in the cemetery. (Photograph by Greg Rodriguez.)

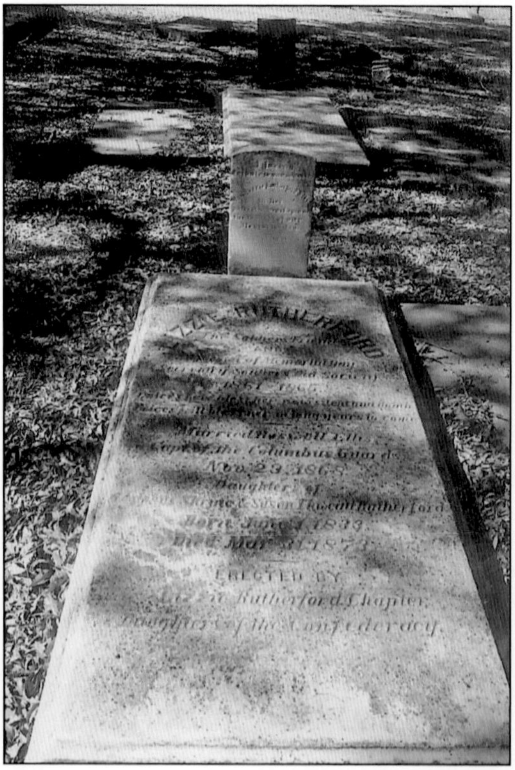

Lizzie Rutherford was the originator of Confederate Memorial Day. Her marker, placed by the Lizzie Rutherford Chapter No. 60, United Daughters of the Confederacy, reads: "A loving tribute to our co-worker, Mrs. Lizzie Rutherford Ellis. In her patriotic heart sprang the thought of our Memorial Day."

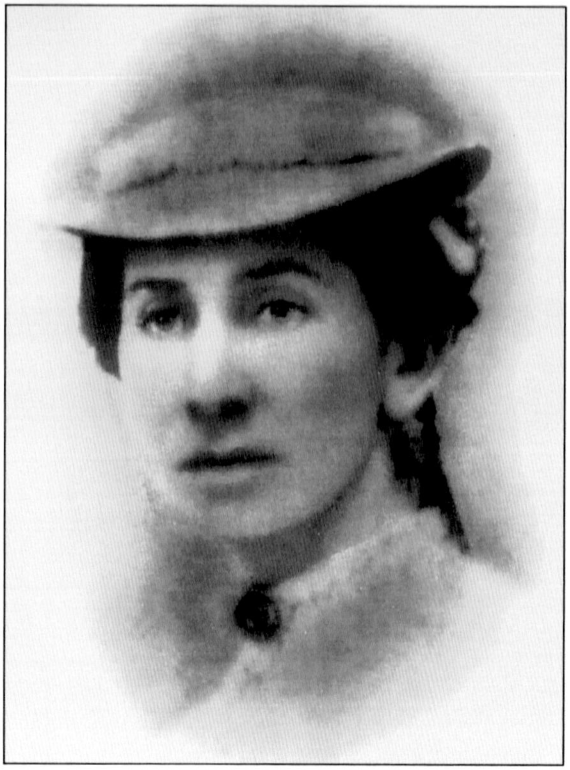

Lizzie Rutherford Ellis died in 1873. Her marker was placed by the members of the United Daughters of the Confederacy chapter named for her. (Courtesy of the Lizzie Rutherford Chapter No. 60, United Daughters of the Confederacy.)

Gen. Henry Lewis Benning, commander of the 17th Georgia Confederate Infantry Brigade, distinguished himself at the Battle of Antietam. A member of the Georgia Supreme Court and the state legislature, Benning was a strong advocate of secession. Fort Benning, on the outskirts of Columbus, is named for him. His marker is inscribed "This was a man." (Courtesy of F. Clason Kyle.)

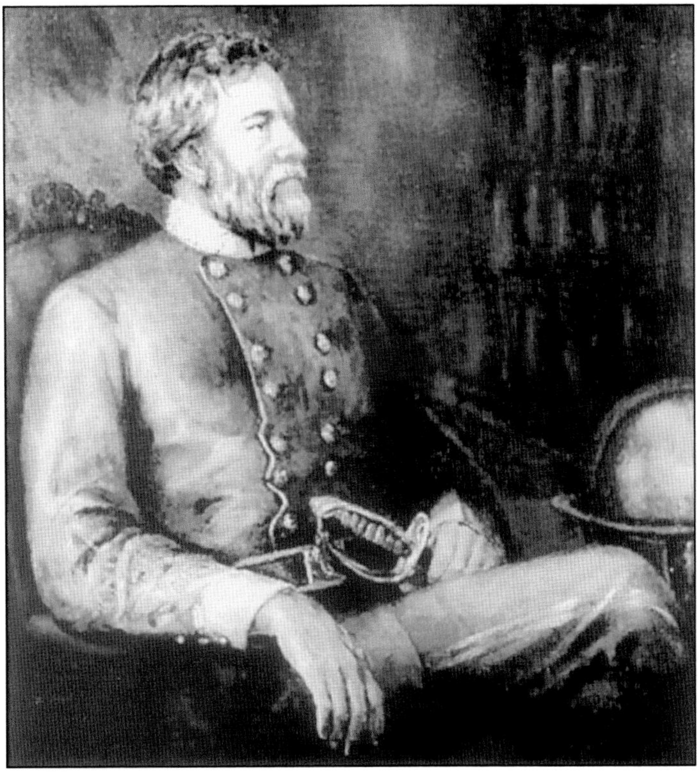

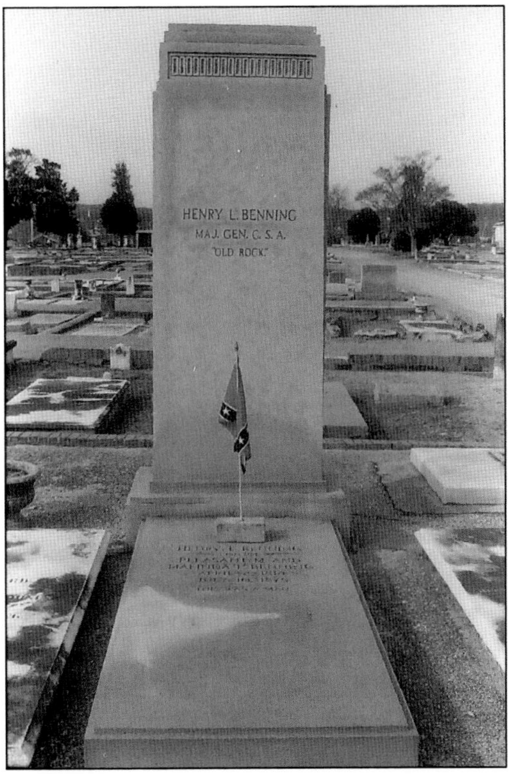

The monument of Gen. Henry Benning draws visitors from all parts of the country who have an interest in Civil War history.

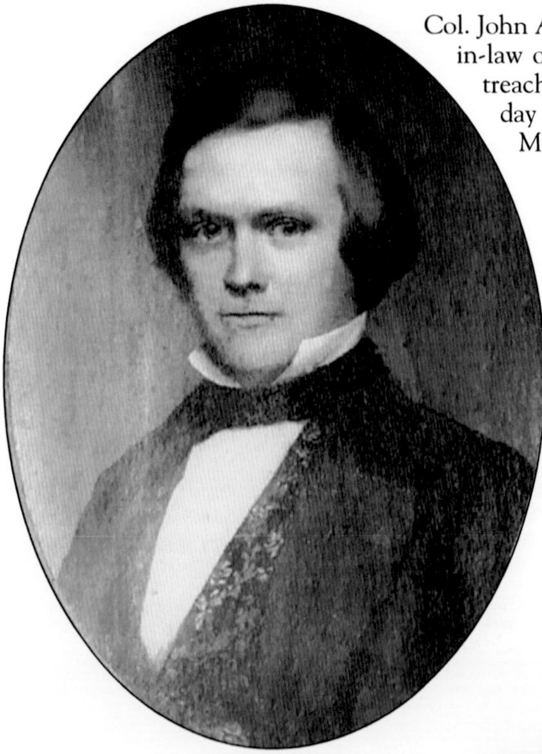

Col. John A. Jones, son of Seaborn Jones and brother-in-law of Gen. Henry Benning, was killed on the treacherous ground of Devil's Den on the second day of the Battle of Gettysburg. (Courtesy of Mimi Pease Childs.)

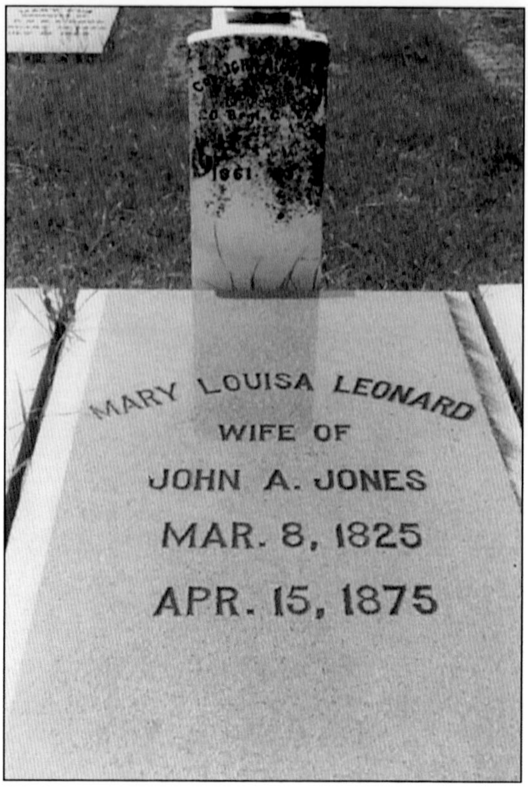

After the war, Colonel Jones's son Leonard traveled to Pennsylvania to bring his father's remains home for burial at Linwood Cemetery. The ship carrying the sacred remains was caught in a ferocious storm. Leonard Jones was rescued but his father's body was lost at sea. A memorial stone was placed at the head of the colonel's wife's tombstone.

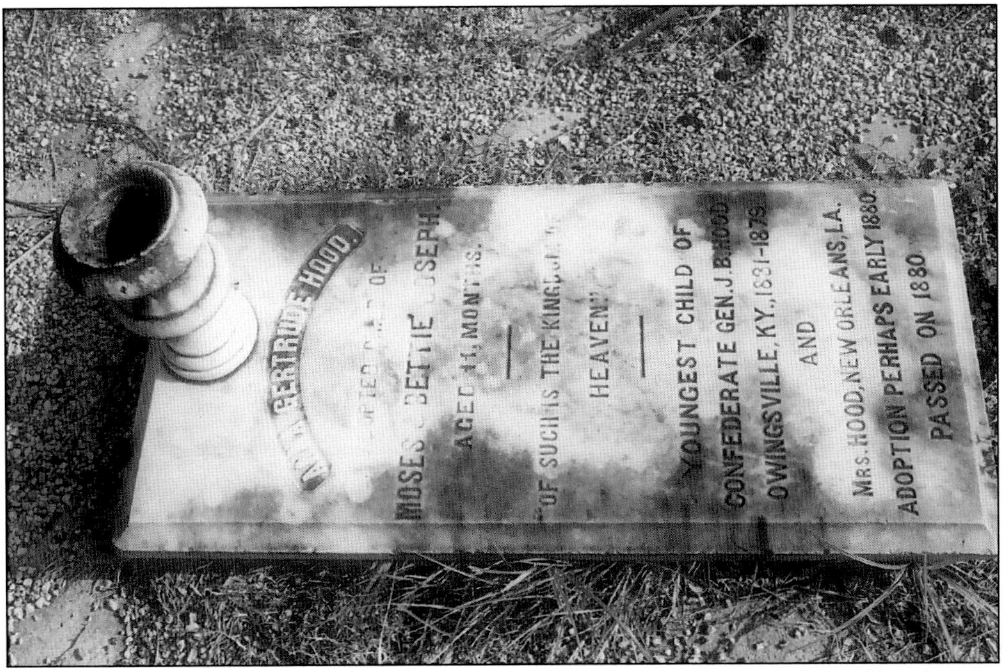

Anna Gertrude Hood was the youngest daughter of Confederate Gen. John Bell and Anna Hennan Hood. In 1879, Anna Gertrude's parents died of yellow fever in New Orleans, leaving 10 surviving children. Anna, only seven months old, was ill. Moses and Betty Howard Joseph of Columbus adopted her. In trying to restore her fragile health, the Josephs took her to Warm Springs, Georgia. She died at the age of 11 months and is buried in Linwood Cemetery.

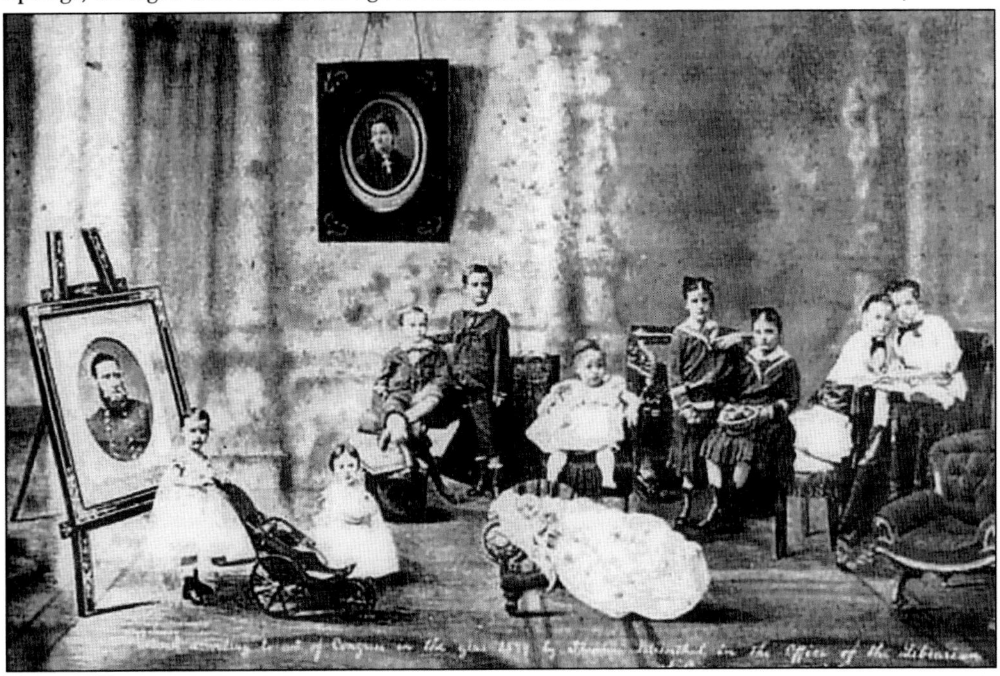

This photograph showing the orphaned Hood children was used by veterans of Hood's Brigade in trying to find homes for the children.

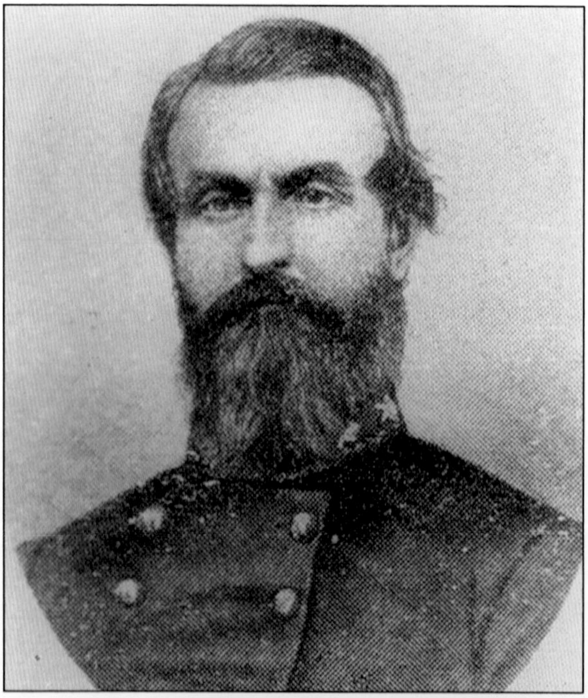

Paul J. Semmes began his military career as captain of the Columbus Guards in 1854. Six years later, he led his men as honor guard for Confederate President Jefferson Davis's inauguration. Semmes later became a brigadier general and was mortally wounded on the second day at the Battle of Gettysburg in 1863 as he led his men through the wheat field. (Courtesy of John D. Kennedy.)

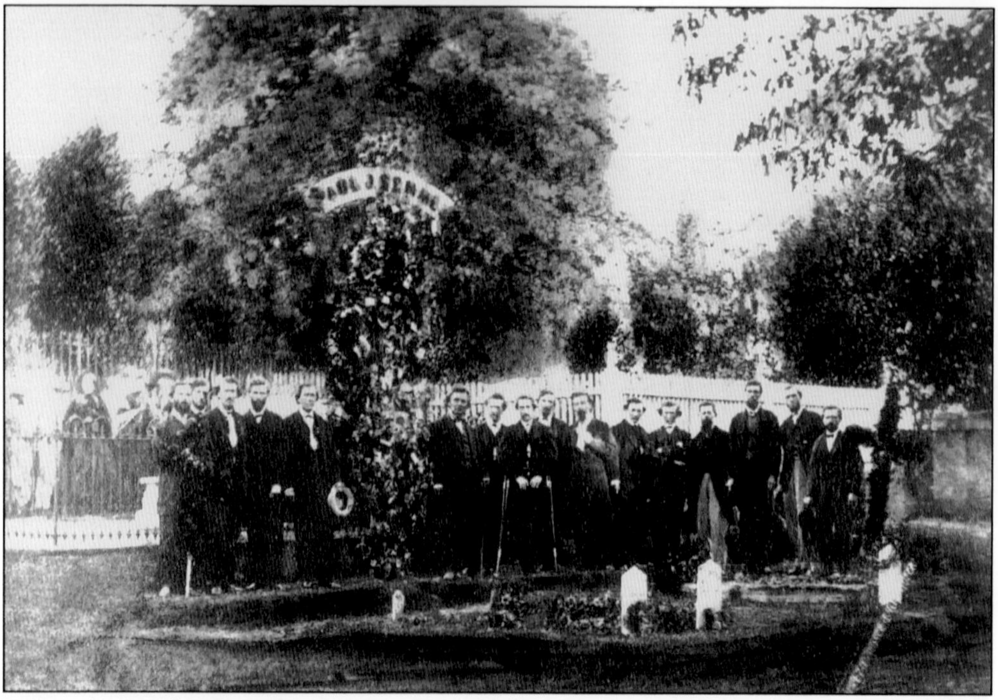

Before the Civil War, Paul Semmes was a lawyer and businessman in Columbus. He was president of the Coweta Falls Textile Mill. After he died, the Columbus City Council made a special appropriation of money to have General Semmes's body brought back home to be buried in Linwood Cemetery. He is interred in the William S. Shepherd lot. (Courtesy of Columbus State University Archives.)

Peyton H. Colquitt, the son of Walter T. Colquitt and brother of Gen. Alfred Holt Colquitt, led the Columbus City Light Guards, known as the Muscogee Volunteers, to Virginia as a captain when the Civil War began. He took with him one of the first swords made by renowned Columbus sword maker Louis Haiman. Colquitt soon became a colonel in the 46th Georgia Regiment. Before the war, Colquitt had made a name for himself in Columbus legal and political circles. He married "the sweetheart of Columbus," Julia Hurt, daughter of Joel Early Hurt of Dinglewood, and she rode off to Virginia with him. (Courtesy of F. Clason Kyle.)

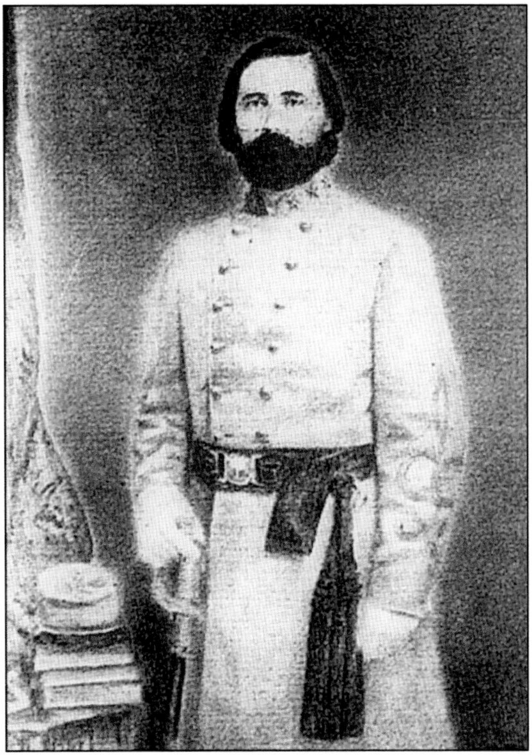

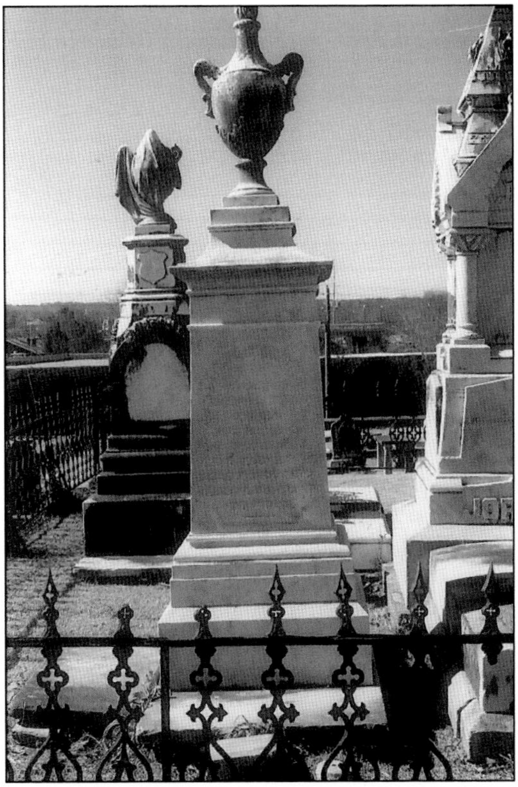

Peyton Colquitt lost his life on September 20, 1863, at Chickamauga, leaving his young bride a widow. He is buried beside her in the Hurt lot.

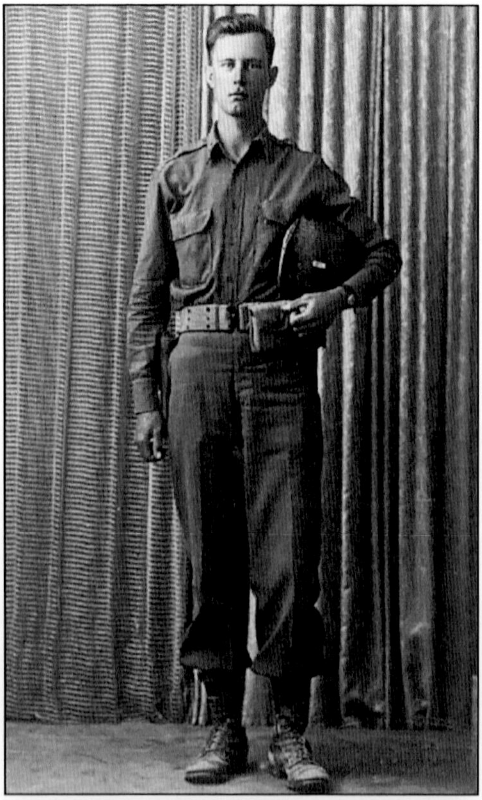

Dan Joseph Morton, son of Fannie and William Gilliam Morton and brother of Annie Morton Morton and Louise Morton Bowers Williams, married Bette Wright before World War II. A graduate of VMI, Captain Morton served as captain of Combat Command A, 2nd Armored Division. Previously, he was an aide to Brig. Gen. Hugh Gaffey, who was on the staff of Maj. Gen. George Patton.

(below, left) Morton was killed in action on July 28, 1944, at Ville Baudon, France, and was buried at the U.S. cemetery in St. Mere Eglise and later removed to St. Laurent, France.

(below, right) In Linwood he is remembered with this memorial stone. (Pictures on this page courtesy of Mr. and Mrs. Joe [Smokey] Bowers. Photograph in France taken by Mrs. Richard Y. Bradley.)

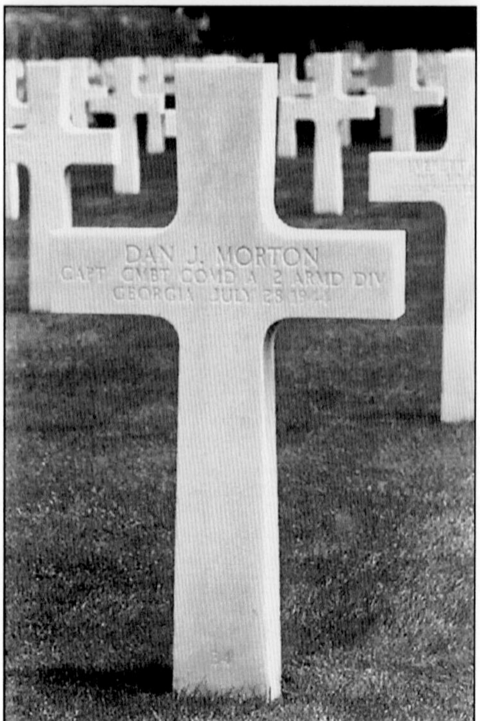

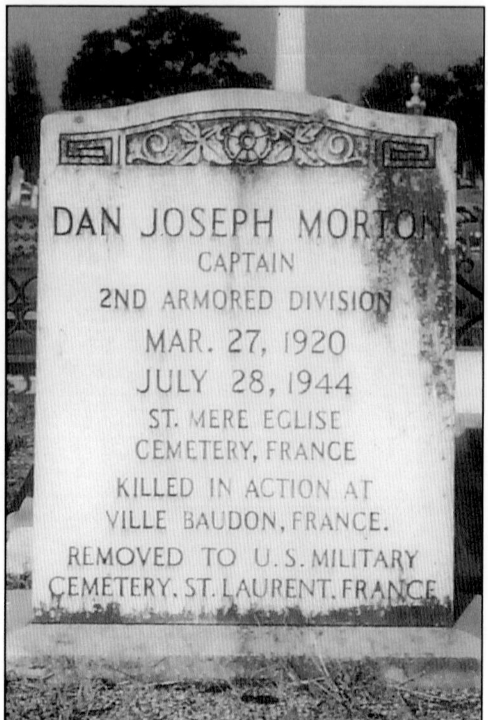

Six

A Bit of History

In a small frontier town that rapidly grew into a thriving industrial city, several residents changed the course of local and even world history. From librarians to suffragettes, from railroad promoters to boat builders, from ice cream makers to soft drink manufacturers, each of these people made their mark on the history of our town and our culture. Sprawling family lots, grand carved monuments, and even humble gravestones memorialize these citizens and their lasting contributions to the civic, economic, and spiritual life of the community.

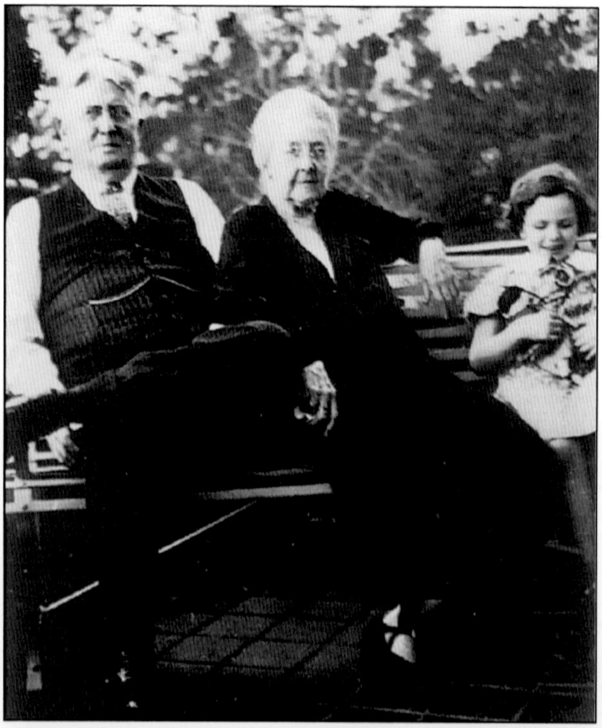

William Clark Bradley arrived in Columbus as a 19-year-old cotton factor. He quickly established himself as an entrepreneur and expanded his business interests to include river navigation, wholesale groceries, fertilizer and textile manufacture, banking, and iron works. In 1919, Bradley and Ernest Woodruff organized a consortium that purchased the Coca-Cola Company. Bradley served as Coca-Cola's chairman from that date until his death in 1947. Pictured are Mr. and Mrs. W.C. Bradley and their granddaughter Betty Turner. (Courtesy of Betty Turner Corn.)

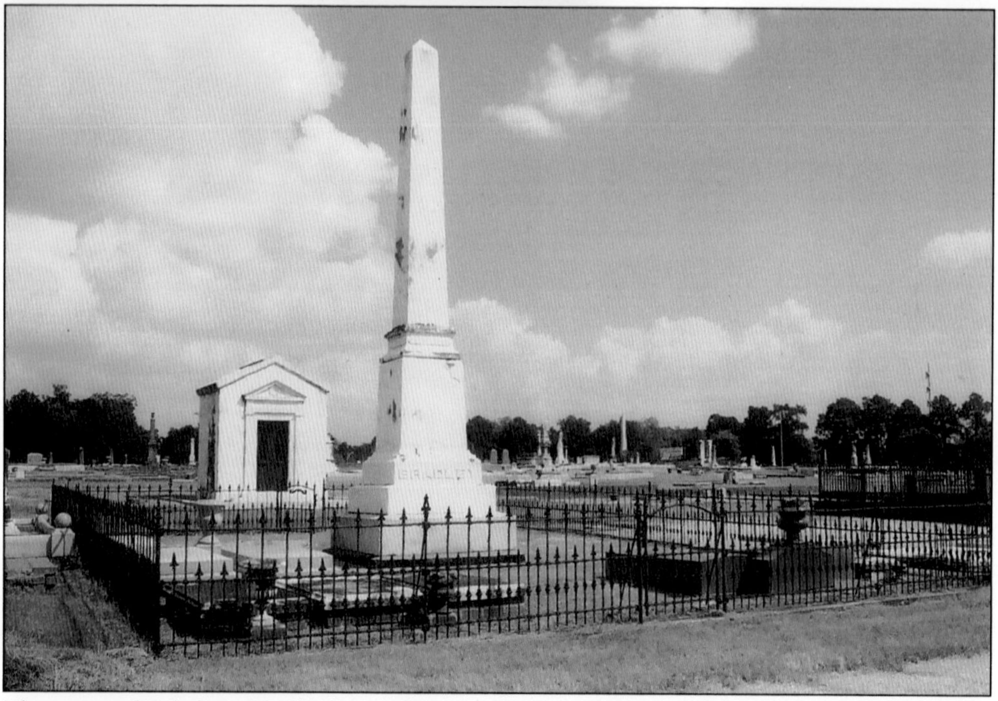

The immaculately kept Bradley lot is a lasting tribute to William Clark and Sarah Hall Bradley. Sarah, daughter of Henry Thomas and Elizabeth Howard Hall, married W.C. Bradley in 1887. Their devoted family life and their charitable endeavors in the religious, civic, educational, and cultural arenas continue to inspire their descendants and benefit all of Columbus.

Henry T. Hall, born in Boston in 1817, came to Columbus in the late 1830s. Both his warehouse and his steamboat were named for Lowell, Massachusetts, the textile center near his birthplace. The *Lowell*, the first steamboat built specifically for the Chattahoochee waters, arrived in Columbus from Ohio via the Ohio and Mississippi Rivers and the Gulf of Mexico in 1839. Hall's daughter Sarah married W.C. Bradley, who kept the steamboats running along the Chattahoochee into the next century. (Courtesy of Minnie Scarbrough Cappel.)

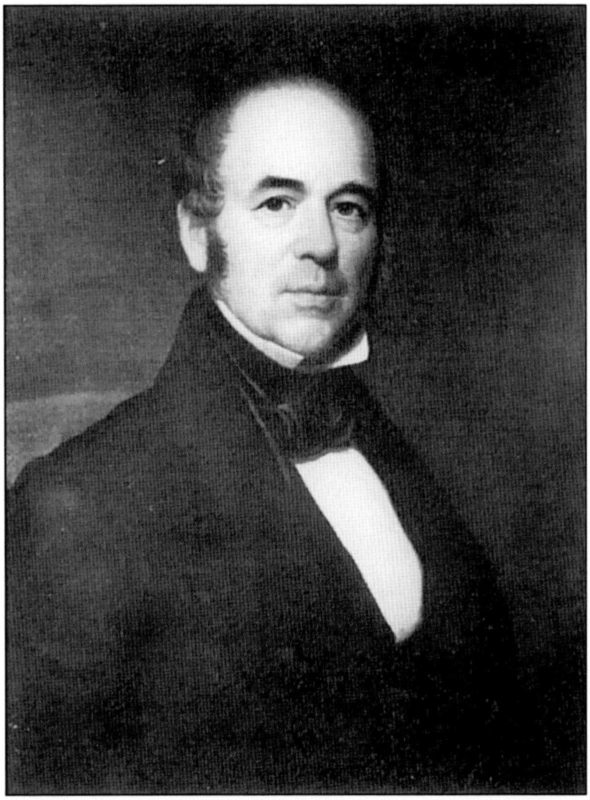

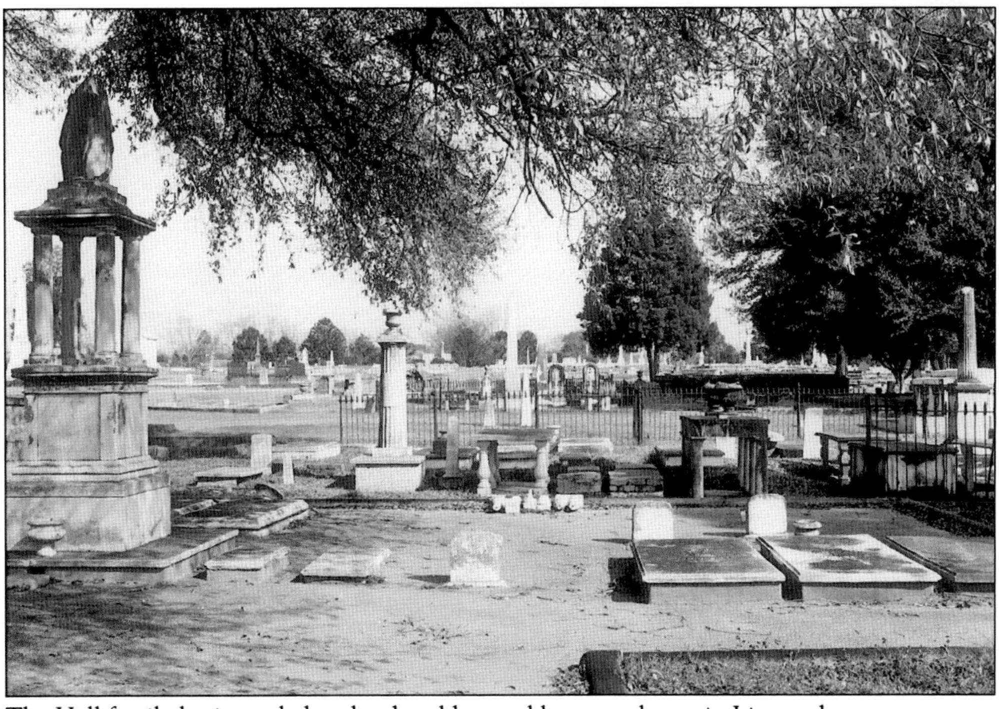

The Hall family lot is nestled under the oldest and largest oak tree in Linwood.

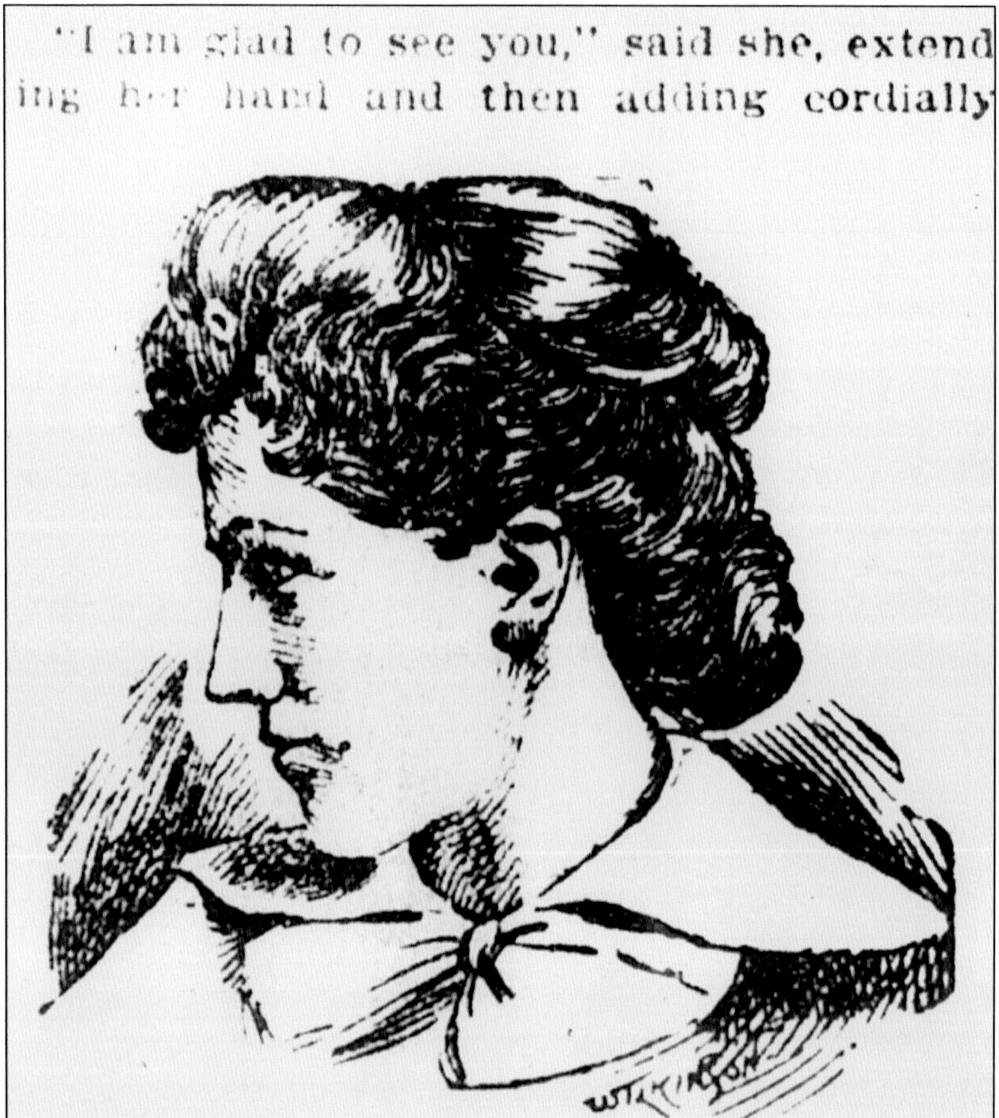

Augusta Howard founded the Woman's Suffrage Association in Georgia, which met in Columbus for four years. It was affiliated with the American Woman Suffrage Association. When in Washington, Augusta spoke before Congress. She persuaded Susan B. Anthony to bring the National Suffragette Convention to Atlanta in 1895, after which Anthony paid a three-day visit to Columbus. Before women received the right to vote in 1920, two suffrage organizations in Georgia joined to form the Woman's League, which later became the League of Women Voters. (Courtesy of Columbus State University Archives.)

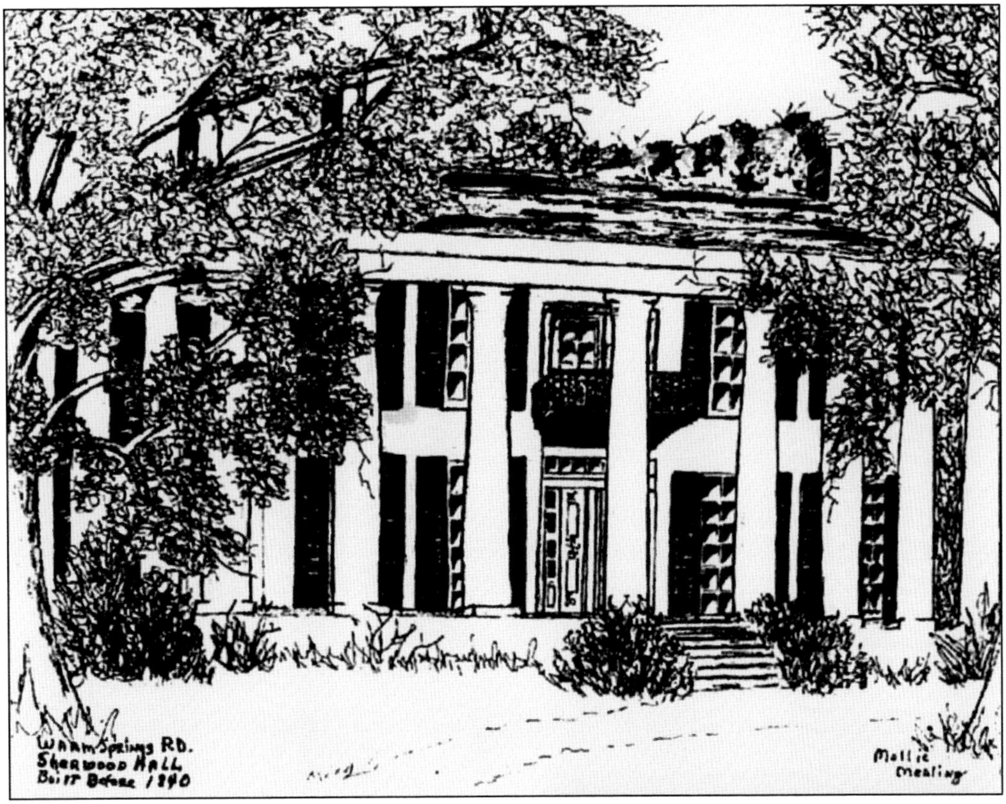

The home where Augusta Howard lived was named Sherwood Hall. Of Greek Revival architecture, it was a showplace because of its magnificent scale and furnishings. (Courtesy of Mollie Mealing.)

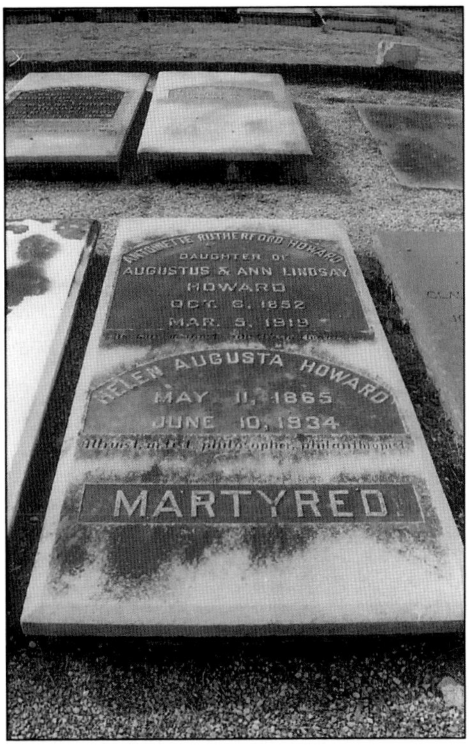

The marker of Augusta Howard reads "Martyred." Her push for women's right to vote was considered radical at the time.

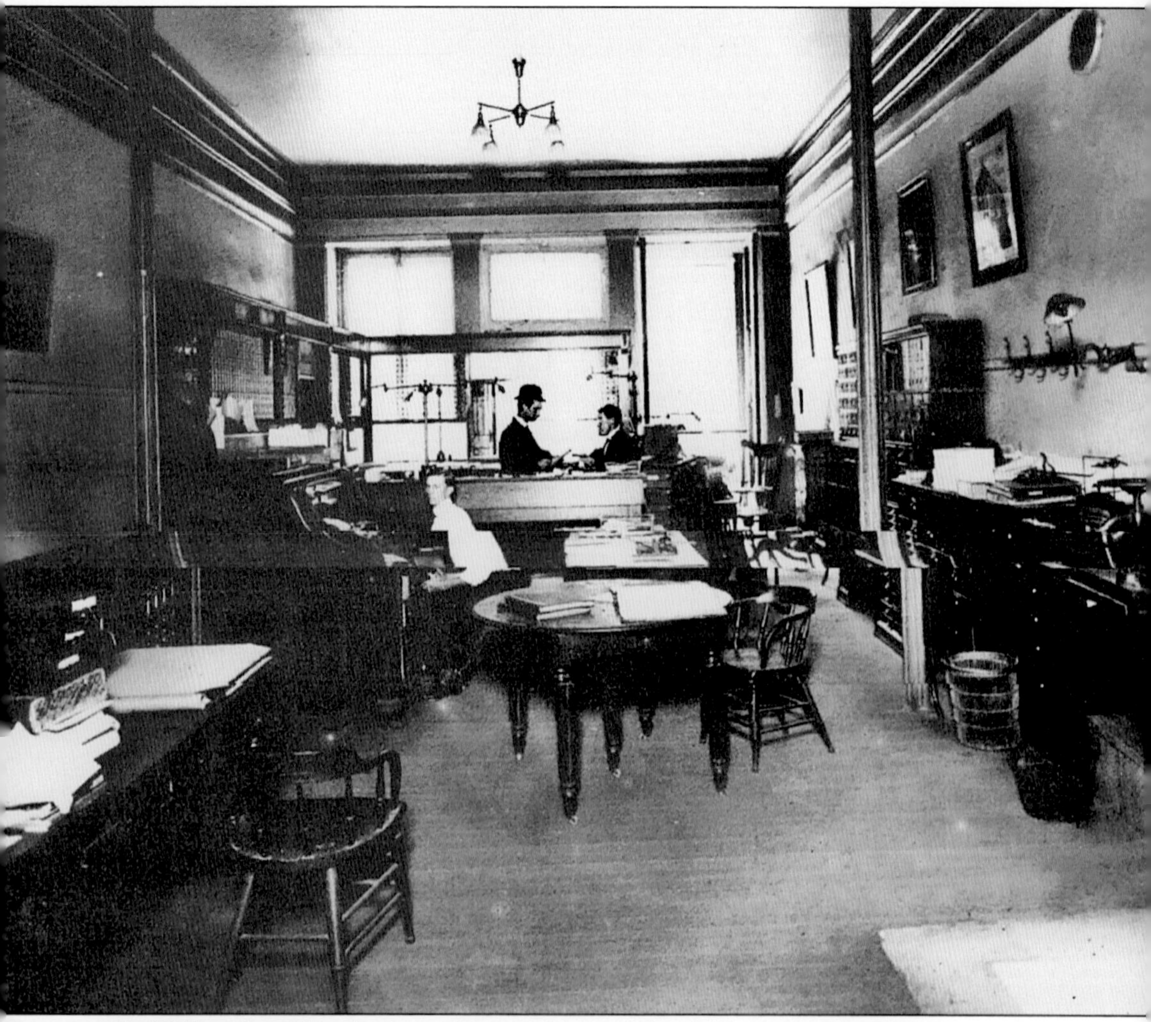

The Willcox-Lumpkin Agency is known as one of the oldest insurance companies in Georgia and continues in business today. Pictured from left to right are William C. Pease Jr., Frank G. Lumpkin, and E.K. Cargill. (Courtesy of F. Clason Kyle.)

In the early 20th century, Frank Grieve Lumpkin was one of the strongest advocates for paving roads, participating with numerous road-building associations to achieve that goal. He raised the money to pave the first roads to Warm Springs and Buena Vista. When he arrived in Columbus, Frank joined the insurance company founded by his grandfather D.F. Willcox in 1848. (Courtesy of Nancy Telfair.)

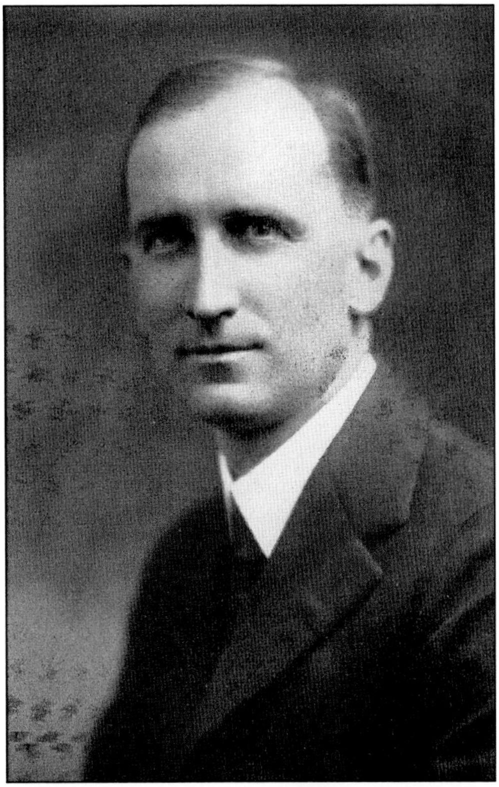

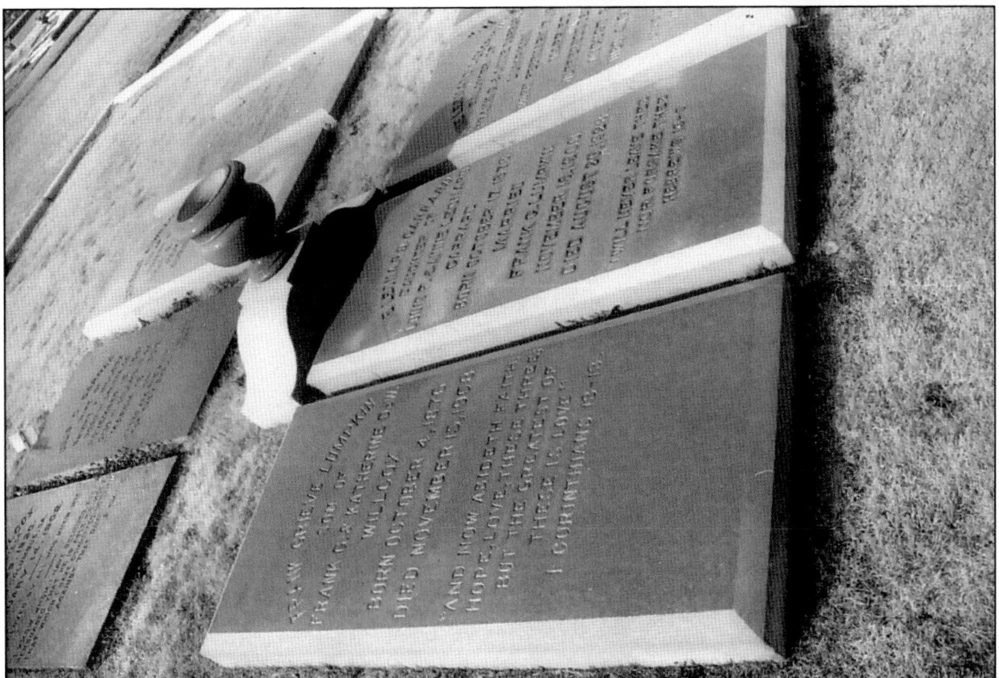

Frank Grieve Lumpkin and Annie Leonard Garrard Lumpkin are buried in the Willcox-Lumpkin family lot.

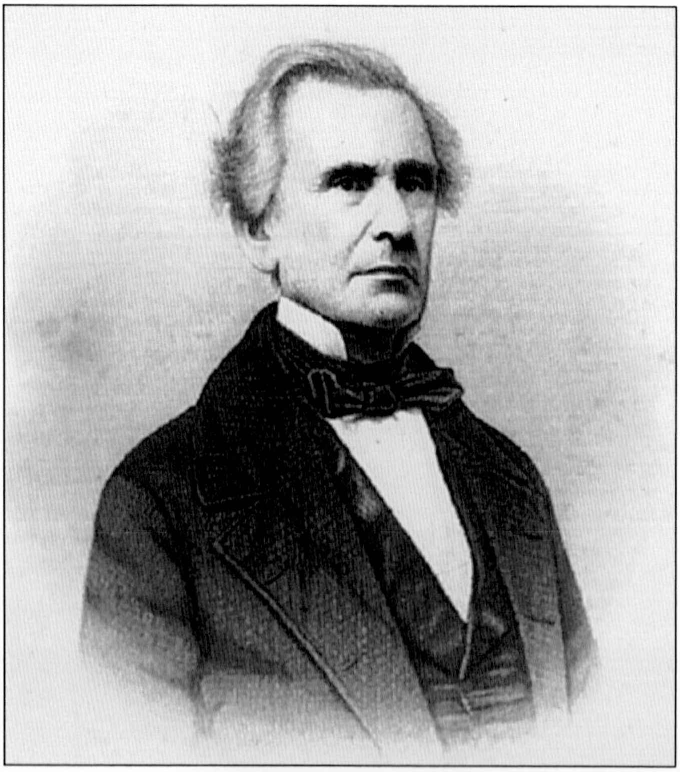

Dr. Lovick Pierce was known throughout Georgia as the "Nestor of Southern Methodism." He lived to be 95 and was known as one of the most influential Methodist ministers the South ever produced. His son George Foster Pierce became a bishop in the Methodist Church. Lovick Pierce has many influential descendants living in Columbus today. (Photograph from *The Life and Times of George F. Pierce*, 1881.)

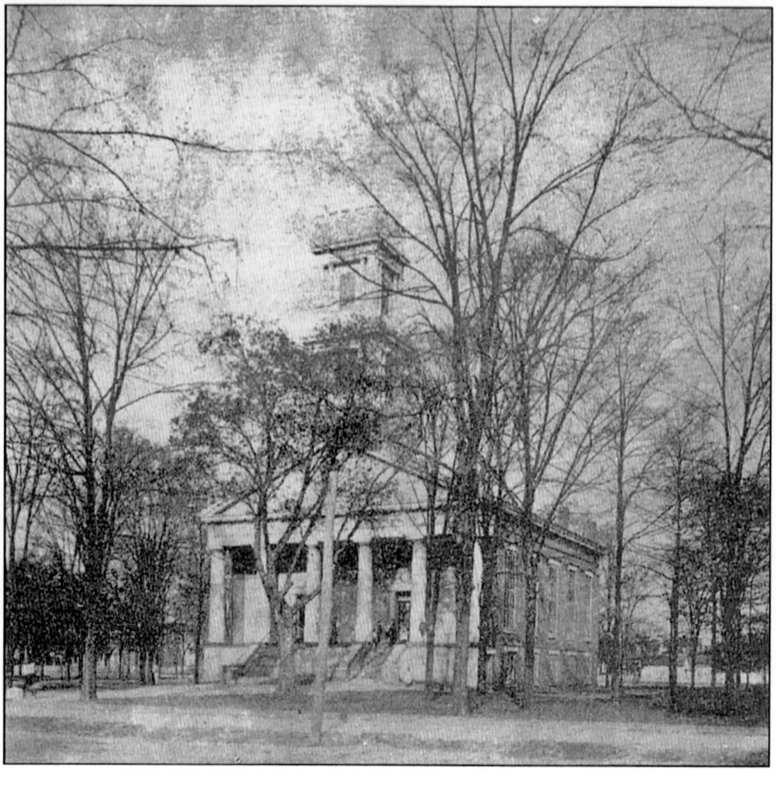

Pierce was pastor of St. Luke Methodist Church in 1836, the first pastor of St. Paul Methodist Church, and presiding elder of the district. Pictured is St. Luke Methodist Church, the first church founded in Columbus. (Courtesy of Columbus Office Supply.)

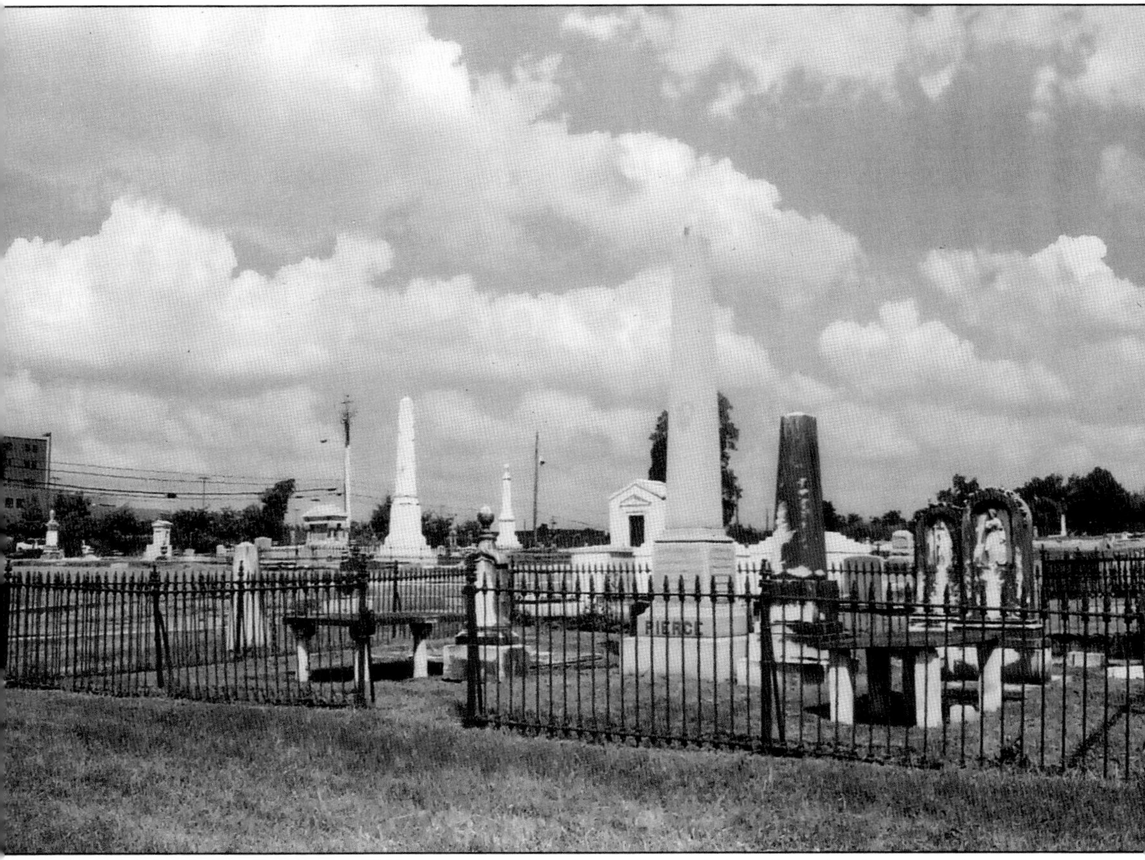

This is the family lot of Lovick Pierce where he, his wife, and their four daughters are buried.

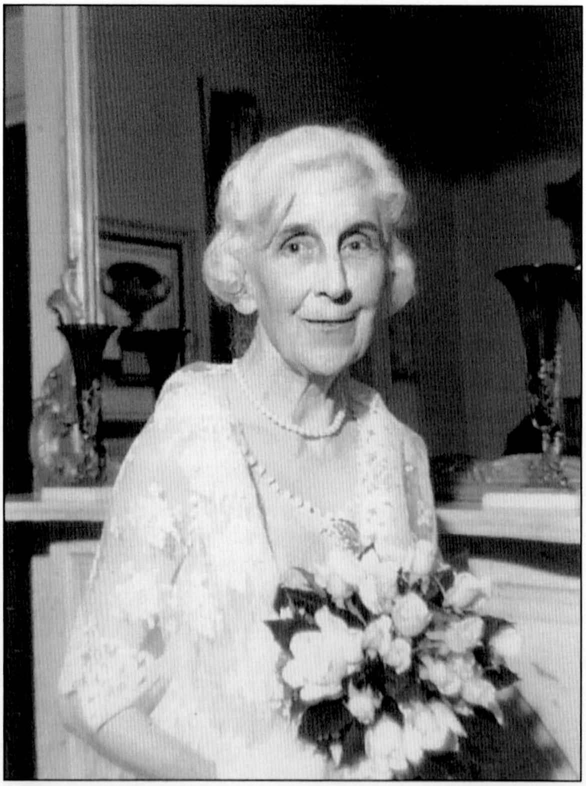

Loretta Lamar Chappell's portrait can be seen hanging in the Columbus Public Library today, honoring her 45 years of service as a city librarian. She was noted for "her charm, love of humanity, and cultural contribution to Columbus through her many years of dedicated library service." She began her work in 1915 at the downtown location of the Carnegie Library and retired in 1962 at the Bradley Memorial Library in Wynnton. She remained active in the preservation of the history of Columbus well into her 80s. (Courtesy of Historic Columbus Foundation.)

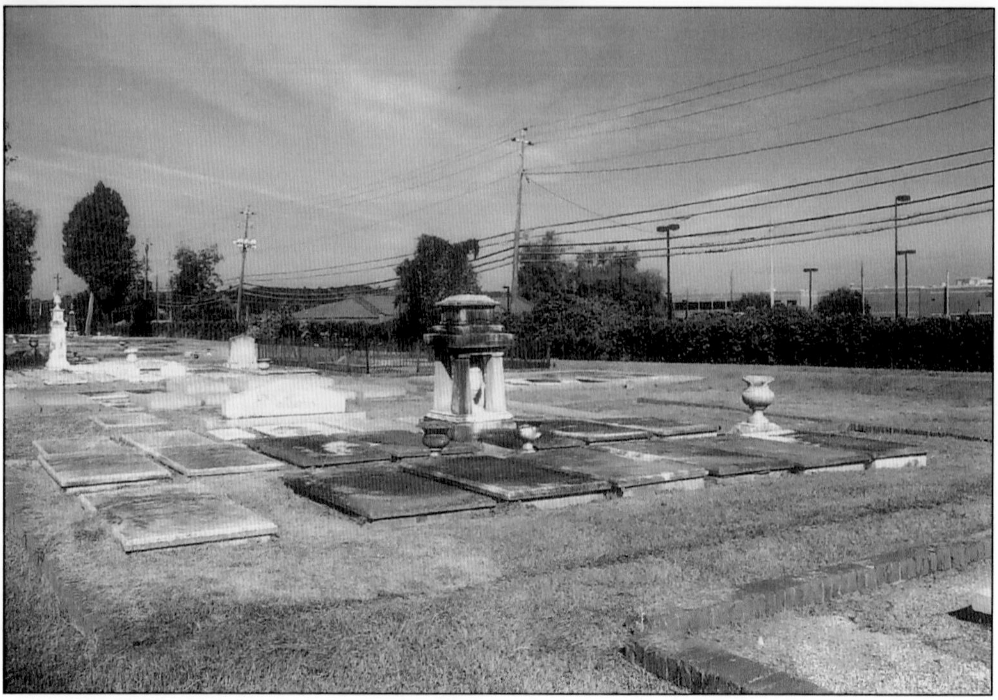

The Chappell family lot is the resting place of many who contributed to the building of Columbus. The Chappell family produced lawyers, senators, college presidents, and authors.

John L. Mustian developed stagecoach lines and railroads. His Muscogee Railroad Company's lines were the very first to reach the city from the east. He purchased the site of the thermal waters near Pine Mountain, later called Warm Springs, and developed the area as a summer retreat for the wealthy. (Courtesy of Columbus Museum.)

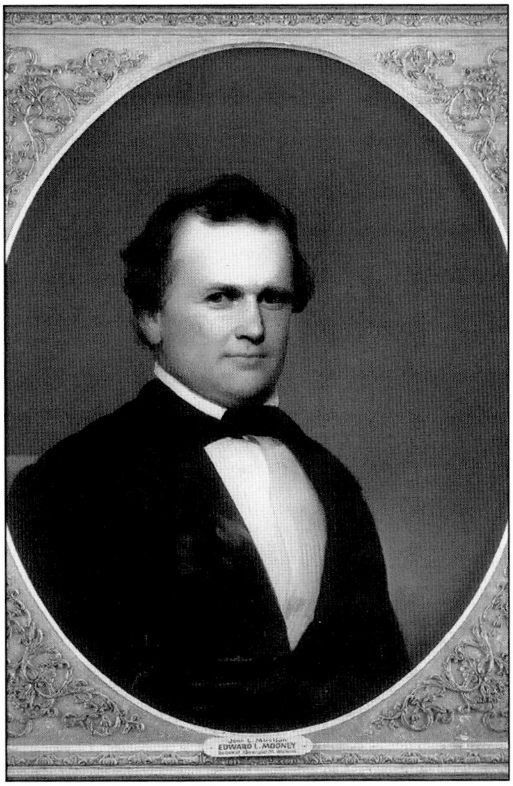

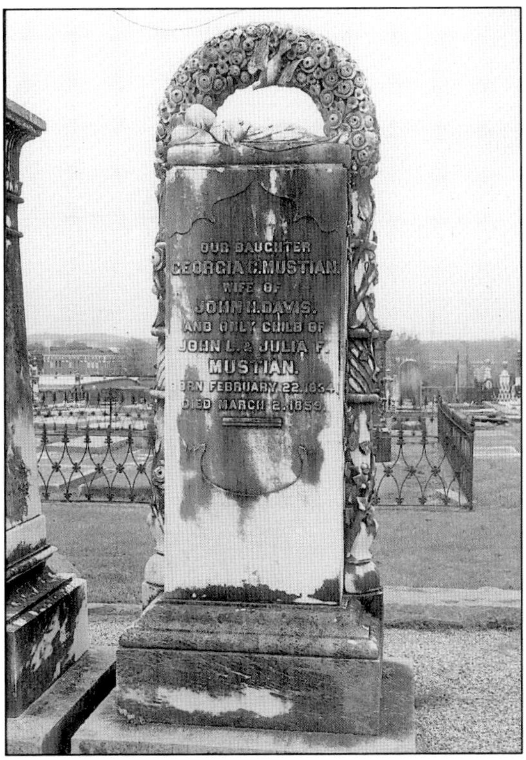

This monument to Georgia Mustian Davis is the most photographed monument in the cemetery. The arched wreath over the reclining figure is indicative of the work of the respected Columbus artisan Henry McCauley; however, the monument is not signed.

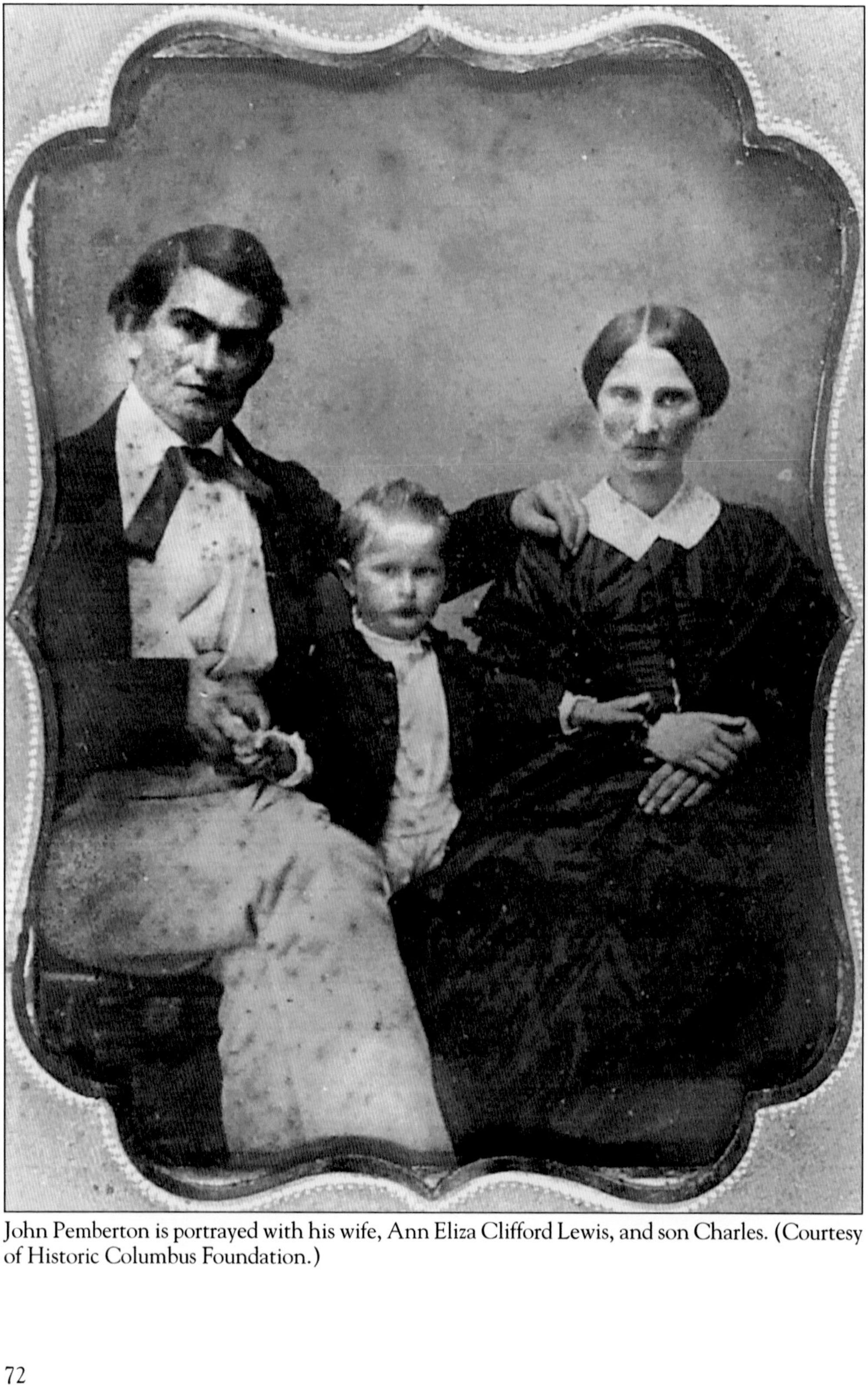

John Pemberton is portrayed with his wife, Ann Eliza Clifford Lewis, and son Charles. (Courtesy of Historic Columbus Foundation.)

John Stith Pemberton invented the formula for Coca-Cola. He was a pharmacist, a dreamer, and an inventor. From his chemical laboratory he manufactured medicines, photographic chemicals, hair dye, perfumes, and cosmetics. From his soda fountain he tested many flavors of soft drinks and tonic, seeking public acceptance. "French Wine of Coca," a headache cure, eventually became the Coca-Cola formula. In 1870 Pemberton moved to Atlanta, and it was there in 1886 that he began marketing Coca-Cola. Following his death two years later, his body was returned to Columbus for burial.

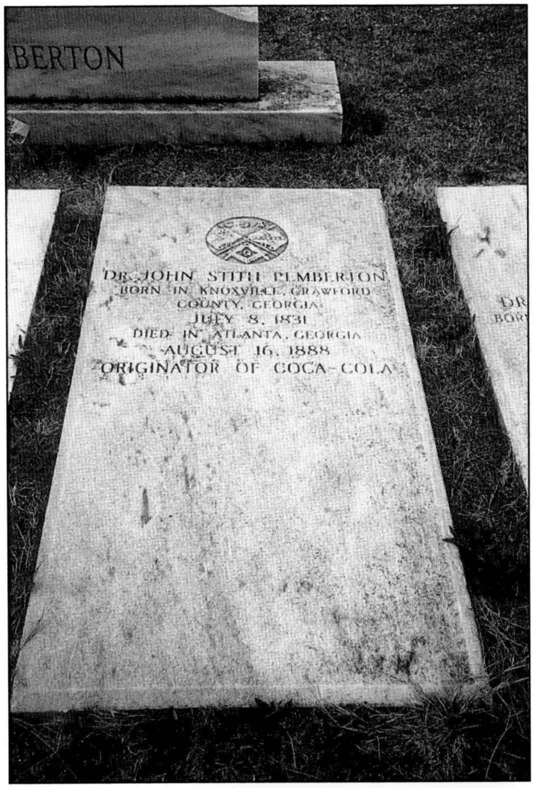

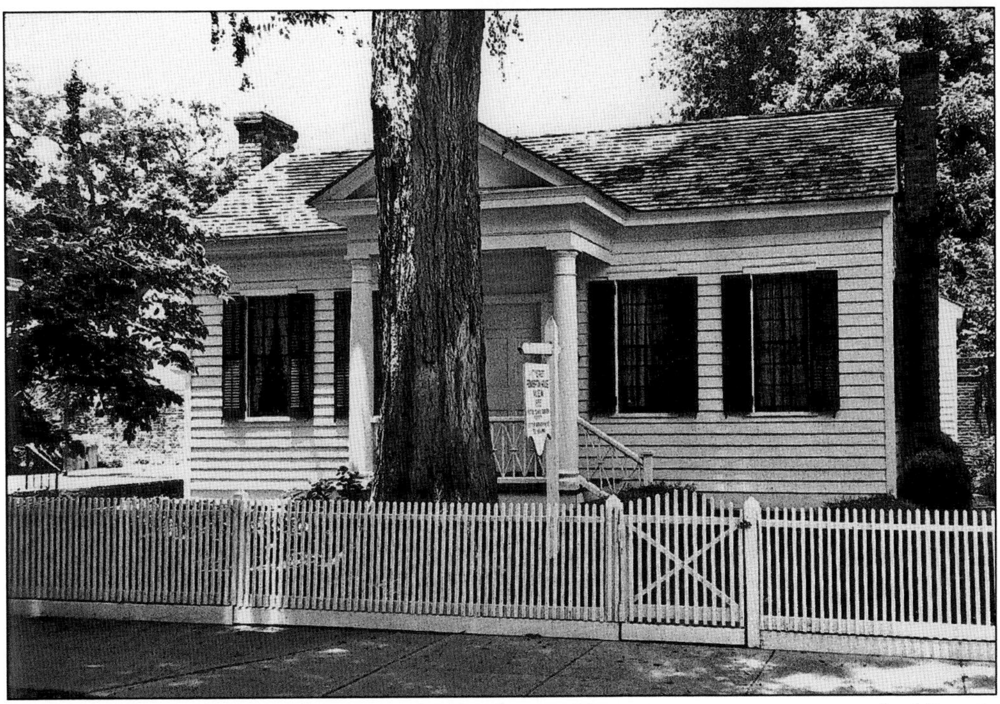

The Greek Revival cottage known as the Pemberton House is now a museum run by Historic Columbus Foundation. (Courtesy of Historic Columbus Foundation.)

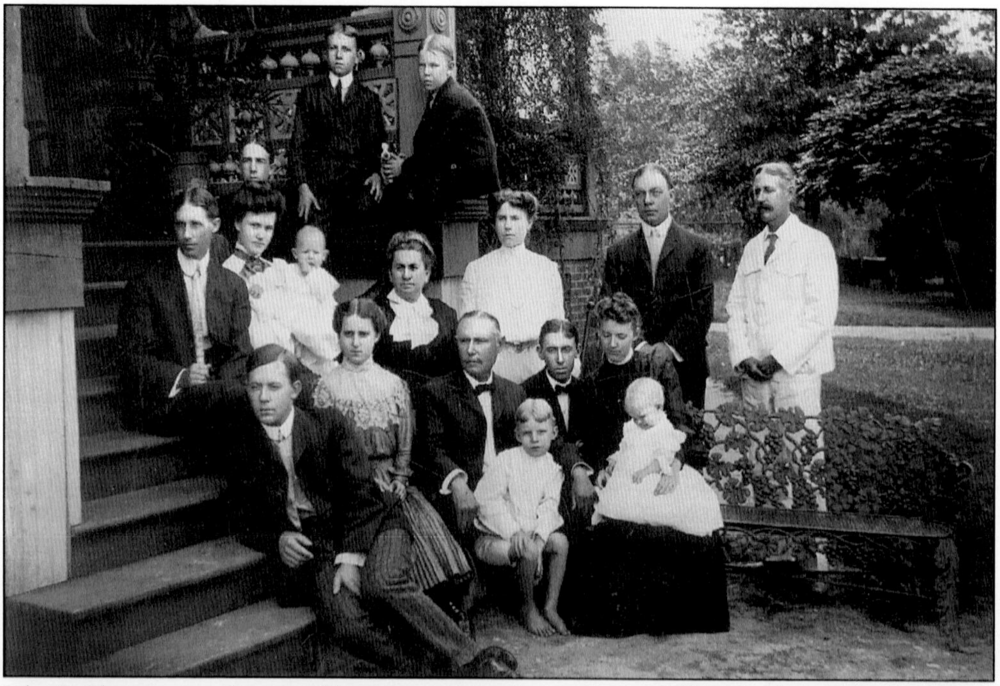

John F. Flournoy was born in Wynnton and fought in the Civil War. In the 1880s, he created the Columbus Railroad Company, which provided electricity for homes, businesses, streetlights, and streetcars. The company instituted streetcars that ran on the "Belt Line" to Wynnton by Wildwood (Weracoba) Park, which he also created. His related real estate ventures developed the Wynnton suburbs from the 1880s to the 1930s. This Flournoy family portrait was taken on the steps of their home Hillcrest, which stands today. (Courtesy of Mr. and Mrs. Murray Calhoun III.)

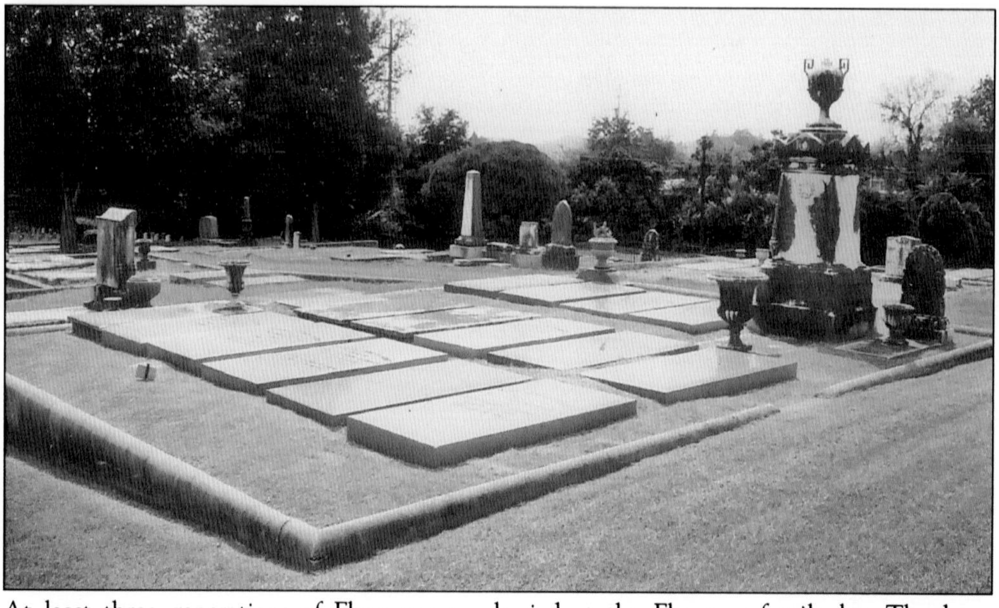

At least three generations of Flournoys are buried at the Flournoy family lot. The large monument, carved by Henry McCauley, is for John Manley Flournoy, father of John Francis.

Francis Xavier Profumo operated a confectionery store at 12–14 Tenth Street. His best known sweet was ice cream, which was said to be the best townspeople had ever eaten. He sold the confection in pints and quarts, to be taken home in returnable containers. His recipe has remained a closely guarded family secret. Pictured are Francis Xavier and his daughter Mary. (Courtesy of F. Clason Kyle.)

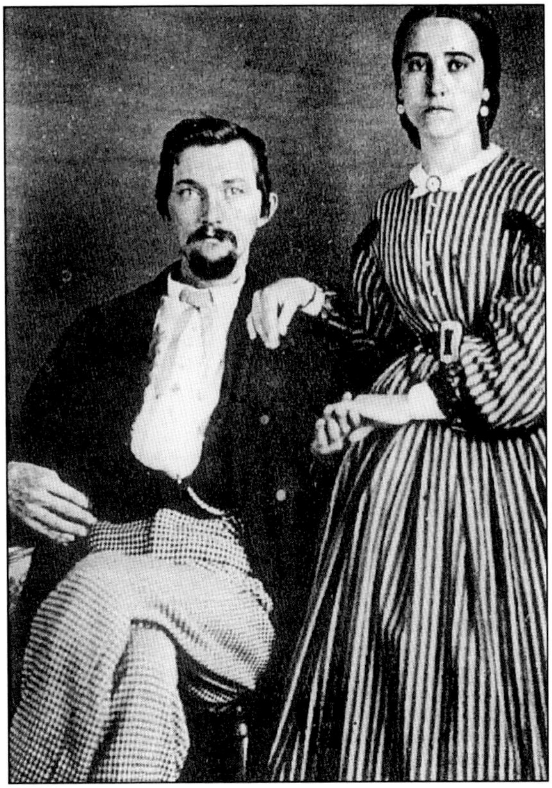

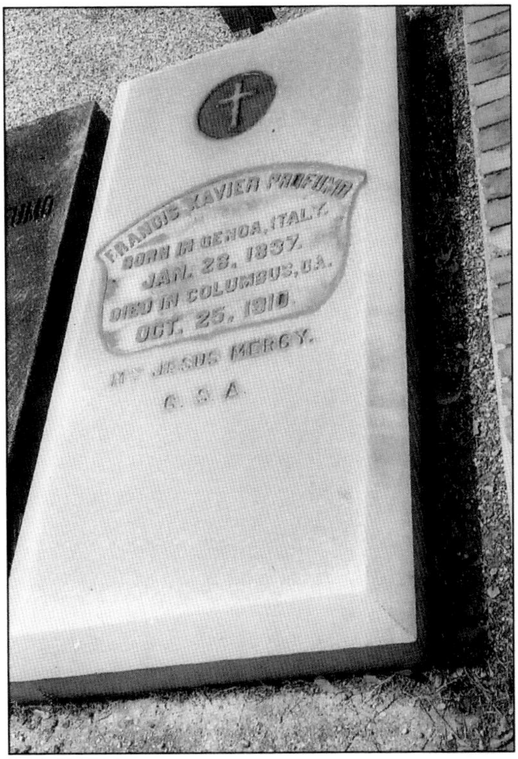

Francis X. Profumo was born in Genoa, Italy, on January 28, 1837, and died in Columbus, Georgia, on October 25, 1910, at the age of 73. His wife and all four children are also buried in this lot.

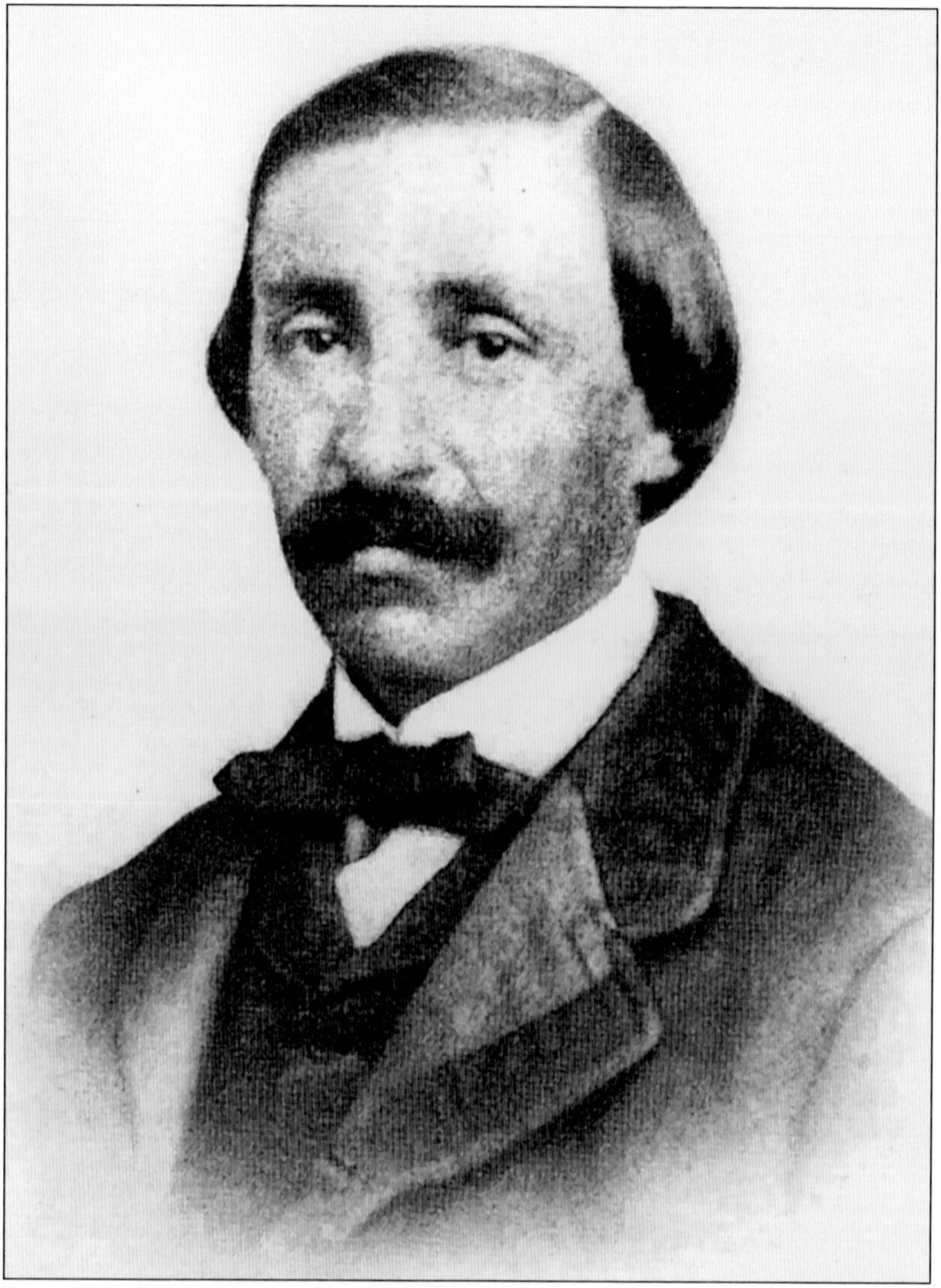

With roots in Prussia as a tinsmith, Louis Haiman and his brother Elias founded one of the largest sword-making companies in the Confederacy. Their factory, located on Franklin Street (now Fourteenth Street) near Oglethorpe (now First Avenue), manufactured swords, bayonets, and pistols for the Confederacy. It was burned when Maj. Gen. James H. Wilson raided Columbus at the end of the Civil War. After the war, Haiman organized the Southern Agricultural Works, which produced farm implements in Columbus and later in Atlanta.

This marker stands where Haiman had his sword factory.

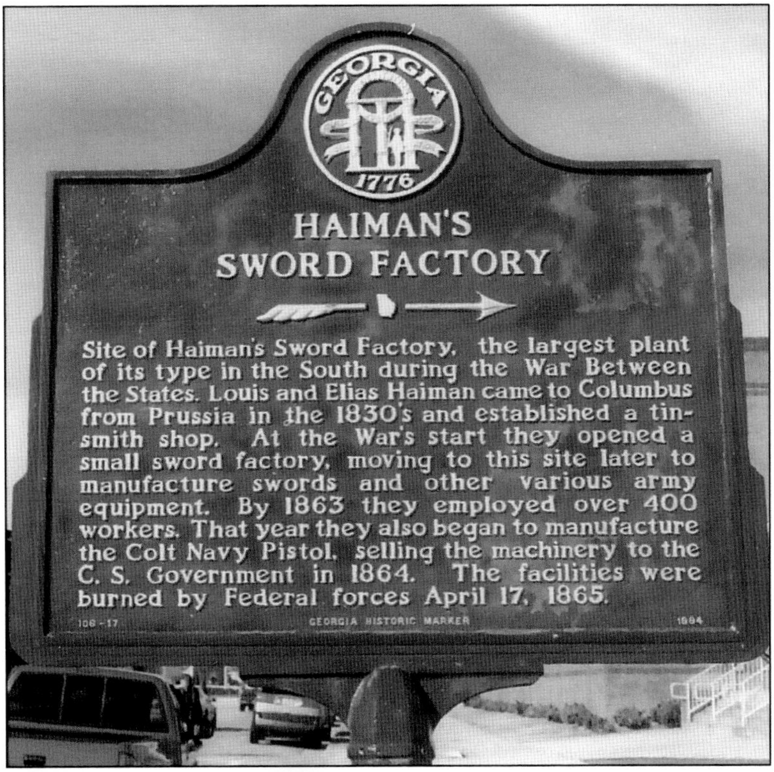

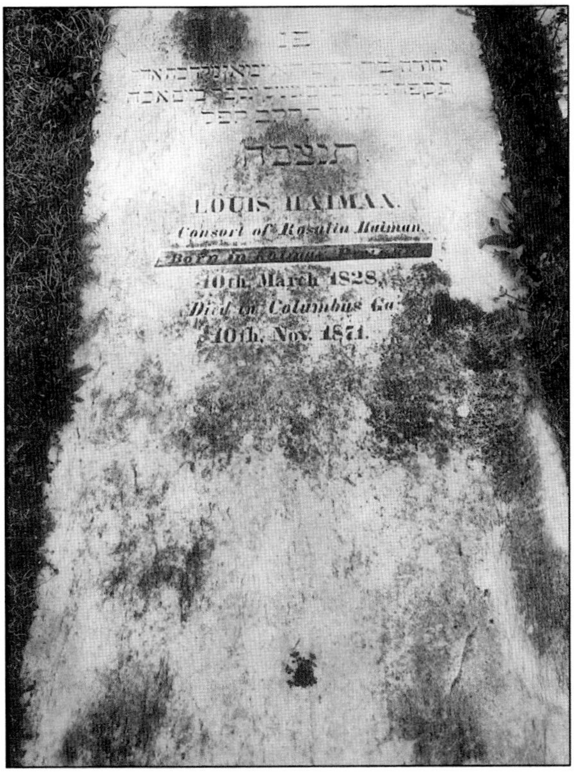

Louis Haiman was born March 10, 1828, and died November 10, 1871. Haiman's grave is the most noted in the Jewish section of the cemetery.

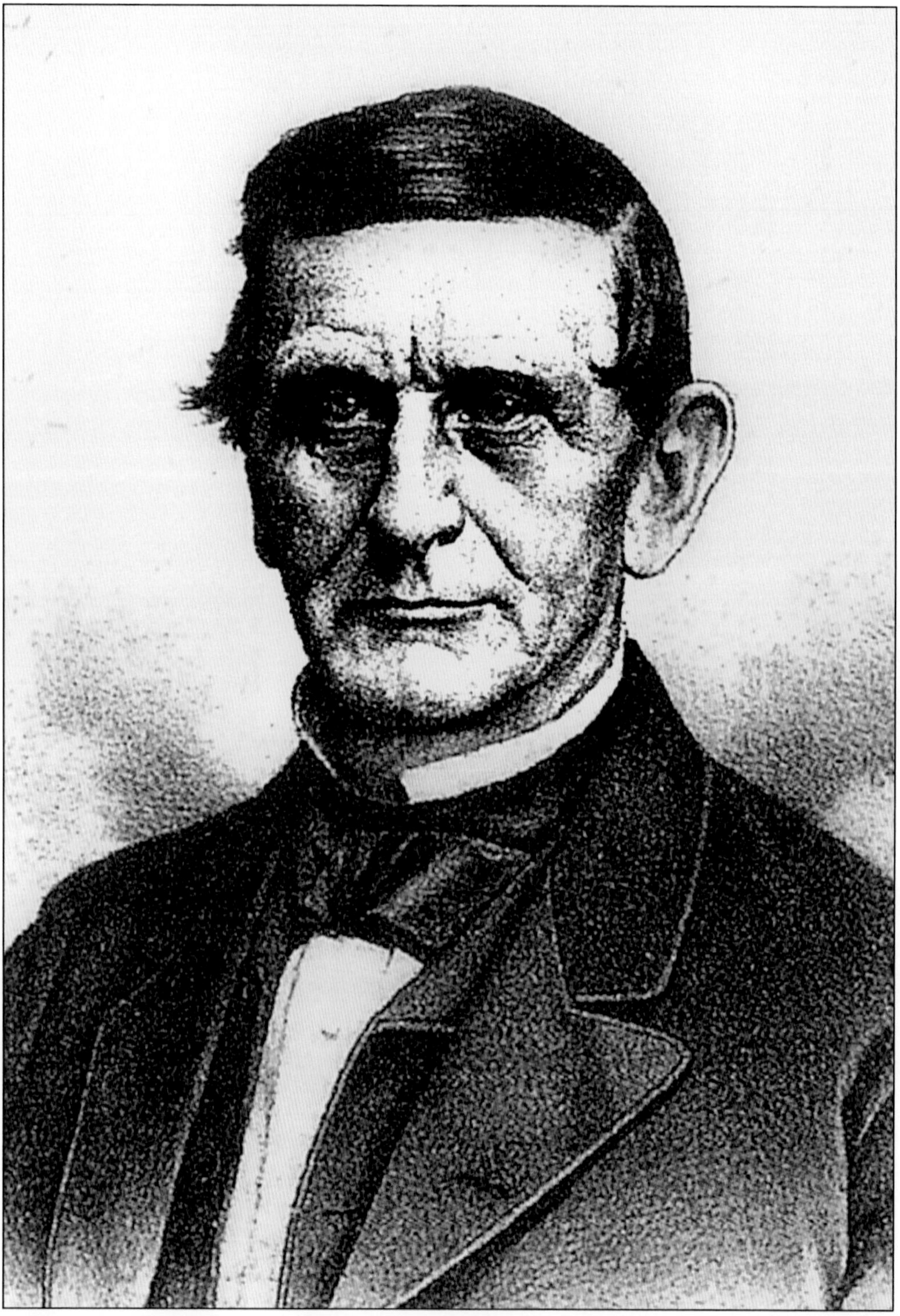

William H. Young was involved in many enterprises in Columbus, one of these being the Georgia Home Insurance Company. He, along with others, started this company as a "stock fire insurance company." (Courtesy of Columbus State University Archives.)

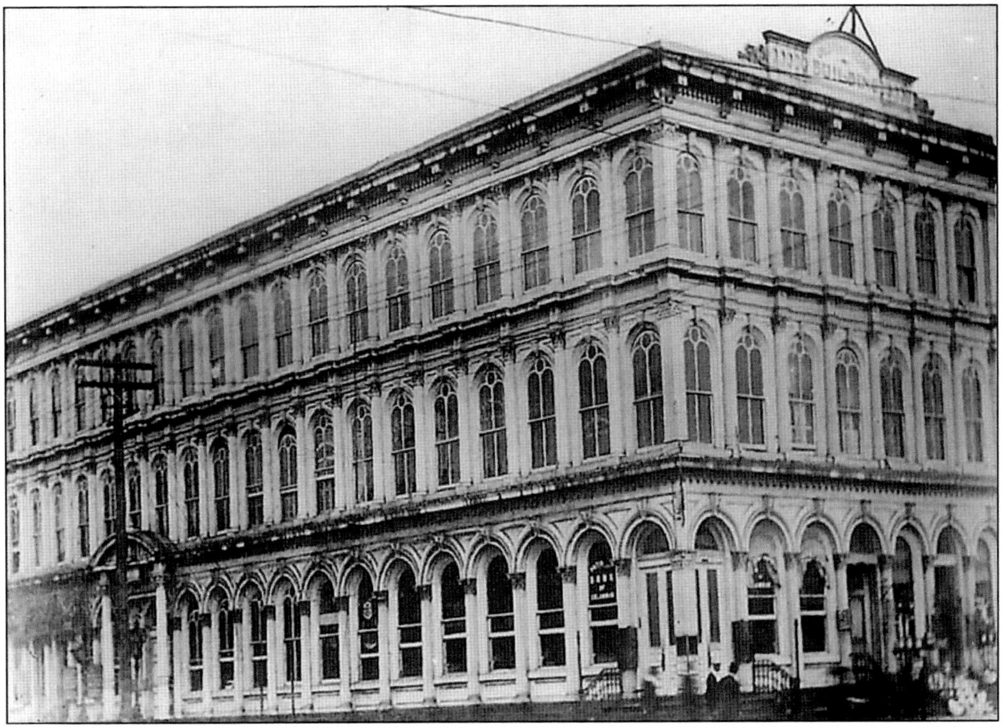

Mr. Young designed this building, completely fabricated of iron, to house the offices of the insurance company. Still in use today, its main tenant is the architectural firm of Hecht Burdeshaw Johnson Kidd and Clark. (Courtesy of Historic Columbus Foundation.)

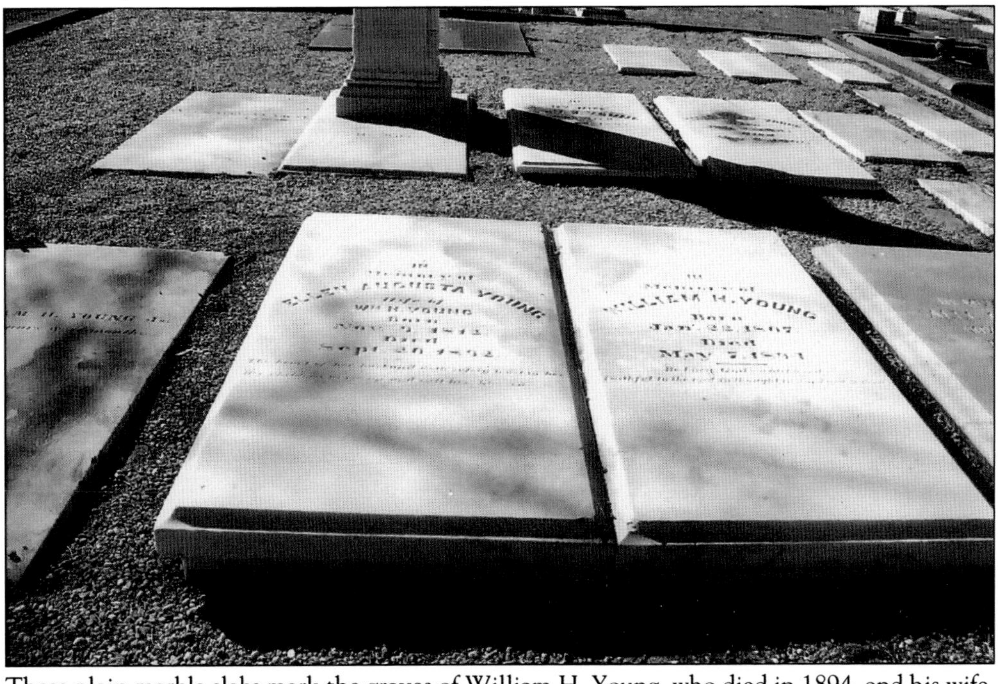

These plain marble slabs mark the graves of William H. Young, who died in 1894, and his wife, Ellen Hall Young, who died in 1892.

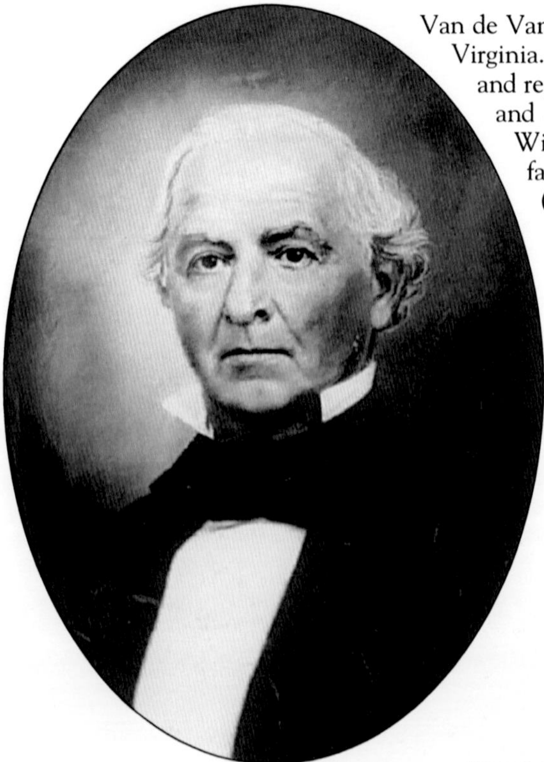

Van de Van Leonard was born in 1790 in Petersburg, Virginia. He came to the Columbus area after 1831 and represented the area as both a representative and state senator. The Van Leonards lived in Wildwood, a house built by Matthew Evans, father of noted author August Evans Wilson. (Courtesy of Mimi Pease Childs.)

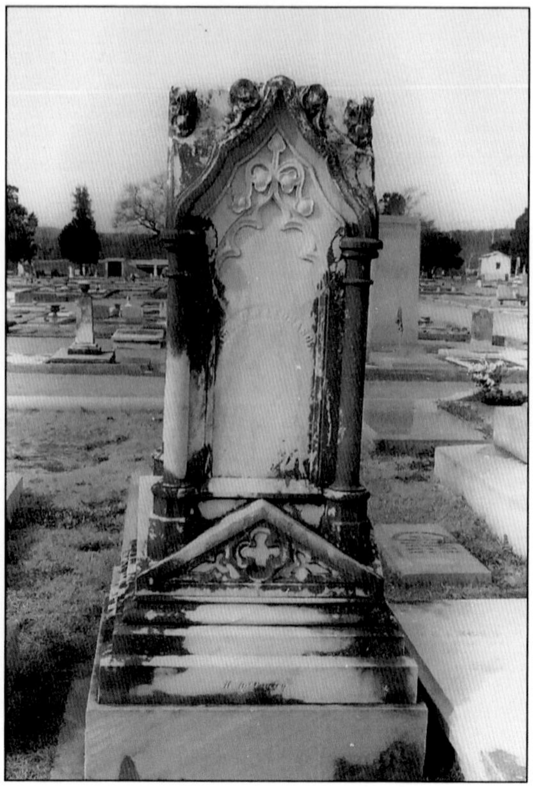

Van de Van Leonard's monument is in the Garrard lot and was carved by Henry McCauley.

James Johnson, Georgia's 28th governor, was appointed provisional governor by Andrew Johnson after the Civil War ended. James Johnson lived in the Columbus area at the time. He died in 1891 and was buried in Linwood. (Courtesy of Georgia Capitol Museum, Office of Secretary of State.)

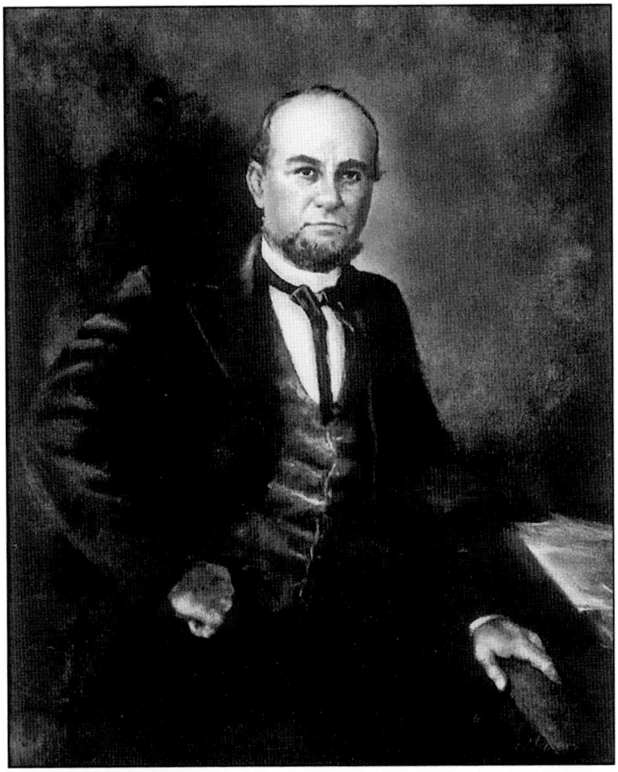

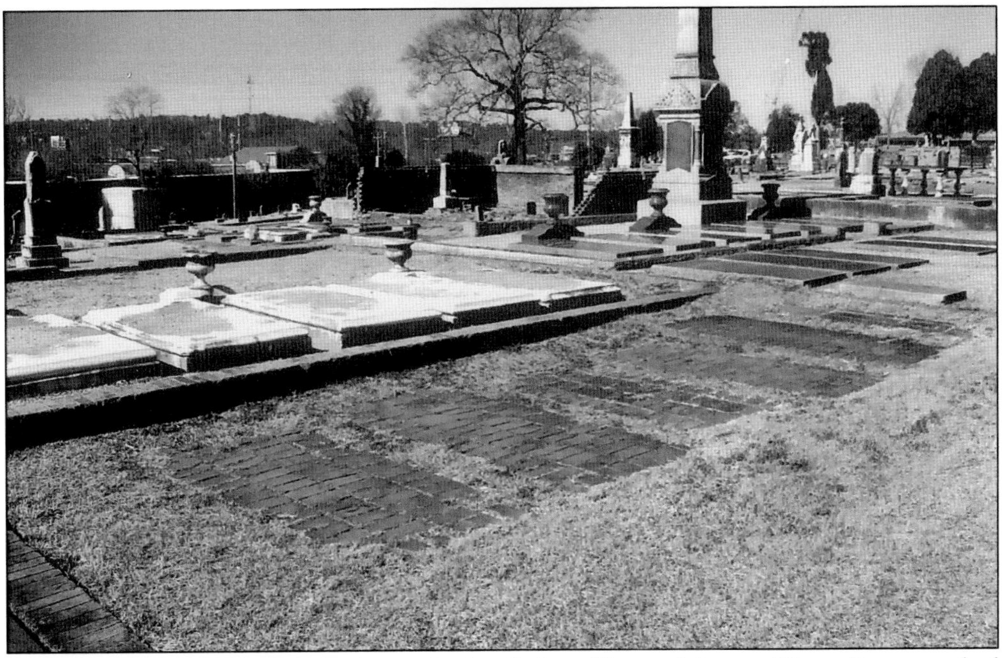

According to cemetery records, this is the family lot of James Johnson. These five unmarked brick slabs are a sampling of many such graves in Linwood. In the past, when vaults were made of brick, the graves were bricked over as well. In many cases, as in the Johnson lot, no markers were ever placed on the graves.

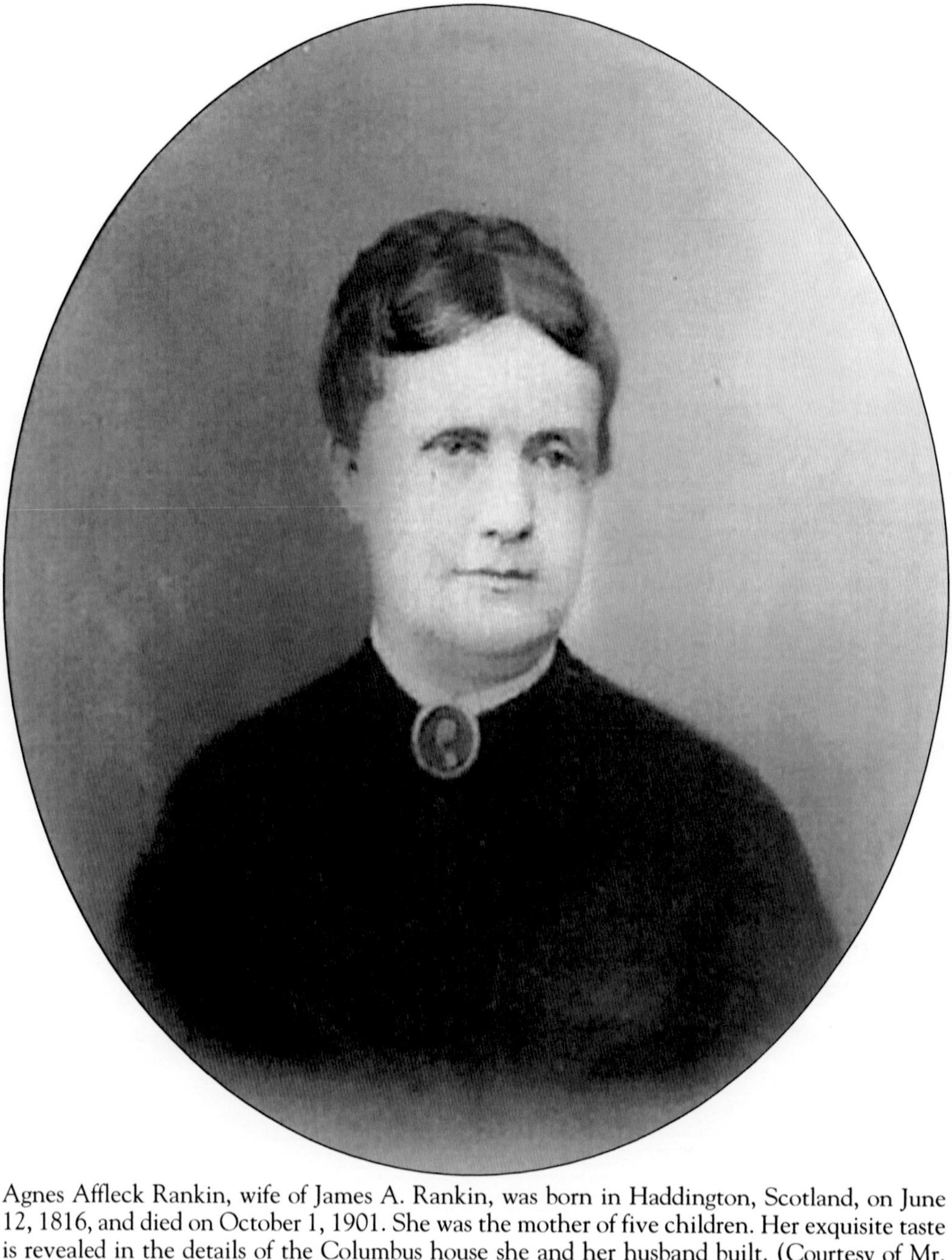

Agnes Affleck Rankin, wife of James A. Rankin, was born in Haddington, Scotland, on June 12, 1816, and died on October 1, 1901. She was the mother of five children. Her exquisite taste is revealed in the details of the Columbus house she and her husband built. (Courtesy of Mr. and Mrs. John Walden.)

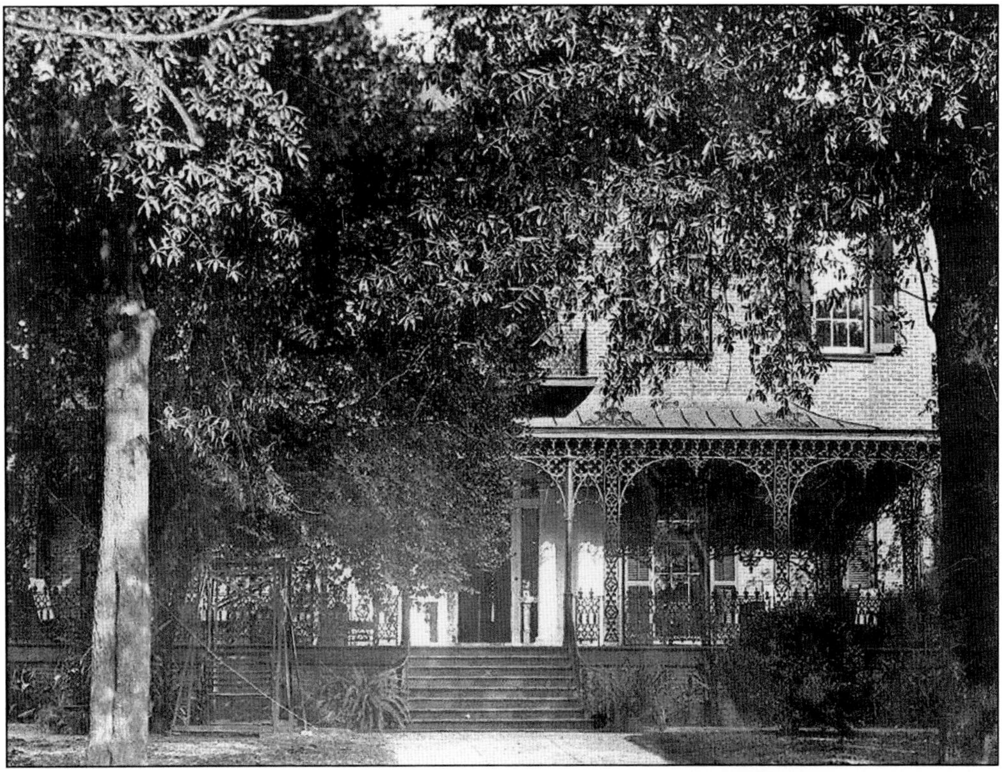

The home James Rankin began building in the 1850s for his family was not finished until after the Civil War. Mr. and Mrs. Rankin traveled to Scotland annually and purchased many of the furnishings there. The Rankin House is now the office of Historic Columbus Foundation. (Courtesy of Mr. and Mrs. John Walden.)

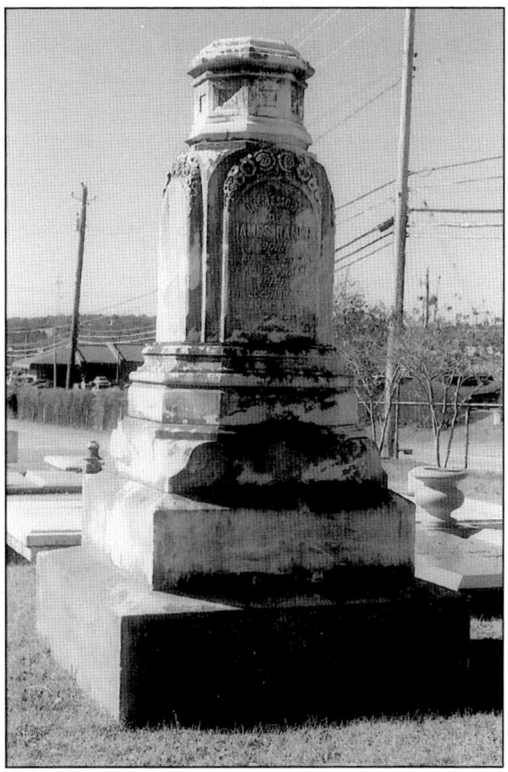

James A. Rankin, as well as his wife, hailed from Scotland; he was born in 1806 and died in 1880. He owned several properties in Columbus. One that bears his name today, the Rankin Building, houses the Uptown Columbus Museum and uptown classrooms for Columbus State University.

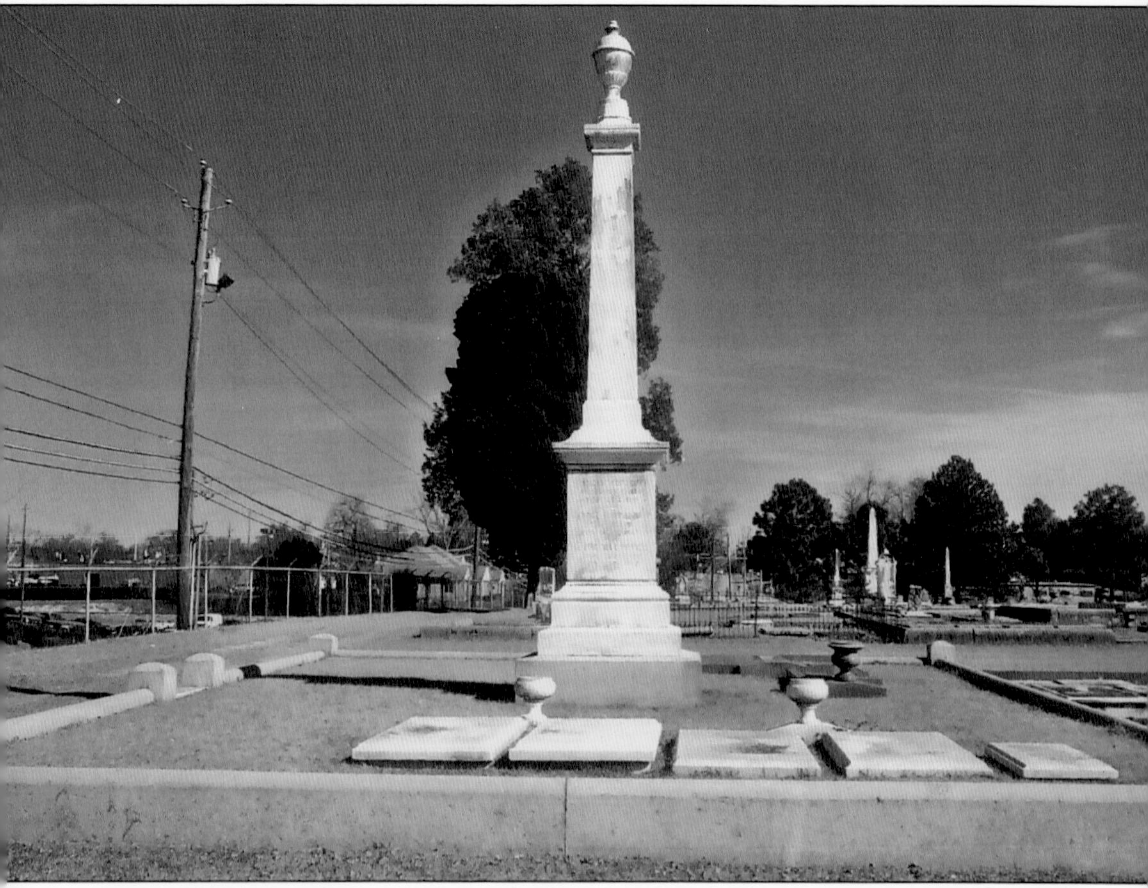

George Waldo Woodruff moved to Columbus in 1847. He was the president of Empire Mills, which played an important role in providing wheat and corn for the Confederate Army. Woodruff's descendants have influenced the commercial, educational, and cultural growth of Georgia.

George Waldo Woodruff was born in 1824 in Connecticut and died in 1911. He is shown with his ear trumpet.

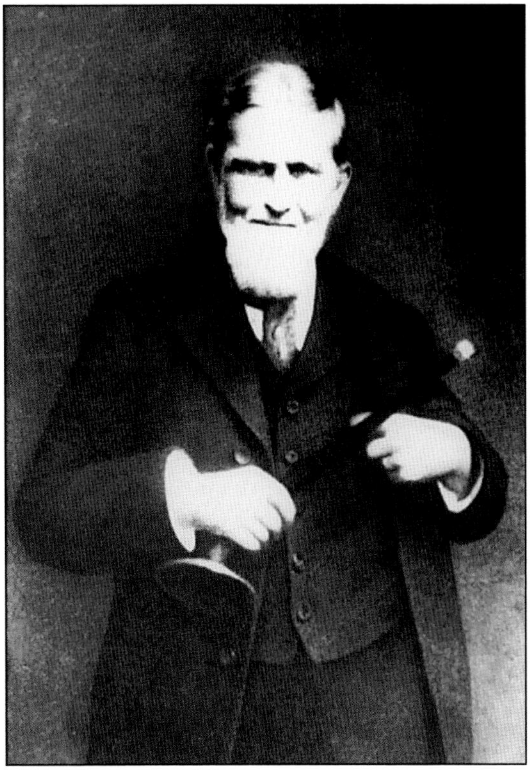

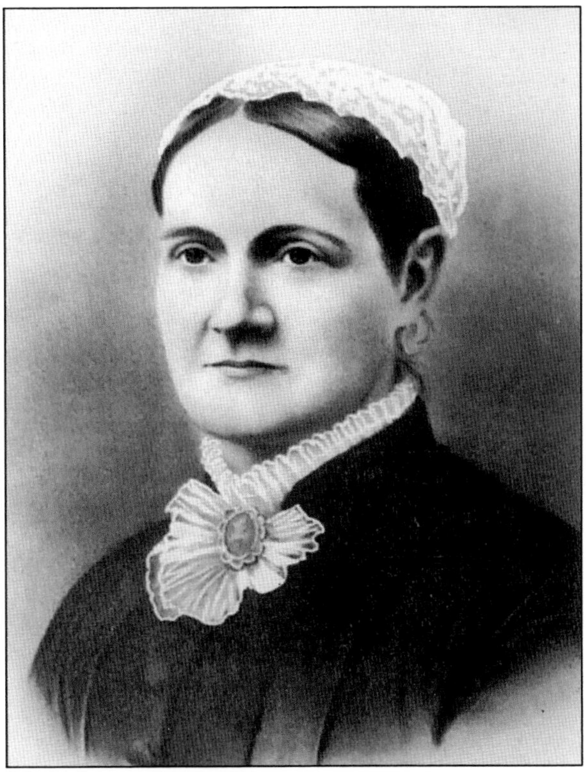

Virginia Lindsay, who was born in 1829 and died in 1911, married George Waldo Woodruff in 1850. They had six children: Annie Bright (Mrs. Joel Hurt); Henry Lindsay, who married Johnnie Kyle; Ernest, who married Emily Caroline Winship; George Sherwood; Virginia (Mrs. O.T. Howard); and Francis Woodruff. (Photographs on this page courtesy of Mr. and Mrs. Clifford Swift III.)

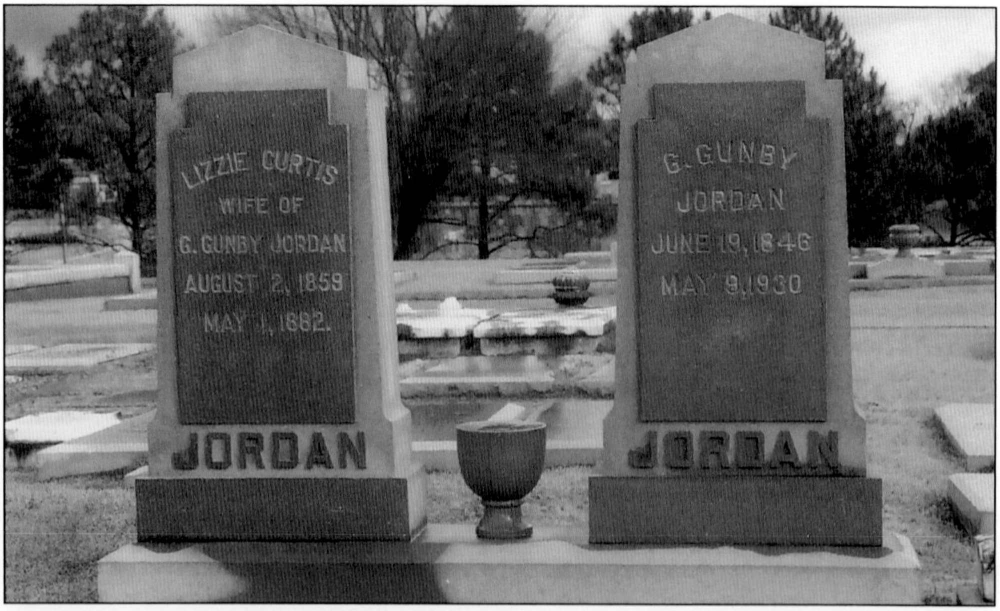

George Gunby Jordan, born in 1846 in Sparta, Georgia, joined the Confederate Army at age 17 as a private in Nelson's Rangers. Following the war, he came to Columbus and, from an initial position as a clerk in a wholesale firm, he moved into leadership positions in the business and political world. He married Lizzie Curtis of Columbus in February 1861. She died the following year after having given birth to a son, Ralph Curtis Jordan. Her husband never remarried and is buried beside her in the Jordan family lot.

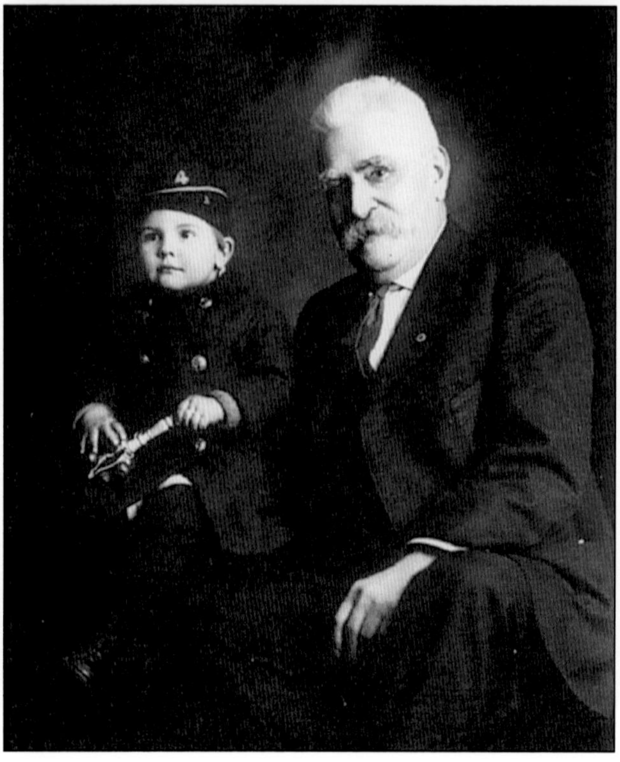

Pictured are George Gunby Jordan and his grandson, G. Gunby Jordan II, who grew to share the business acumen and dedication to community of his grandfather. (Courtesy of F. Clason Kyle.)

Mulford Jordan, born October 7, 1918, was the son of Mr. and Mrs. Ralph Curtis Jordan and grandson of Mr. and Mrs. G. Gunby Jordan. He attended the Kent School in Connecticut and graduated from Yale in 1940. In January 1942, he graduated from Officer Candidate School at Fort Benning and in the same month married Miss Sarah Smith of Atlanta. (Courtesy of Katherine Jordan Waddell.)

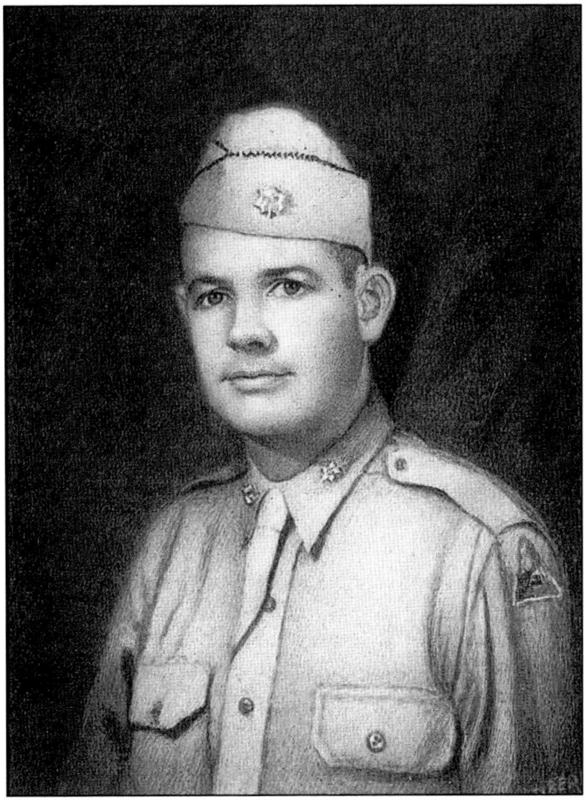

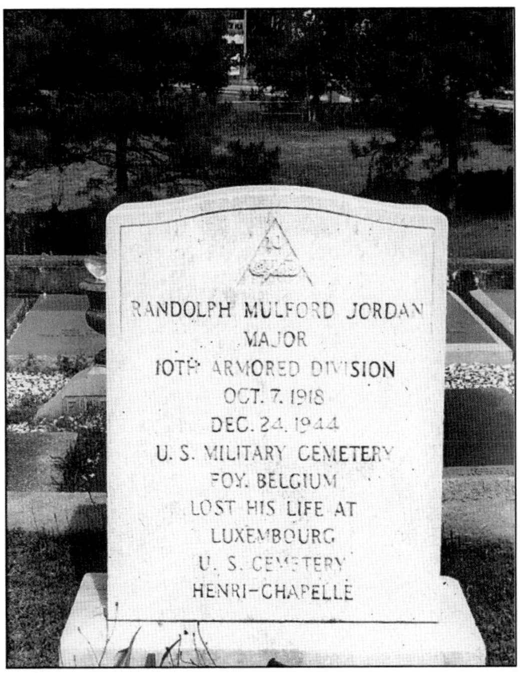

In September 1944, after serving as aide de camp to Maj. Gen. W.H. Morris Jr., Maj. Mulford Jordan was assigned to the staff of the 10th Armored Division in Germany, serving as G-3Air, the operations officer over air operations. Major Jordan was on an air reconnaissance mission when his plane went down over Luxembourg on Christmas Eve. He is buried in the U.S. Cemetery in Henri-Chapelle, Belgium, and his memorial stone is in Linwood. (Photograph by Lisa Cheatham.)

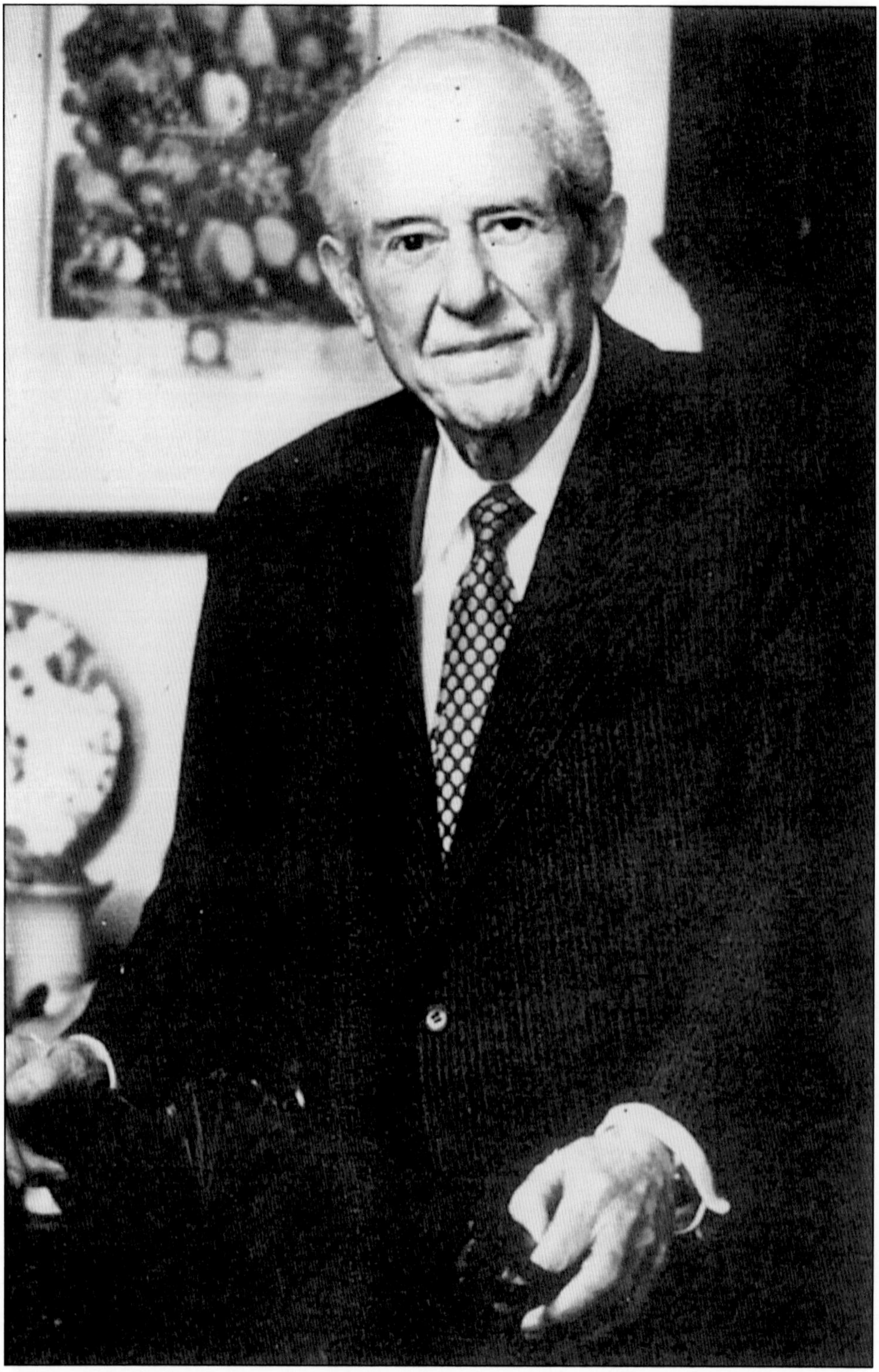

Philip Trammell Shutze, born in 1890, became one of America's finest architects. The Swan House in Atlanta is one of his designs. (Courtesy of F. Clason Kyle.)

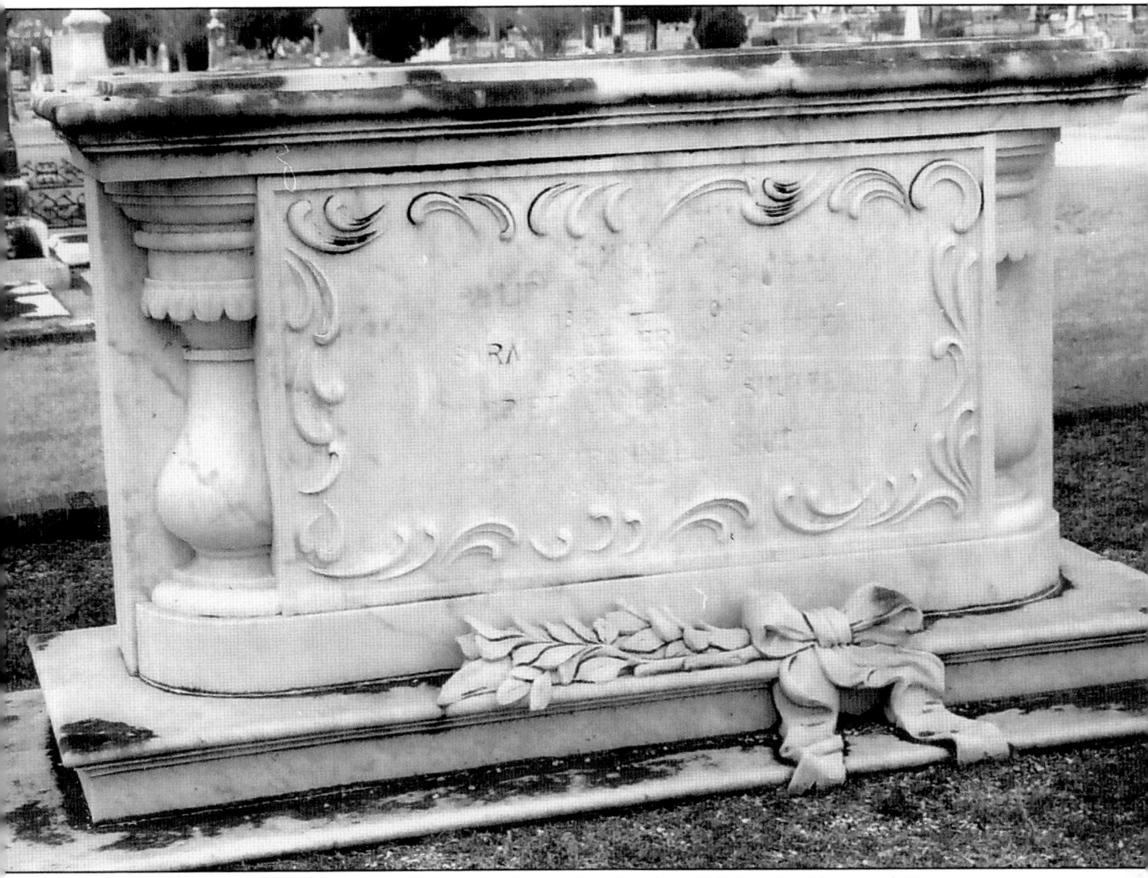

Shutze died in 1982 at the age of 92 and is buried in his family's lot in Linwood Cemetery.

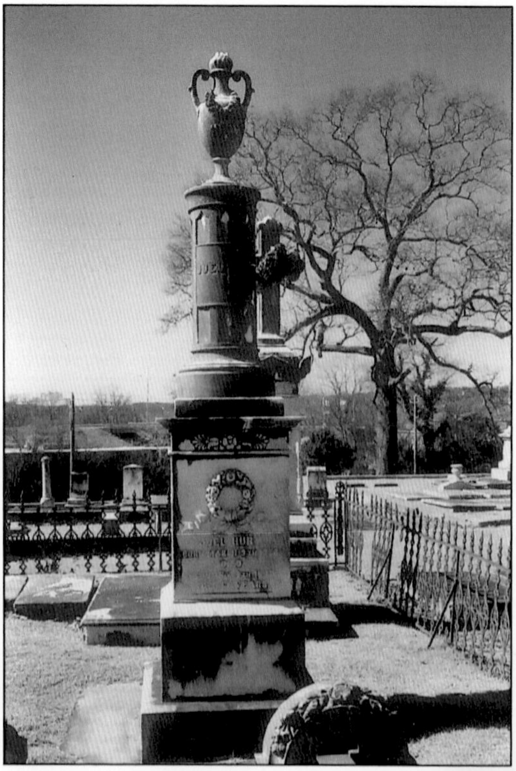

Joel Early Hurt was born in Putnam County, Georgia, in 1821 and died in Columbus in 1865. His monument was carved by Henry McCauley.

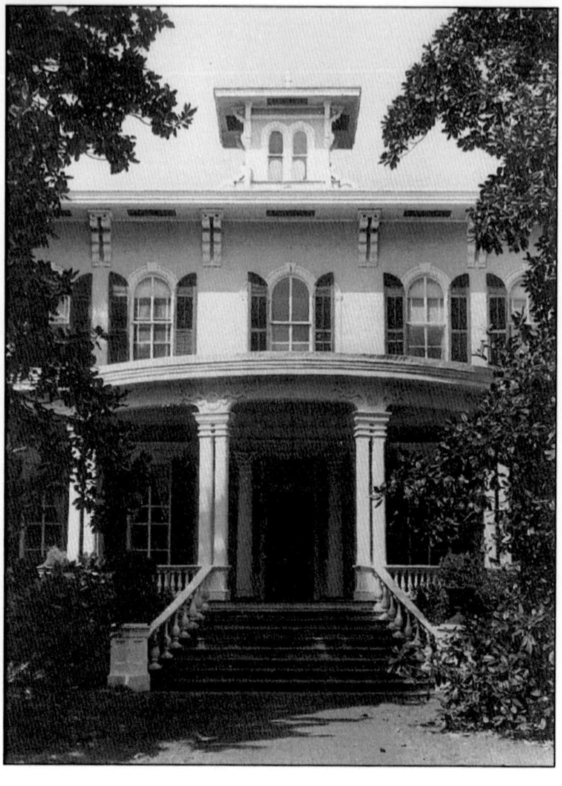

Joel Early Hurt built this home, Dinglewood, in the 1850s for his wife Frances and daughter Julia. Styled as an Italian villa, it has been beautifully preserved and is on the National Register. (Courtesy of Columbus State University Archives.)

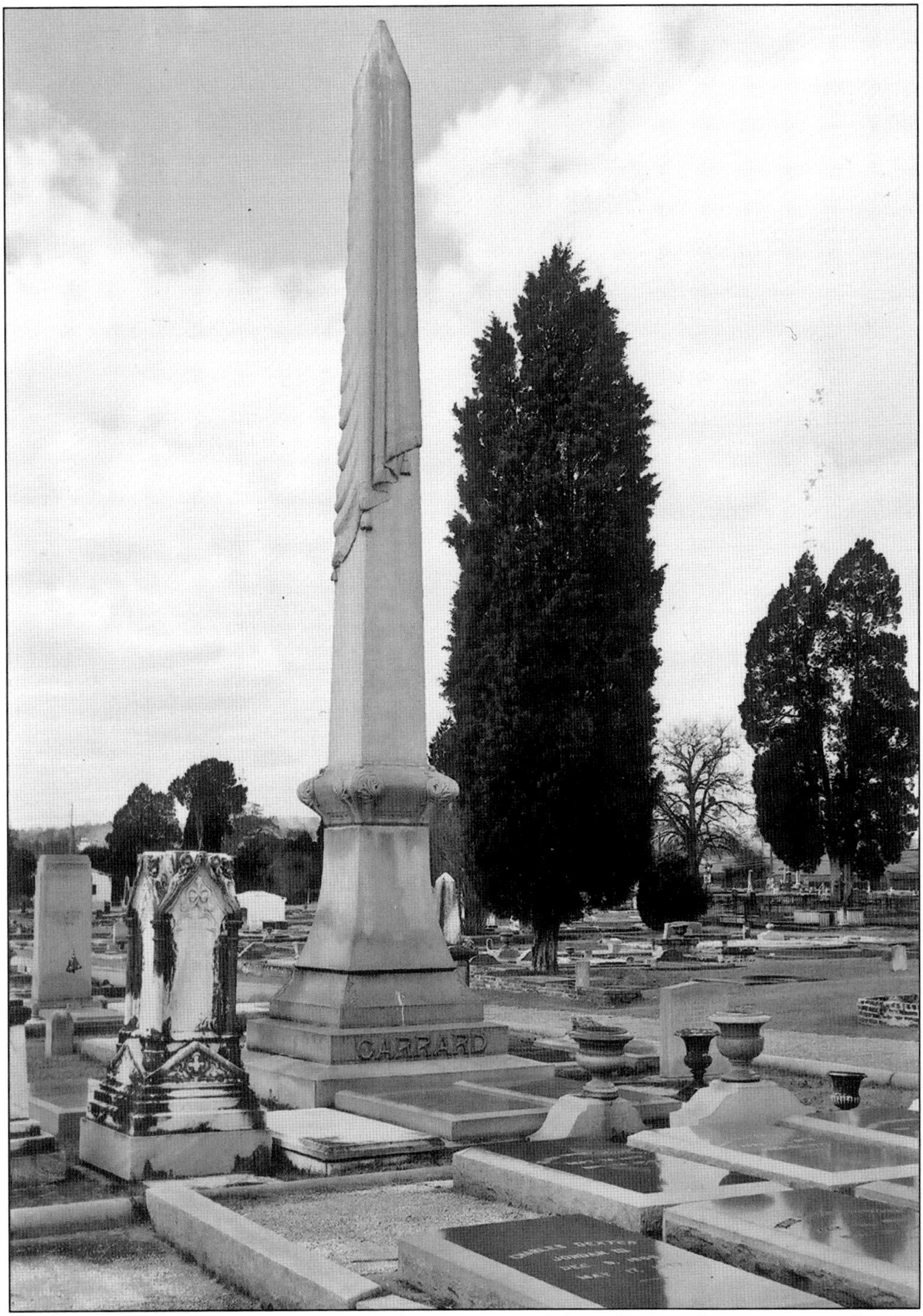

The obelisk marking the Leonard-Garrard lot is one of the tallest in the cemetery and is the landmark that draws visitors to the adjacent family lot of Seaborn Jones and his son-in-law, Gen. Henry Lewis Benning. These families are connected by the marriage of Van Leonard's daughter Mary and Seaborn Jones's son John.

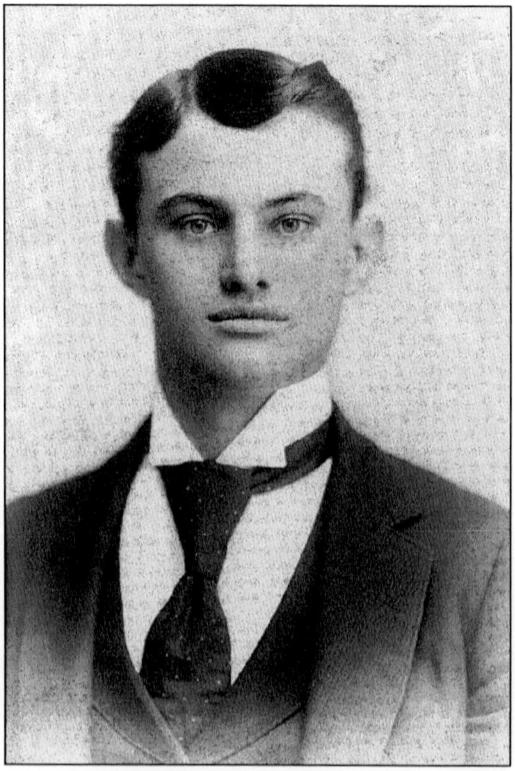

Louis Ford Garrard, born in Columbus in 1847, died in 1908 shortly after his wife's death. He served in Nelson's Rangers with such courage that Gen. Robert E. Lee publicly acknowledged his actions. A Harvard Law graduate, he was active in politics and served as speaker of the Georgia House of Representatives in 1882–1883. In the hard economic period after the Civil War, Garrard protected the property of General Benning's daughters with his own financial resources.

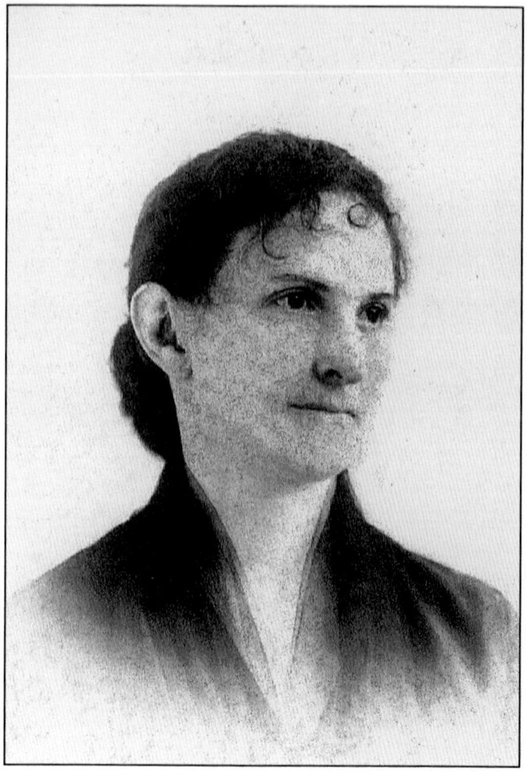

Annie Foster Leonard, daughter of Van de Van Leonard, married Louis Ford Garrard in 1868. Known as "Little Auntie" and "Sweet Annie of Wildwood," she was beloved by family and friends. She opened her home at Wildwood for family occasions, including weddings. (Photographs on this page courtesy of Mimi Pease Childs.)

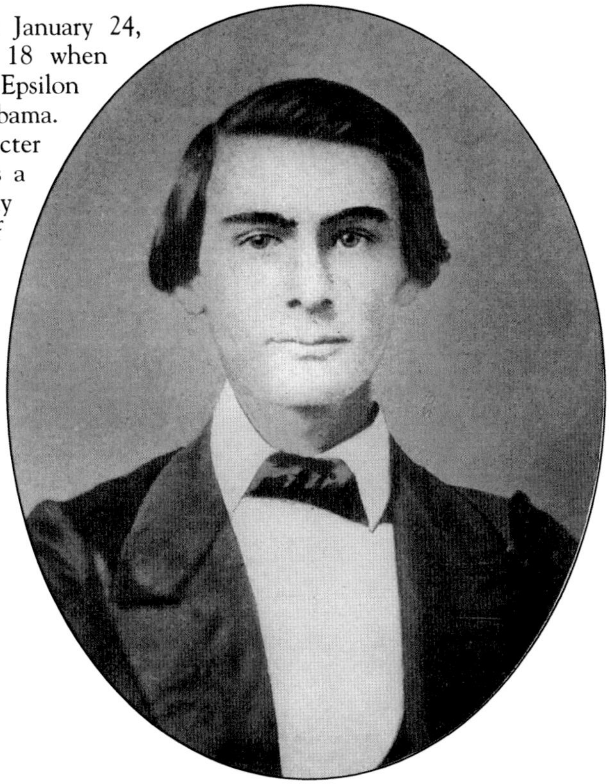

Born in Tuscaloosa, Alabama, on January 24, 1838, Noble Leslie DeVotie was 18 when he organized the Sigma Alpha Epsilon fraternity at the University of Alabama. A young man of sterling character and superior intellect, DeVotie was a chaplain in the Confederate Army when he drowned off the coast of Alabama in 1861. His father, Dr. James H. DeVotie, was pastor of First Baptist Church of Columbus. Noble was buried at Linwood Cemetery next to his brother Howard. One flat slab marks both graves. (Photograph from William C. Levere's *The History of the Sigma Epsilon Fraternity*, Vol. 1, Chicago, 1911.)

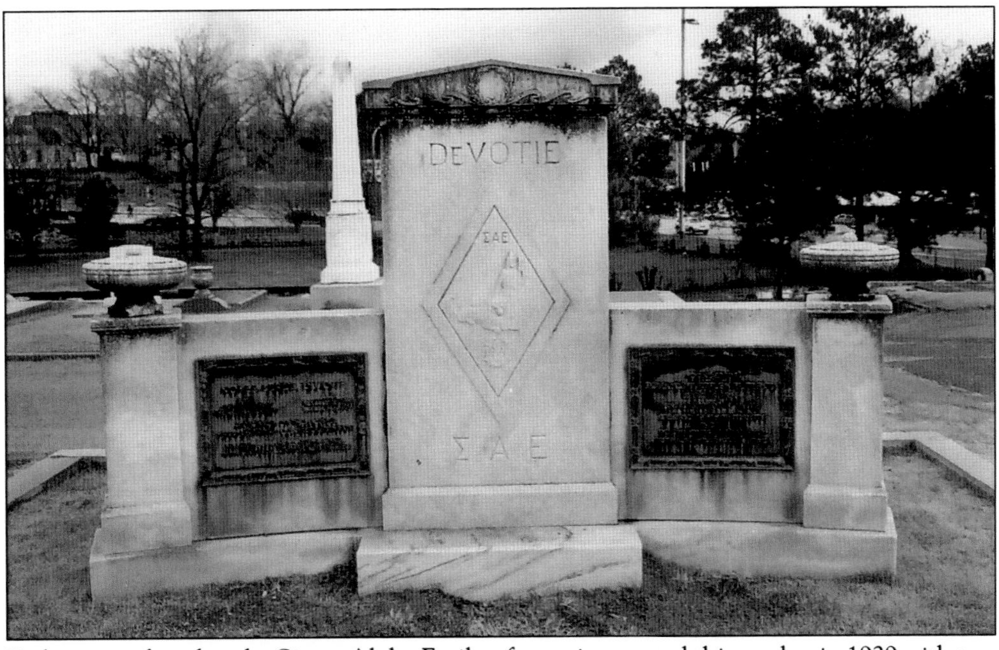

To honor its founder, the Sigma Alpha Epsilon fraternity erected this marker in 1929 with two inscriptions: "To one whose life was brief but whose influence is lasting" and "Greater love had no man than this, that a man lay down his life for his friends." The SAE fraternity is the largest in the United States, and many members have made pilgrimages to this site.

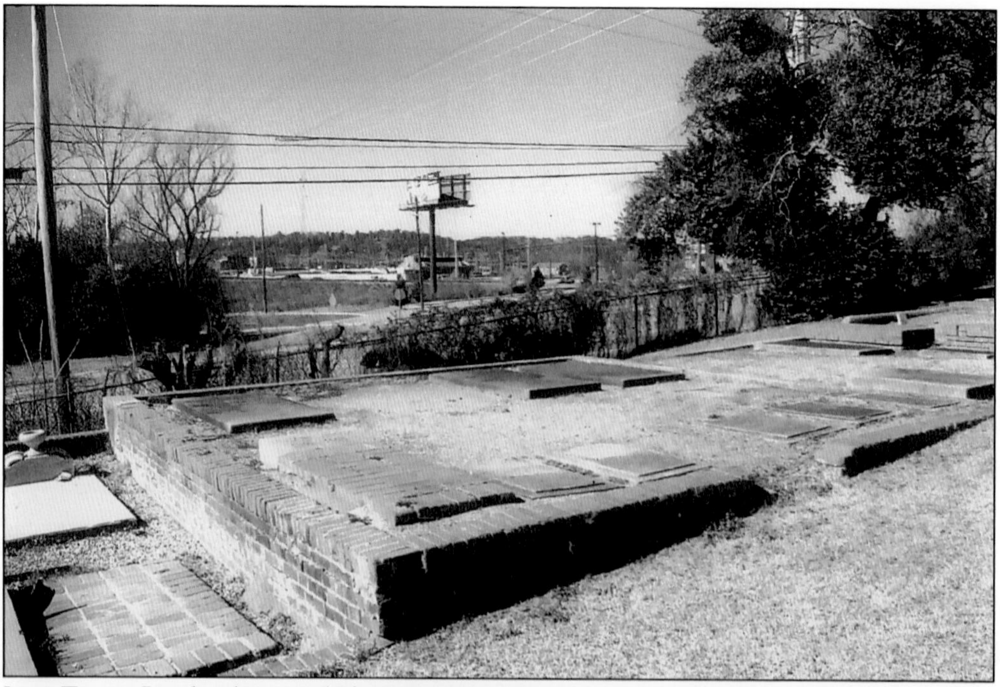

Isaac Turner Brooks, the son of Isham Brooks and Lezina Daniel Brooks, was born October 15, 1818, in Putnam County, Georgia. He married Mary Frances Wynn, and in the 1850s they moved to Columbus, where he became tax collector and clerk of the Superior Court. He died in 1893 and Mary died in 1903.

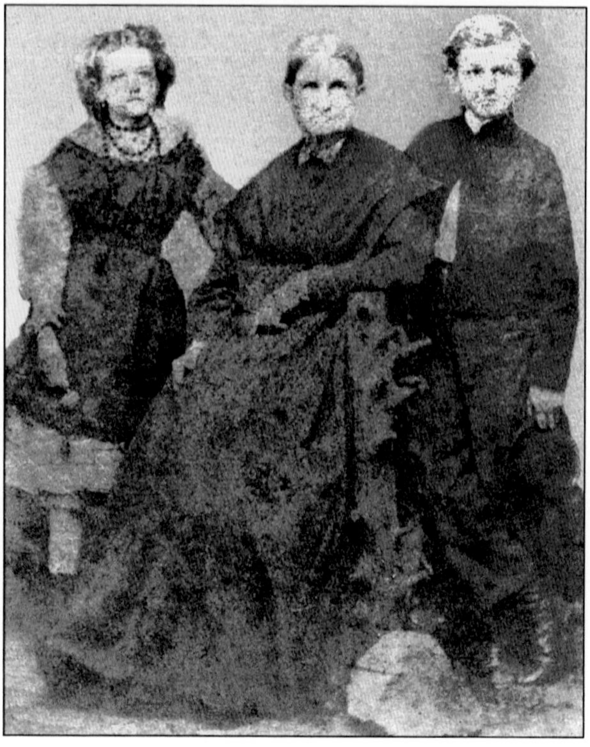

Pictured here are Mary Wynn Brooks and her twin children, Ida Matilda Brooks, who later became Mrs. Isaac Tamblin King, and Isaac Cheney Brooks. (Courtesy of John Sheftall.)

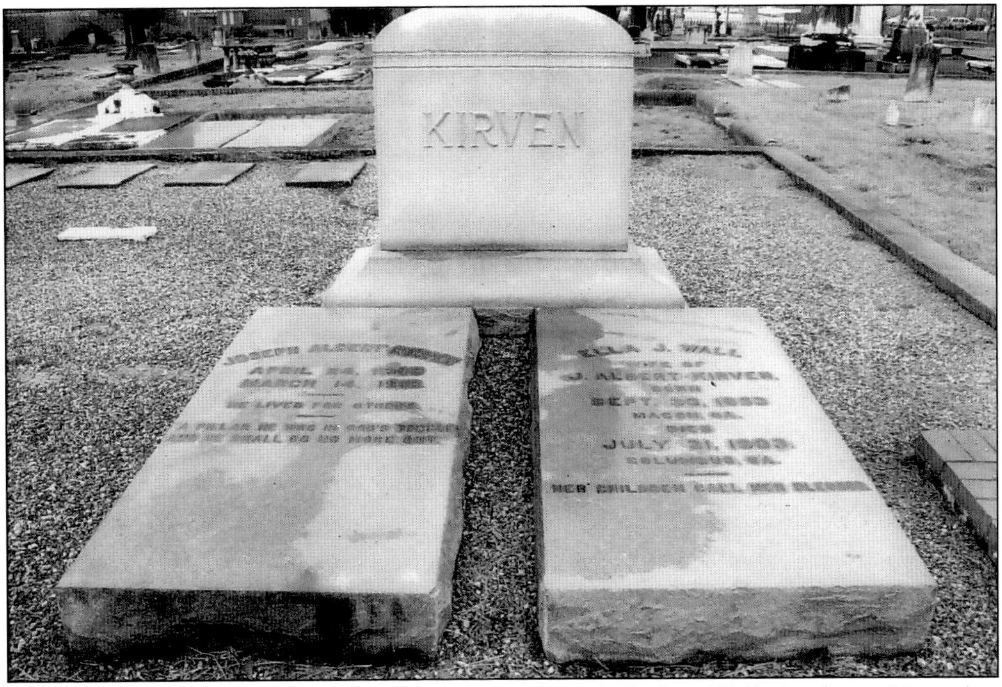

James Albert Kirven, born in Columbus in 1849, married Ella Jane Wall, daughter of Cornelius DuPont and Jane Chelney Wall. He founded the J.A. Kirven Co., a store that provided Columbus citizens everything from a first pair of shoes to a suitcase for a trip abroad. His legacy in public service has continued through the generations of his family. His grandson J. DuPont Kirven Jr. was one of the first benefactors of Historic Linwood Foundation.

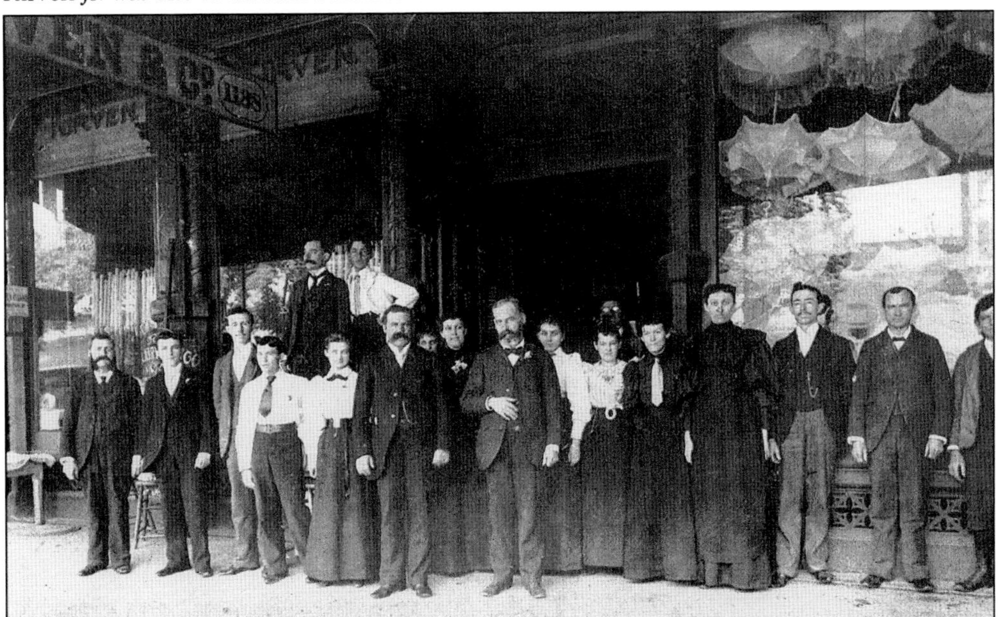

The proprietors and employees of J.A. Kirven and Co. are pictured in 1892. In the right front center is James Albert Kirven and at left front center is his brother Richard Kirven. (Photograph courtesy of Mr. and Mrs. Elliott Kirven.)

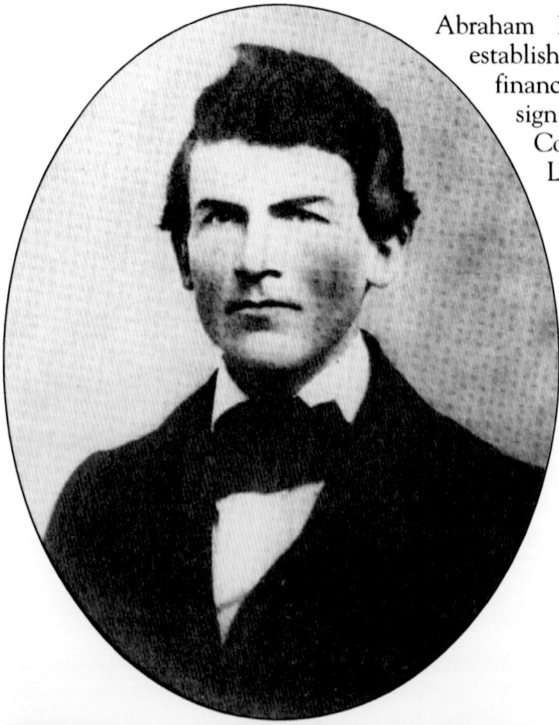

Abraham Illges played a pivotal role in the establishment of industry in Columbus. Offering financial backing and expertise, he played a significant role in a variety of local businesses: Columbus Ice Co., Golden's Foundry, Lummus Cotton Gin Co., City Mills, Columbus Electric and Power, Swift Spinning Mill, Muscogee Manufacturing Co., Georgia Midland and Gulf Railroad, and others. (Courtesy of Virginia Illges Norman.)

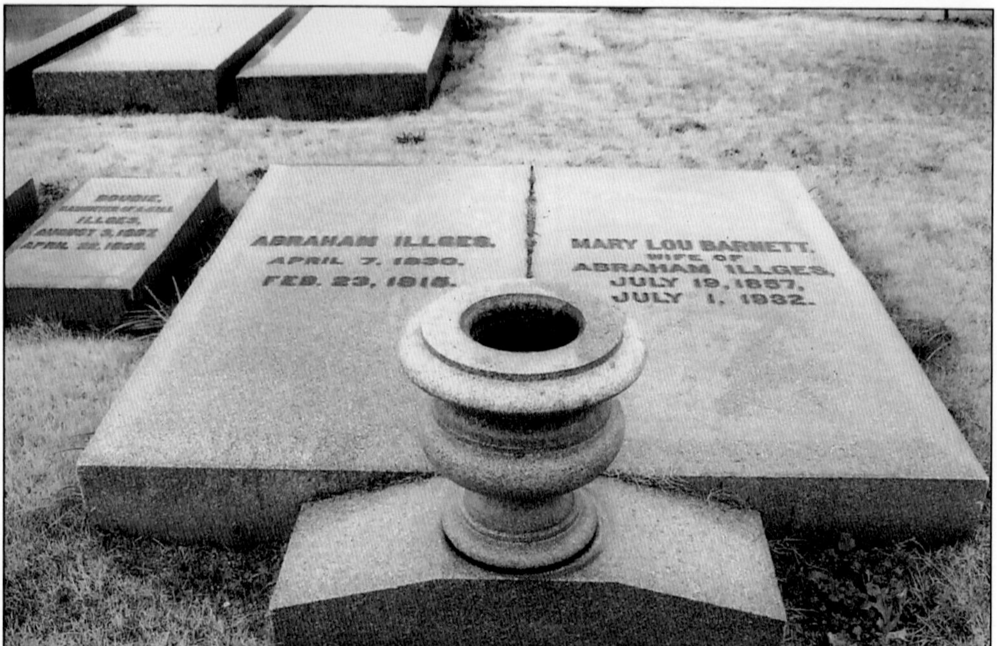

Abraham Illges married Mary Lou Barnett when he was 50 years old. Their seven children grew up happily in the Illges home on Second Avenue. Through marriage, these seven children link the Illges family with a long list of other Columbus families. The modesty of the simple urn marking the burial place of Abraham Illges and his wife is indicative of his life: he gave his name to none of the businesses that profited from his expertise and financial assistance.

Seven

Wrought and Cast Iron Fencing

Linwood Cemetery is fortunate to have many fenced lots that have survived over the years in very good condition. While little is known about the manufacturers of the fencing, we do know that some of the early fences were made in Columbus, perhaps by slave artisans. Although Columbus had several iron foundries, no records of these businesses survive that detail the making of fences for the cemetery. However, some of the early monument carvers advertised that they "would provide Wrought Iron and Wire Railing." Henry McCauley was the sole agent in Columbus for the New York Wire Railing Company. Andrew T. Elledge and John T. Norman, in business together as the Marble and Granite Works, advertised their "iron railings and other enclosures were a specialty."

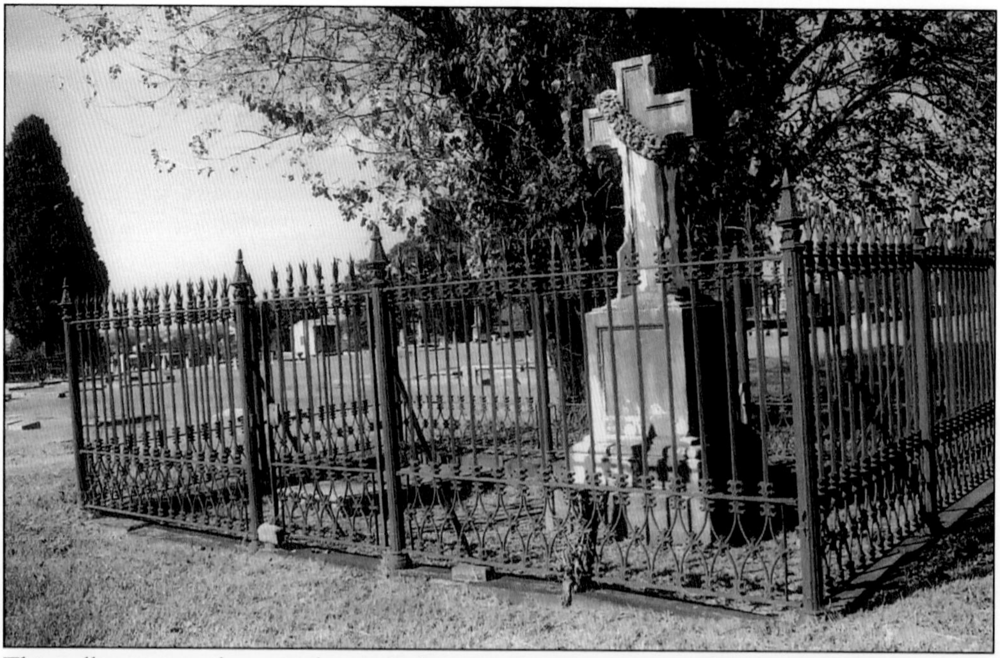

This tall cast iron fence and extraordinary monument are a tribute to the mystique and wealth of Edward Bell Fishburne. Fishburne lived in Columbus but maintained a cotton plantation across the river in Russell County, Alabama. He participated in the Cotton Planters Organization, attending their convention in Macon in 1851 as a delegate. He died in Lumpkin, Georgia, in 1854.

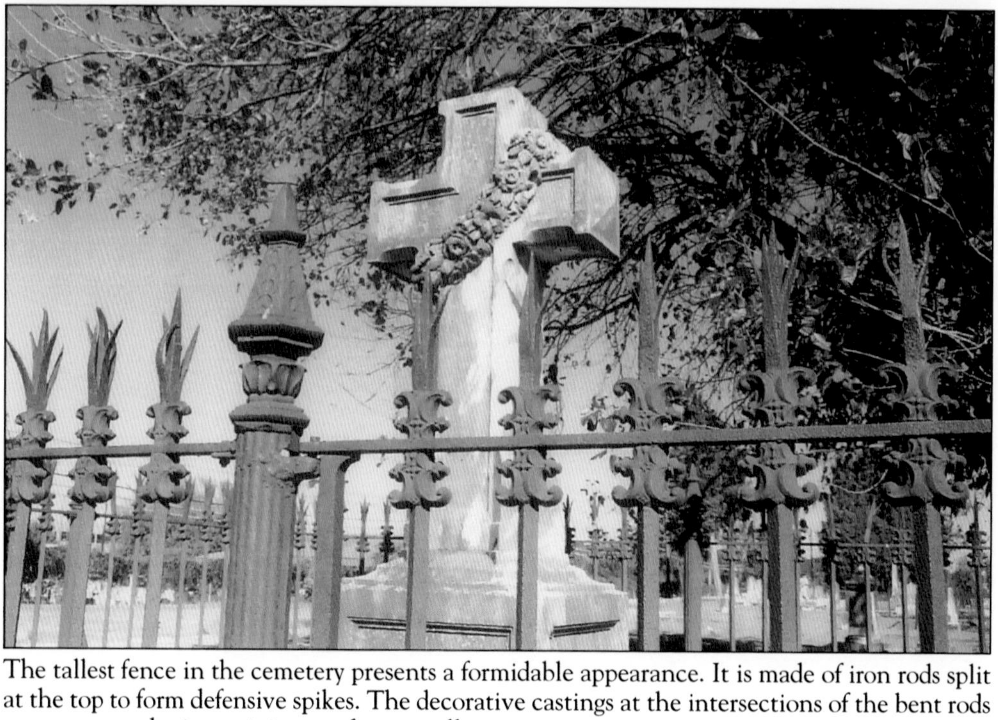

The tallest fence in the cemetery presents a formidable appearance. It is made of iron rods split at the top to form defensive spikes. The decorative castings at the intersections of the bent rods are cast onto the iron, giving a softer overall appearance.

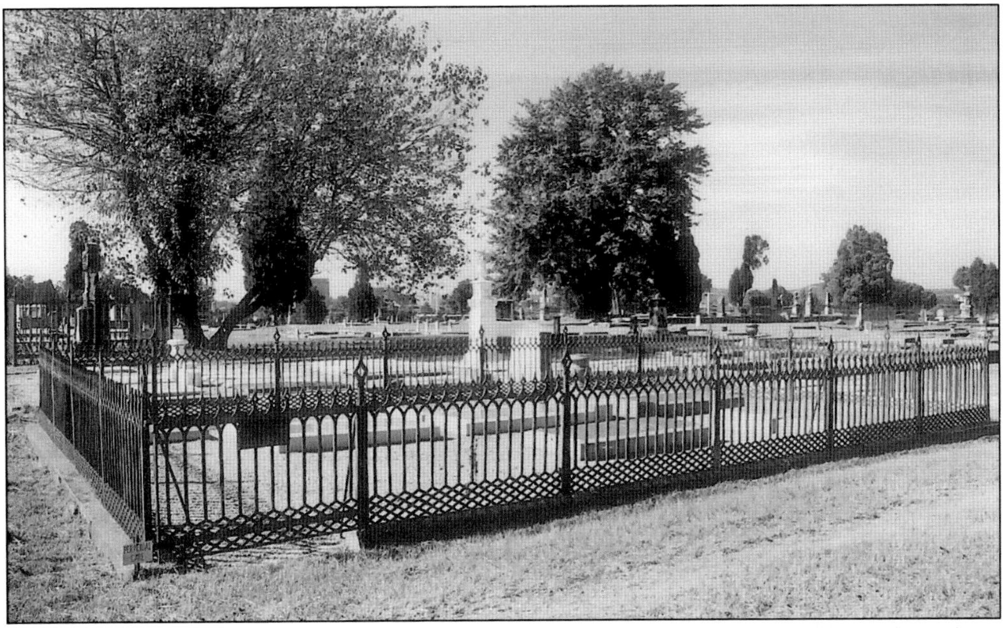

This fence surrounds the lot of the Golden family. Made by Golden's Foundry and Machine Co., it is of heavy cast iron panels with plain newels capped by a spear-shaped design. The bottom has a latticework effect. There are at least three other fences similar to this in the cemetery. The patriarch of the Golden family, George Jasper Golden, and his wife Sara Poitevent are buried here. George was superintendent and a shareholder in the Columbus Iron Works.

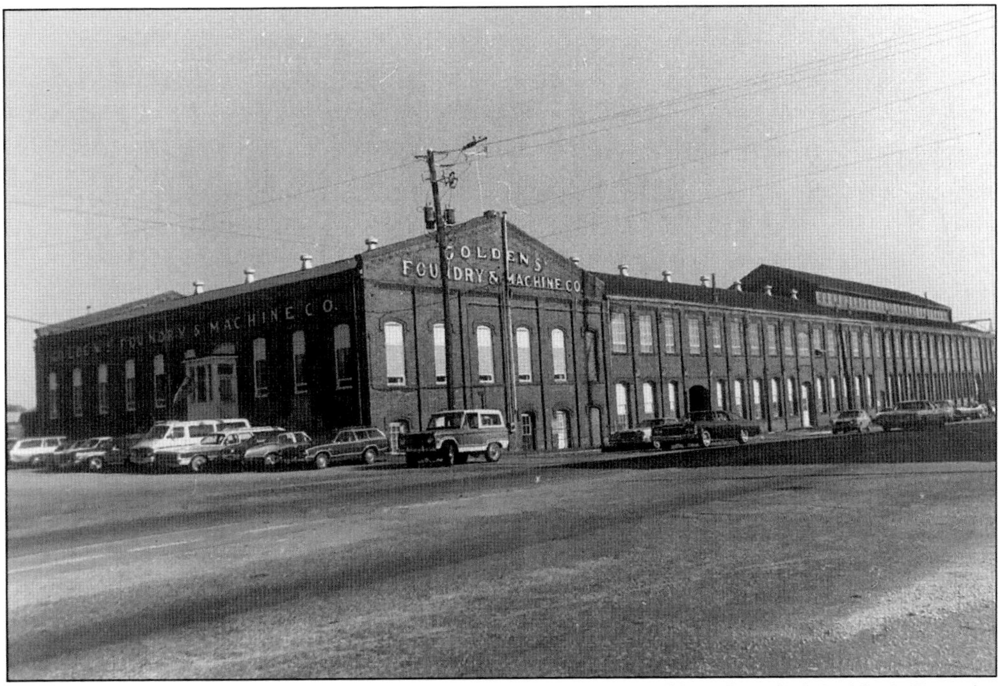

George Golden's sons, Theodore Ernest and John Poitevent Golden, founded Golden's Foundry in 1882. (Courtesy of Columbus State University Archives.)

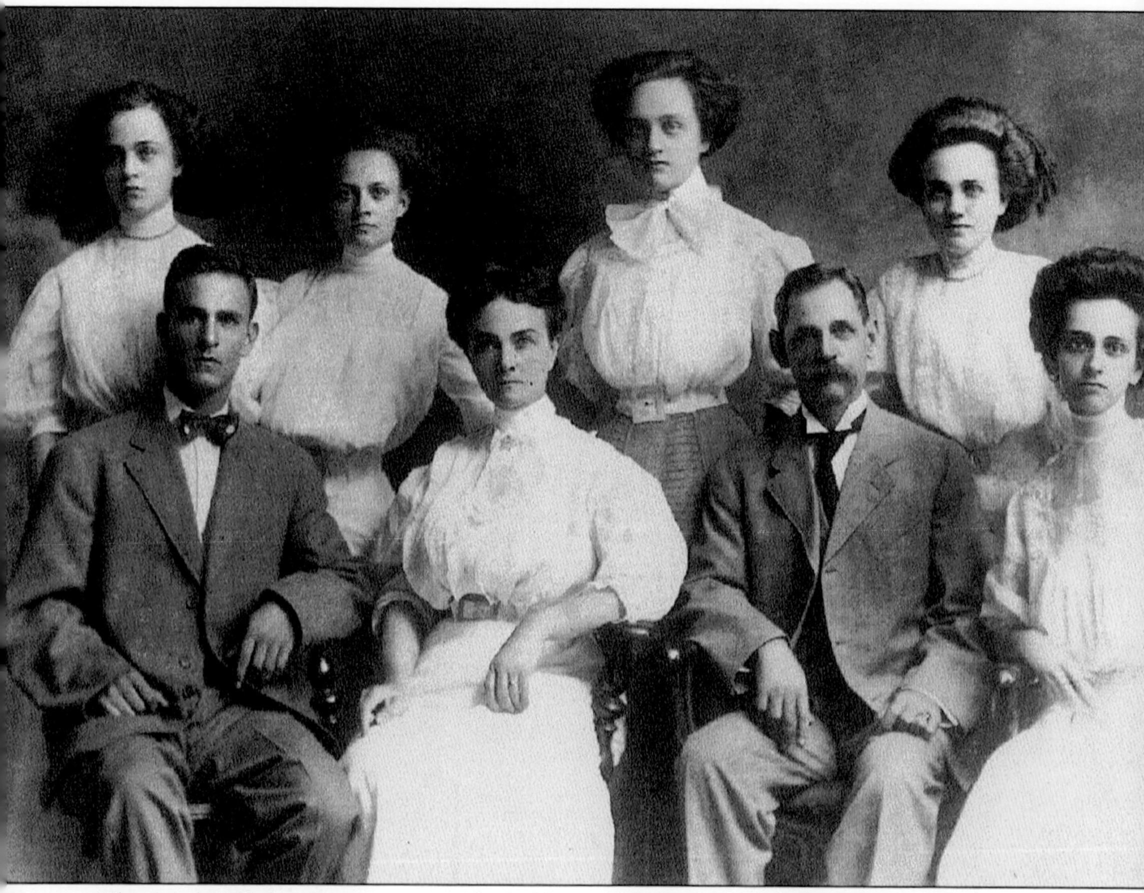

The family of John Poitevent and Ida Golden are, from left to right, (front row) George Jasper Golden Jr., Ida Blau Golden, John Poitevent Golden, and Lucile (Mrs. Benjamin Hill Fletcher); (back row) Leonora (Mrs. Henry Smith), Kathleen (Mrs. William Clark Pease), Vera (Mrs. Richard Dawson Gay Jr.), and Sara. (Courtesy of Poitevent Golden Pease Jr.)

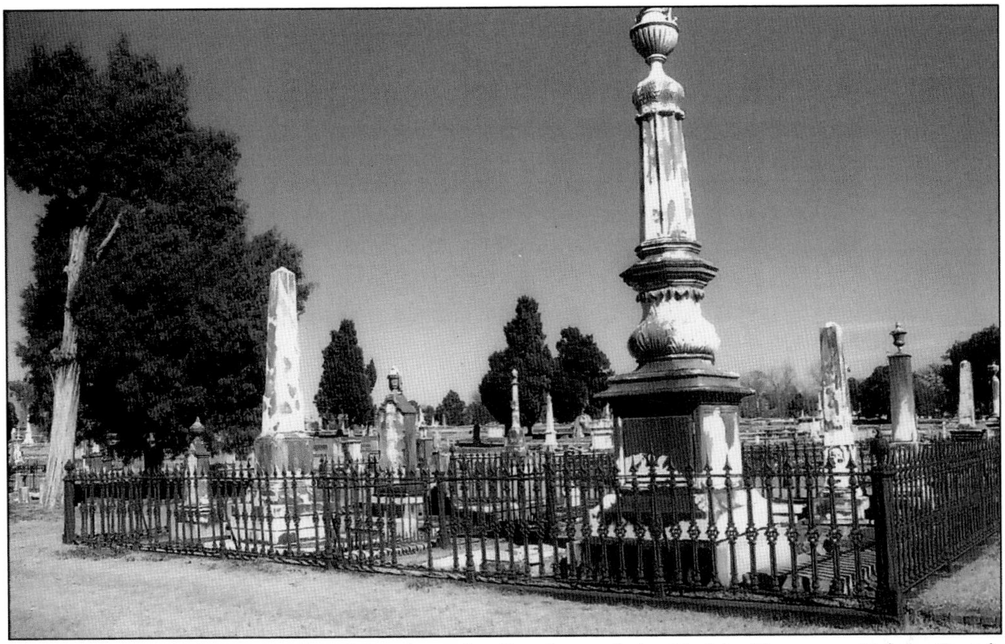

These two lots belong to related families, the Smiths and the Redds. Hampton Sidney Smith is the patriarch of the family, buried in the northern half of the Smith-Redd lot. Smith owned a warehouse capable of holding 14,000 bales of cotton. He was in the commission business, selling cotton for local planters and supplying them with necessaries not produced on the plantation. William A. Redd, whose grave is found in the Smith-Redd lot, was a businessman who supported education in Columbus and Troup County, Georgia.

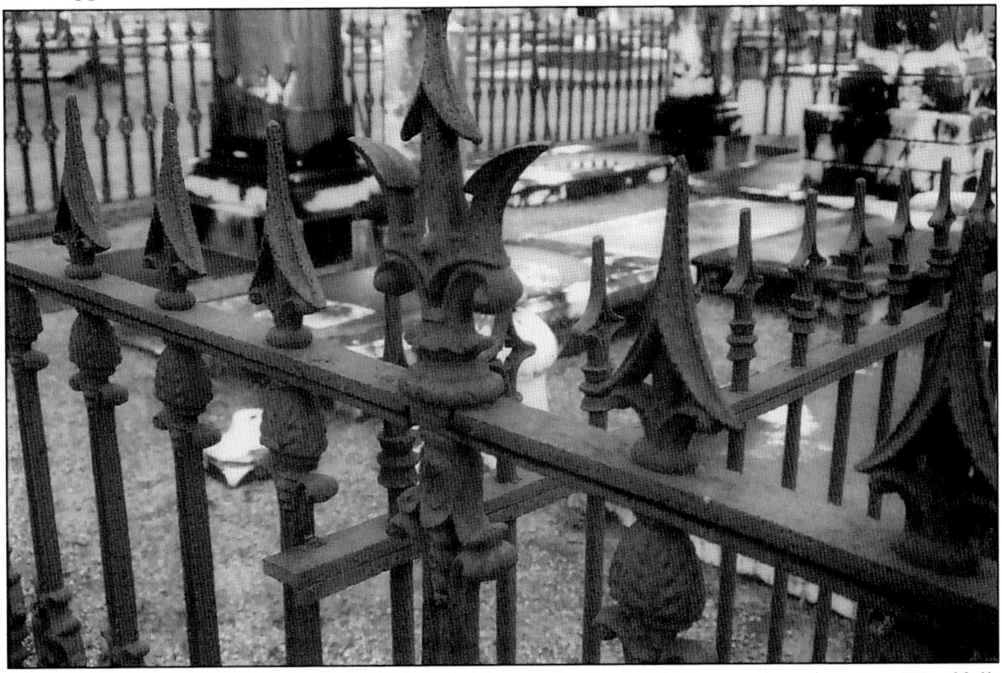

These lots were originally surrounded by one fence similar in design to the adjoining Woolfolk lot, but they were later divided in the middle by a fence of a different design.

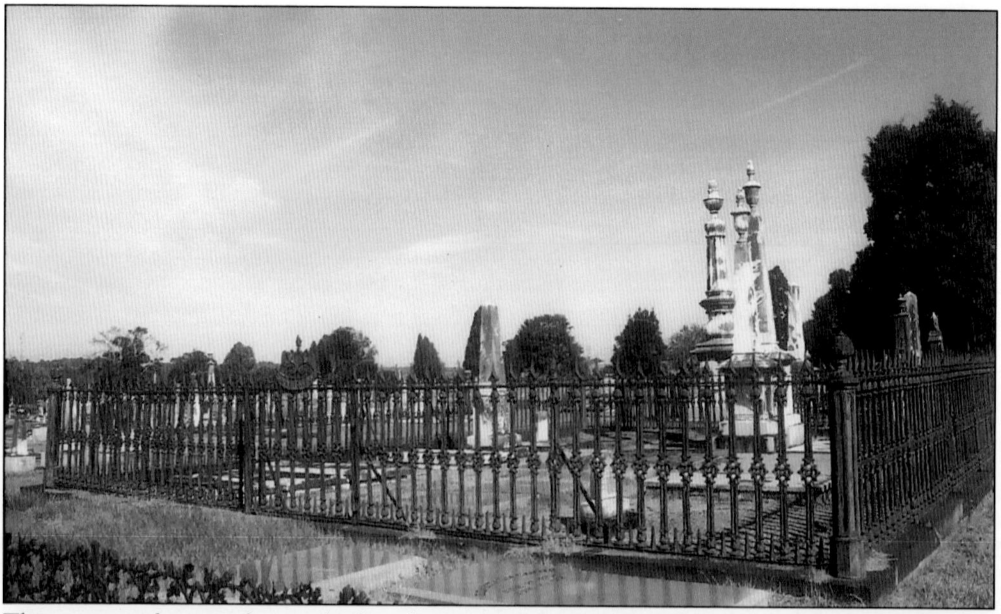

This cast iron fence with very thick pickets topped with spears has a classical design midway up the picket. The fence surrounds the lot of the John Woolfolk family. Inside, several unmarked brick slabs for children and adults are scattered among other tall and elaborate monuments. The first burial in the lot was Margaret Woolfolk in 1853. John Woolfolk, the Columbus family patriarch, died in 1861.

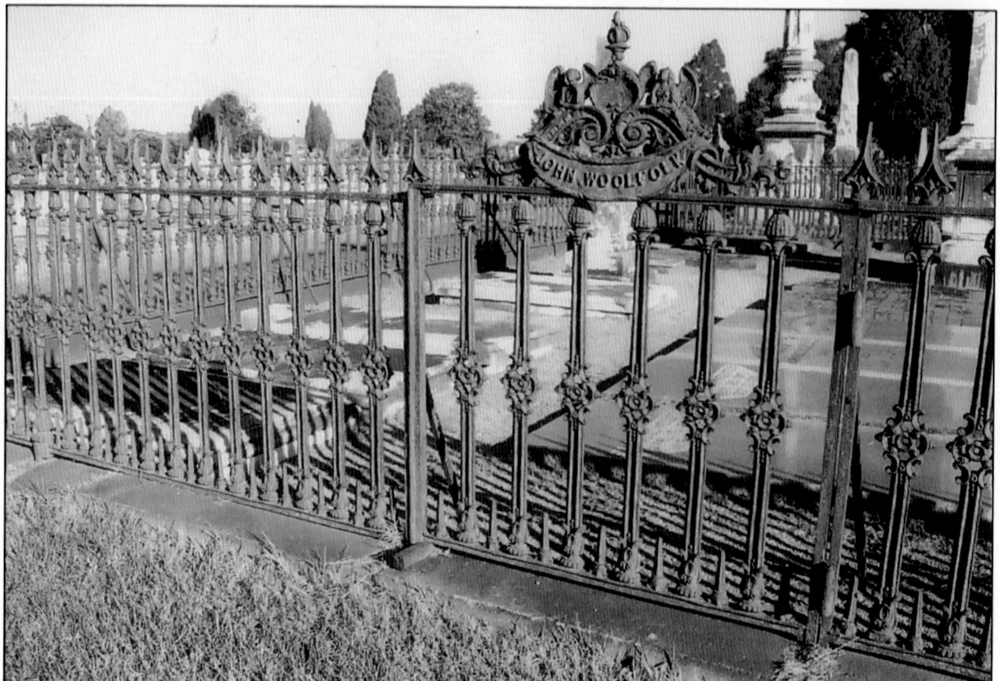

The gate to the Woolfolk lot is adorned with angels supporting a design topped with a burning torch. While many gates have been stolen from the cemetery, this one remains, perhaps because it bears a name.

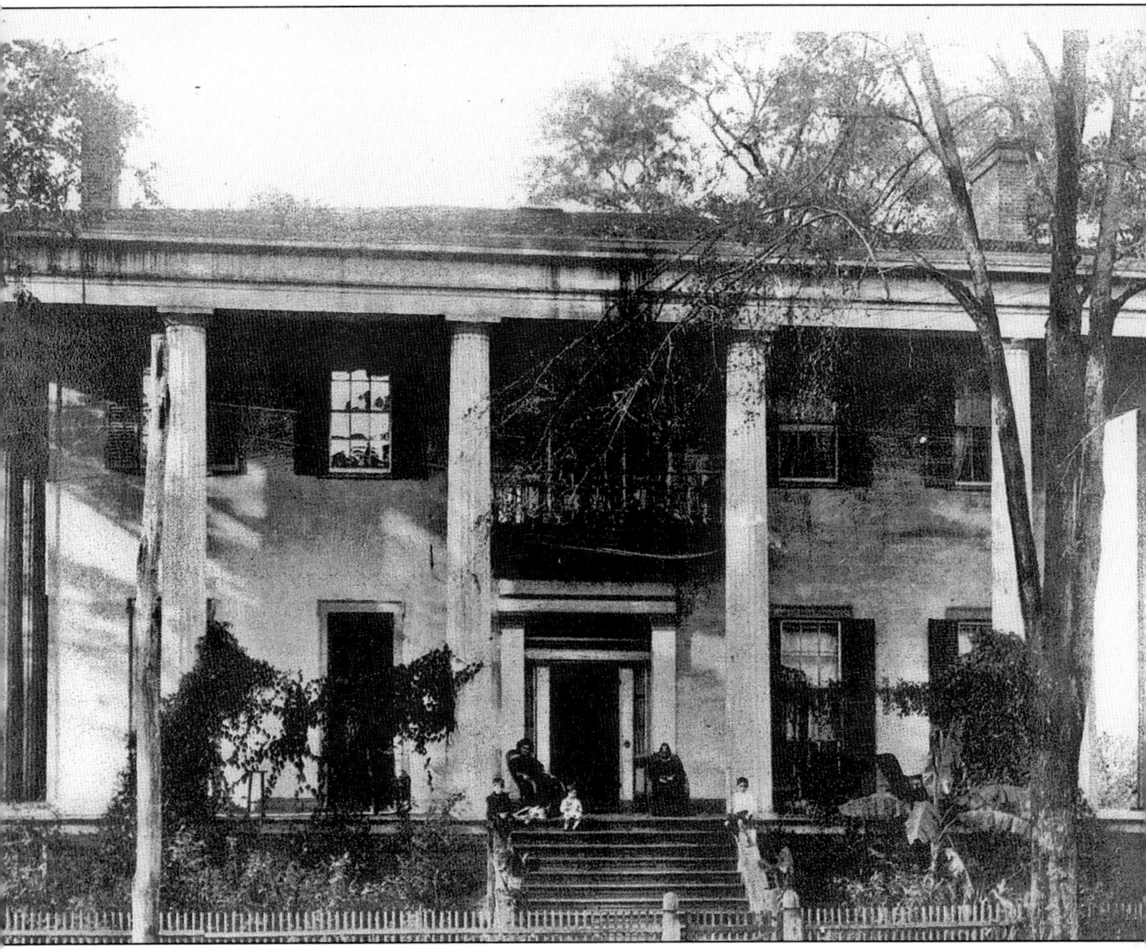

After the Woolfolks came to Columbus in 1831, John developed a cotton plantation eight miles south of the city. The family later lived in a stately mansion in Wynnton. Saved from destruction by Historic Columbus Foundation, the house is now being restored. Pictured here are members of the James Fleming Waddell family, who owned the house after John Woolfolk's death.

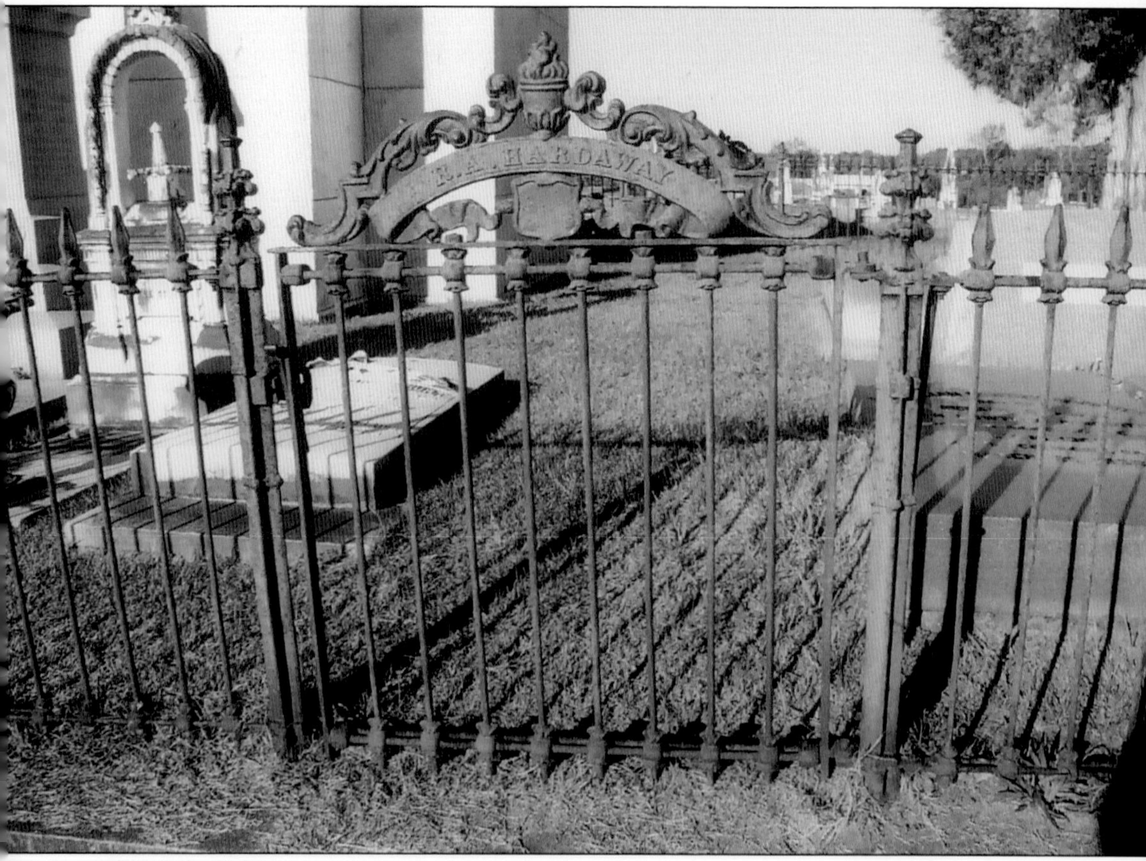

This beautiful gate at the entrance of the fenced lot surrounds four generations of deceased Hardaways. Made of wrought iron rods topped with cast iron spearheads, the fence is anchored with brick pillars.

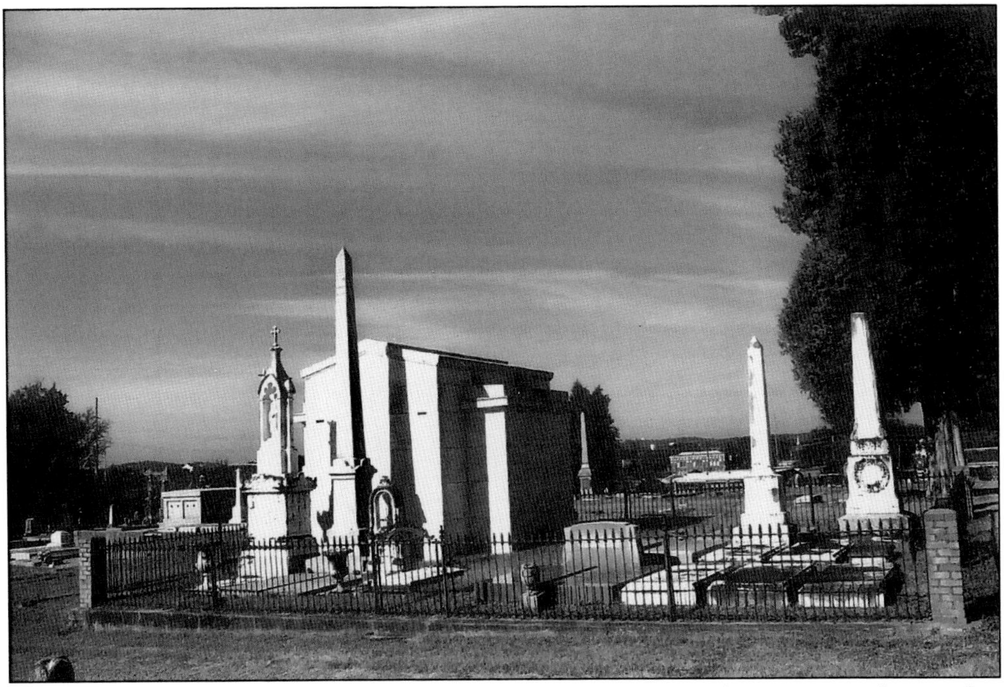

The Hardaway lot holds some of the most ornate monuments in the cemetery, along with a mausoleum. A cast iron bench is placed inside for comfortable viewing and meditation.

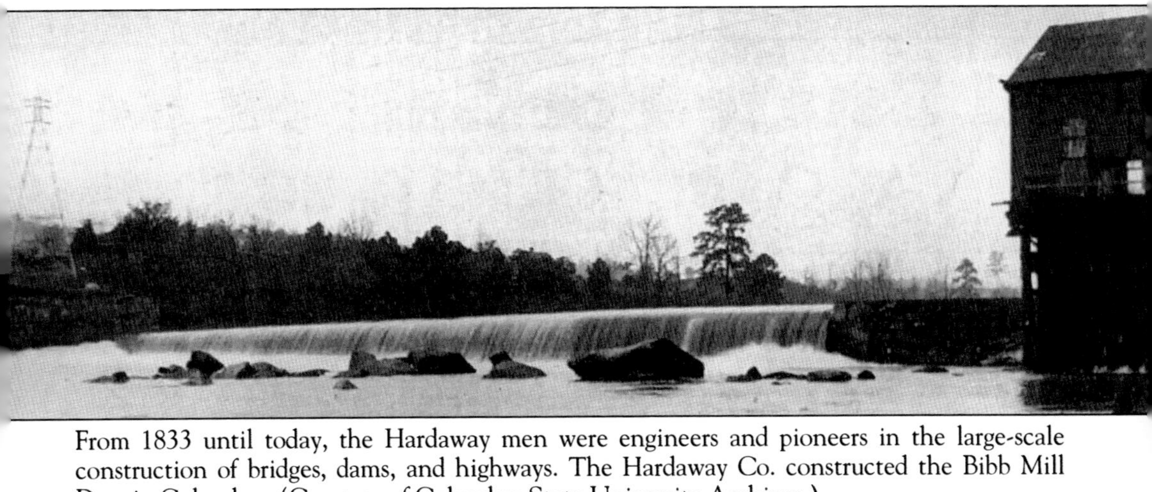

From 1833 until today, the Hardaway men were engineers and pioneers in the large-scale construction of bridges, dams, and highways. The Hardaway Co. constructed the Bibb Mill Dam in Columbus. (Courtesy of Columbus State University Archives.)

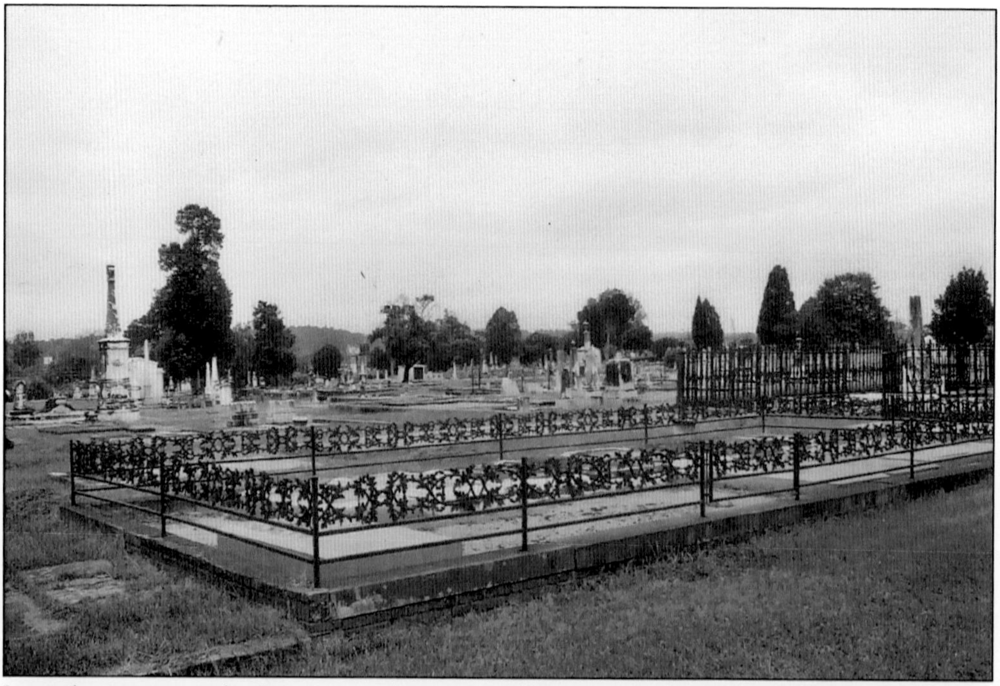

In stark contrast to the fencing, tombstones, and monuments in the other 19th-century lots, this fence has low panels of cast iron oak leaves and acorns. Martin J. Crawford is buried here with his family. He was a practicing lawyer and a judge of the Superior Court. His marble slab, with rounded decorated corners, reads, "How many hopes lie buried here." There are no rising monuments in the lot. All the graves are marked by marble and granite slabs.

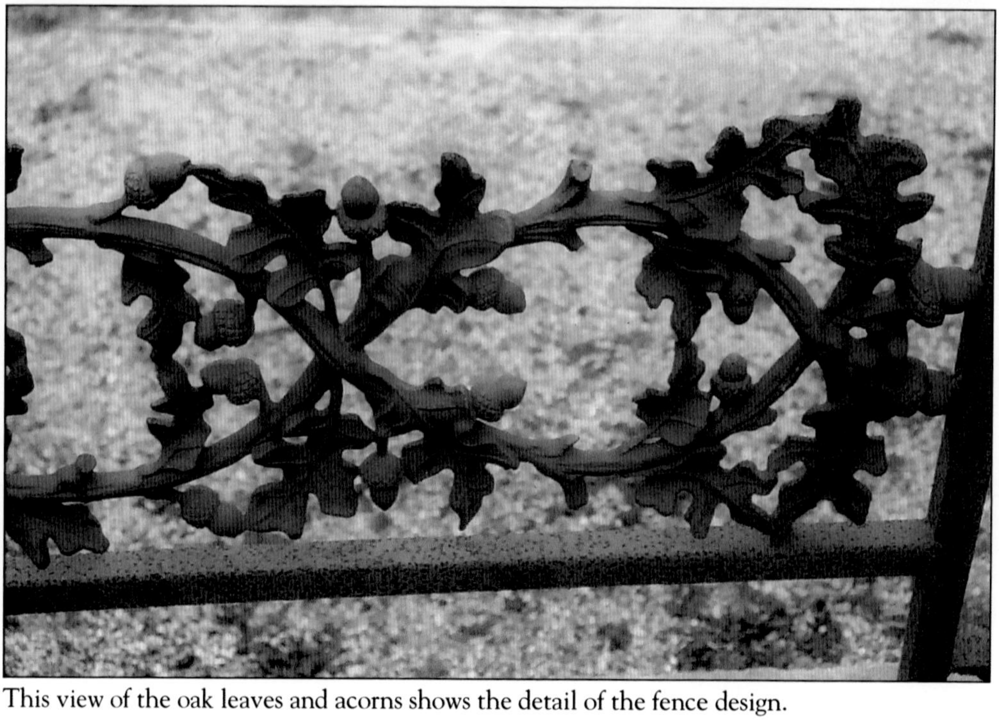

This view of the oak leaves and acorns shows the detail of the fence design.

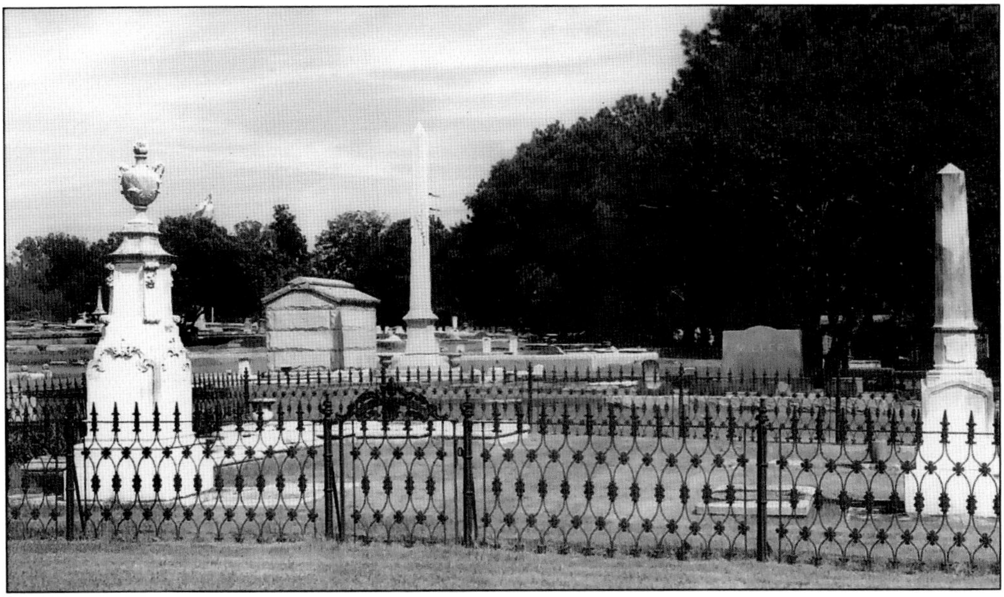

The Nathaniel Nuckolls lot, one of the largest in the cemetery, is surrounded by a drawn wire fence that bends and weaves. It is decorated with cast iron rosettes at the points of intersection and cast iron tips on the pickets. Nathaniel was a prosperous businessman in Columbus and the patriarch of a large family. He owned one of the original town lots in Columbus but later lived in Alabama for a while before he died at his home in Linwood, a suburb now incorporated into Columbus.

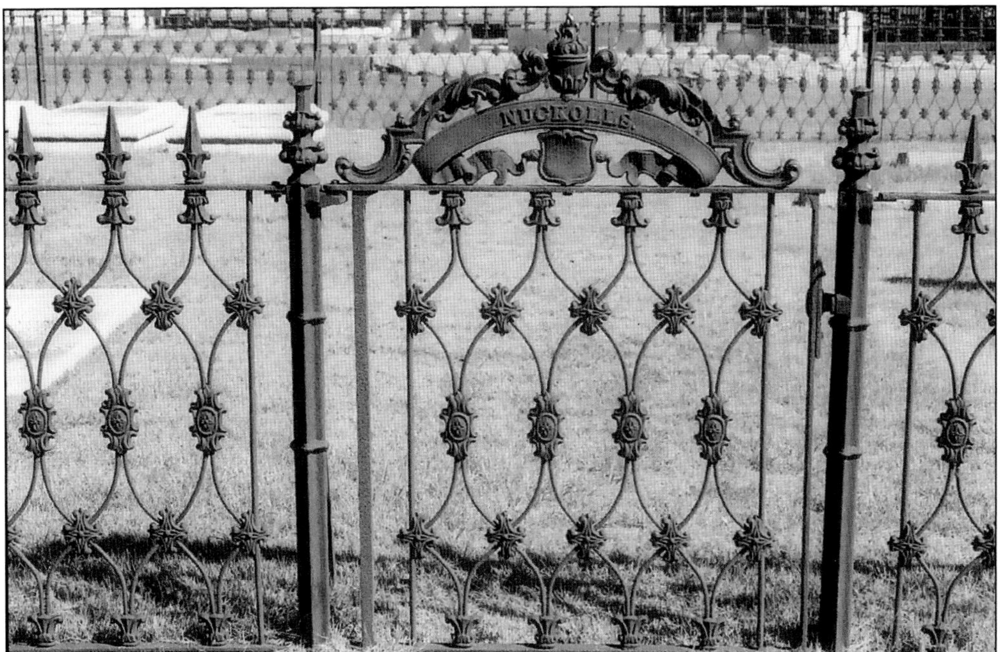

A closer view of the Nuckolls gate shows the detail of the rosettes. A burning torch is held up by scrollwork above the family name. Although the fence design is different, the decoration at the top of the gate is identical to the Hardaway gate.

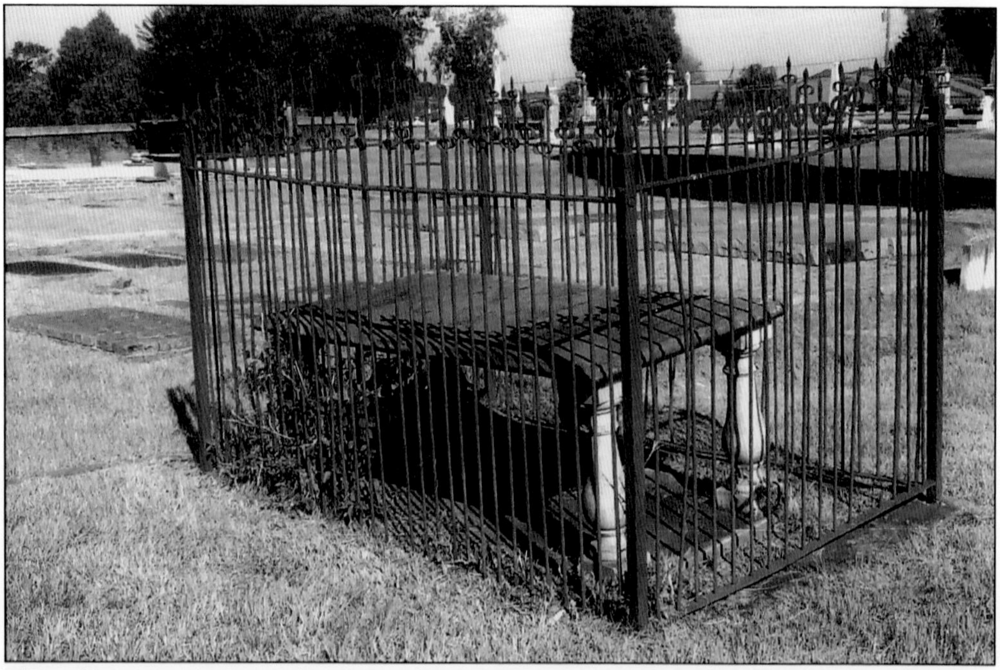

This tabletop tomb covers the grave of Eaton Flewellen, who died in 1839. Only a few years earlier, he had come to Tallapoosa District, Alabama, to grow cotton. He was unmarried, leaving his estate to his sister and her five children, who lived in eastern Georgia. Although placed here with loving thoughtfulness, today this tall wrought iron fence with no opening seems to symbolize loneliness and solitude.

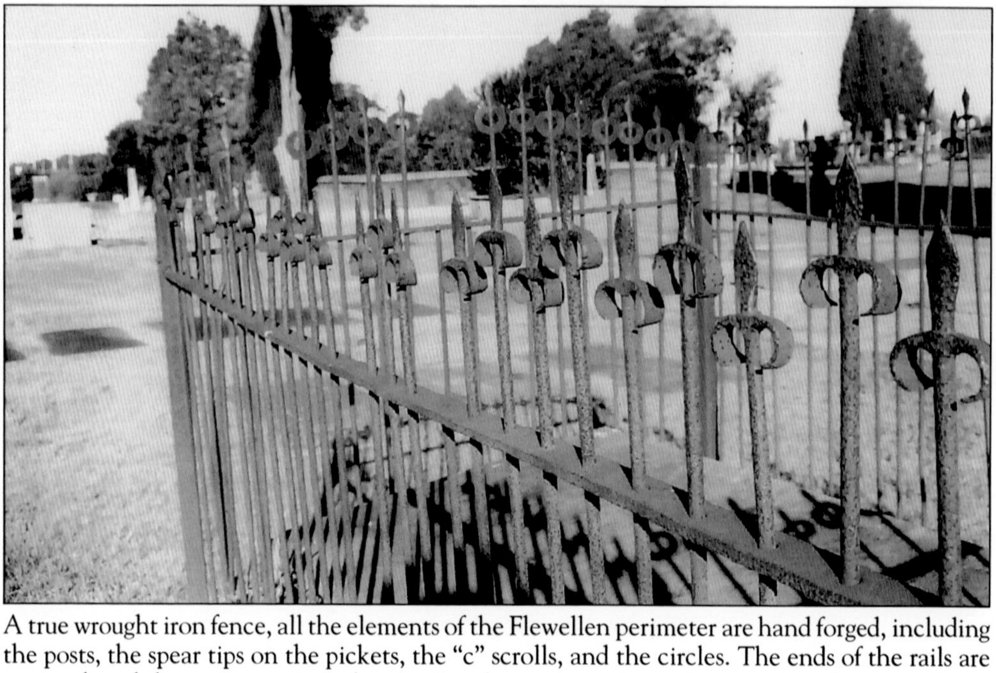

A true wrought iron fence, all the elements of the Flewellen perimeter are hand forged, including the posts, the spear tips on the pickets, the "c" scrolls, and the circles. The ends of the rails are tenoned, and the posts are pierced to receive the tenons, whose tips were then hammered into a rivet head.

Eight

Museum Pieces and the Unusual

Scattered throughout Linwood Cemetery, some grave markers stand out because of their exceptional beauty. Some were carved by local monument carvers, while some were shipped in by rail and steamboat. Replicating these beautiful sculptures today would cost a king's ransom. The cemetery also has markers that do not fit into any specific category. Since markers are usually placed by those who are left behind, it is those individuals who determine what type of marker will tell the story of the deceased. These striking markers, beautiful and unusual, are special enough to warrant their own place in our book.

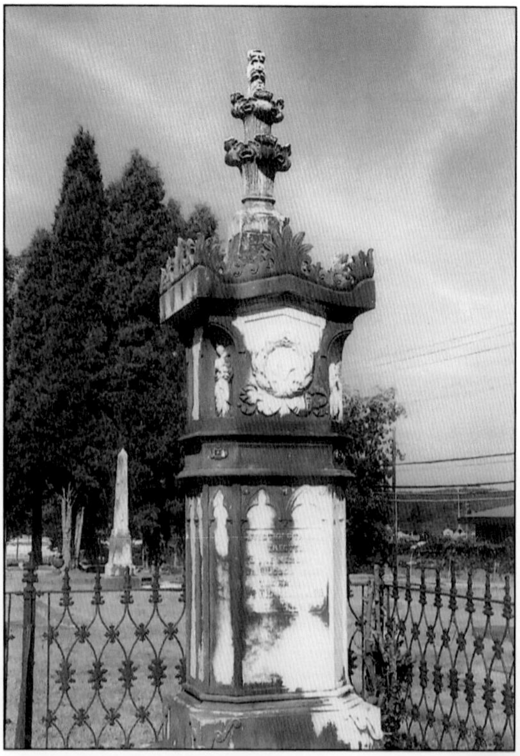

One of the first physicians in Columbus, Dr. Hudson Allen Thornton came to Columbus along with his parents, Jeremiah and Elizabeth Thornton, and his siblings; they were among the first to own city lots. Dr. Thornton participated in both political and civic affairs. In 1832, he served on the City Health Committee and was surgeon of the 60th Regiment of the Georgia Militia. In 1837, he joined the States Rights Auxiliary Association. His wives, Judith, who died in 1829, and Elizabeth, who died in 1837, are buried with him. The unusual monument with four exquisitely carved figures was commissioned by his children. Unfortunately, the monument is not signed by the sculptor.

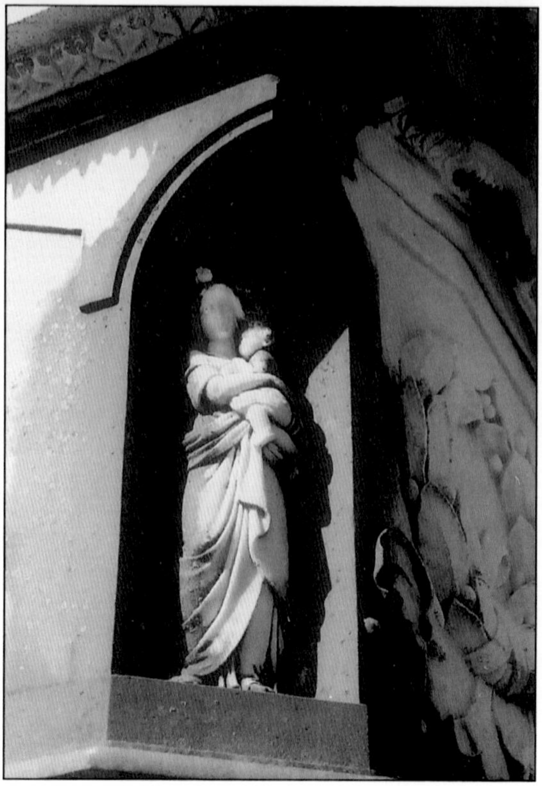

Each corner of the monument has a different figure. This corner, which depicts a mother holding a child, is a symbol of charity.

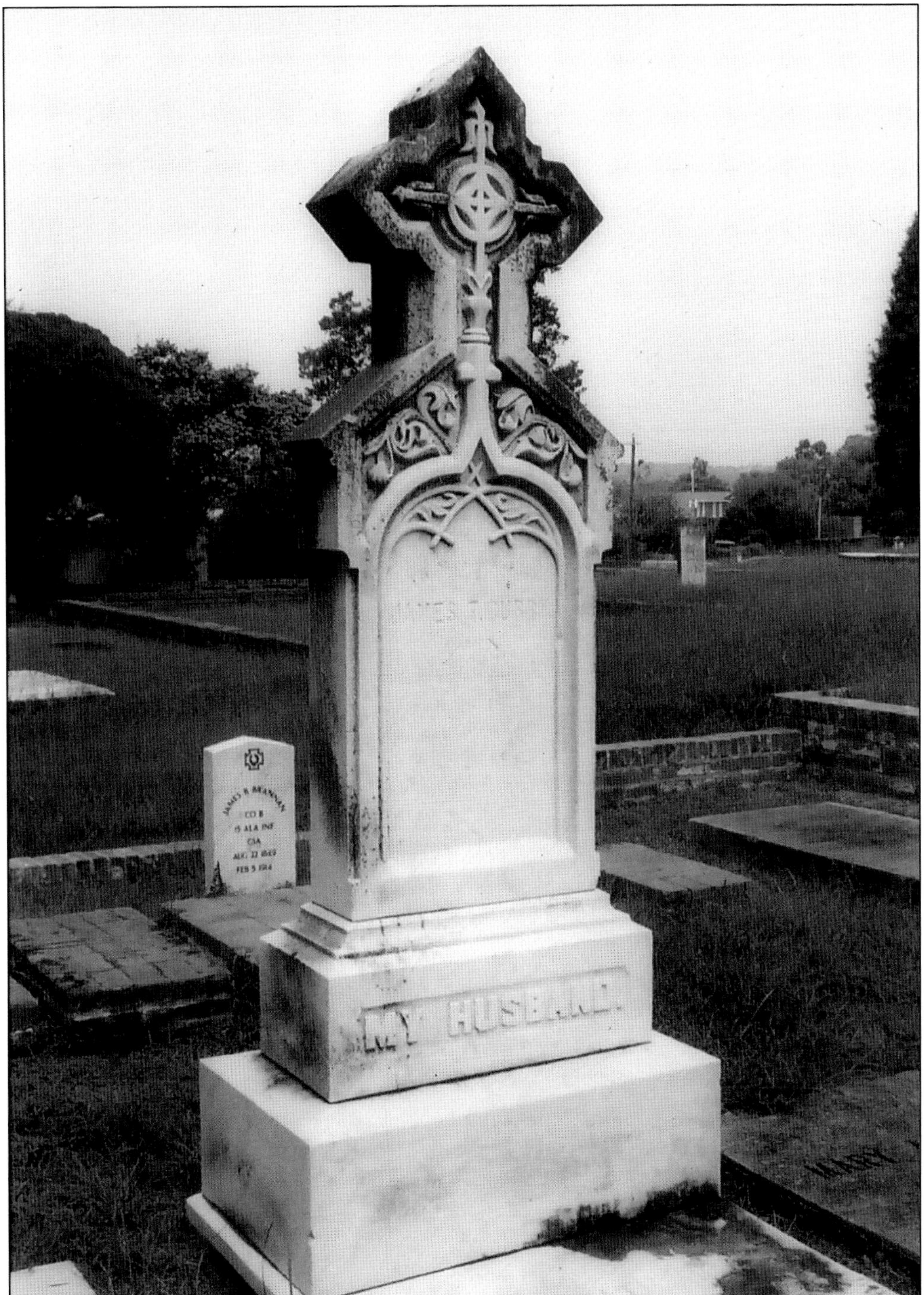

This handsomely carved Celtic cross, the only such design in the cemetery, graces the grave of James T. Curry. Curry, born in London in 1826, came to Columbus in 1851. He worked as a railroad engineer, serving with several different rail lines during his lifetime. With his family, he resided on McIntosh Street, now Fifth Avenue.

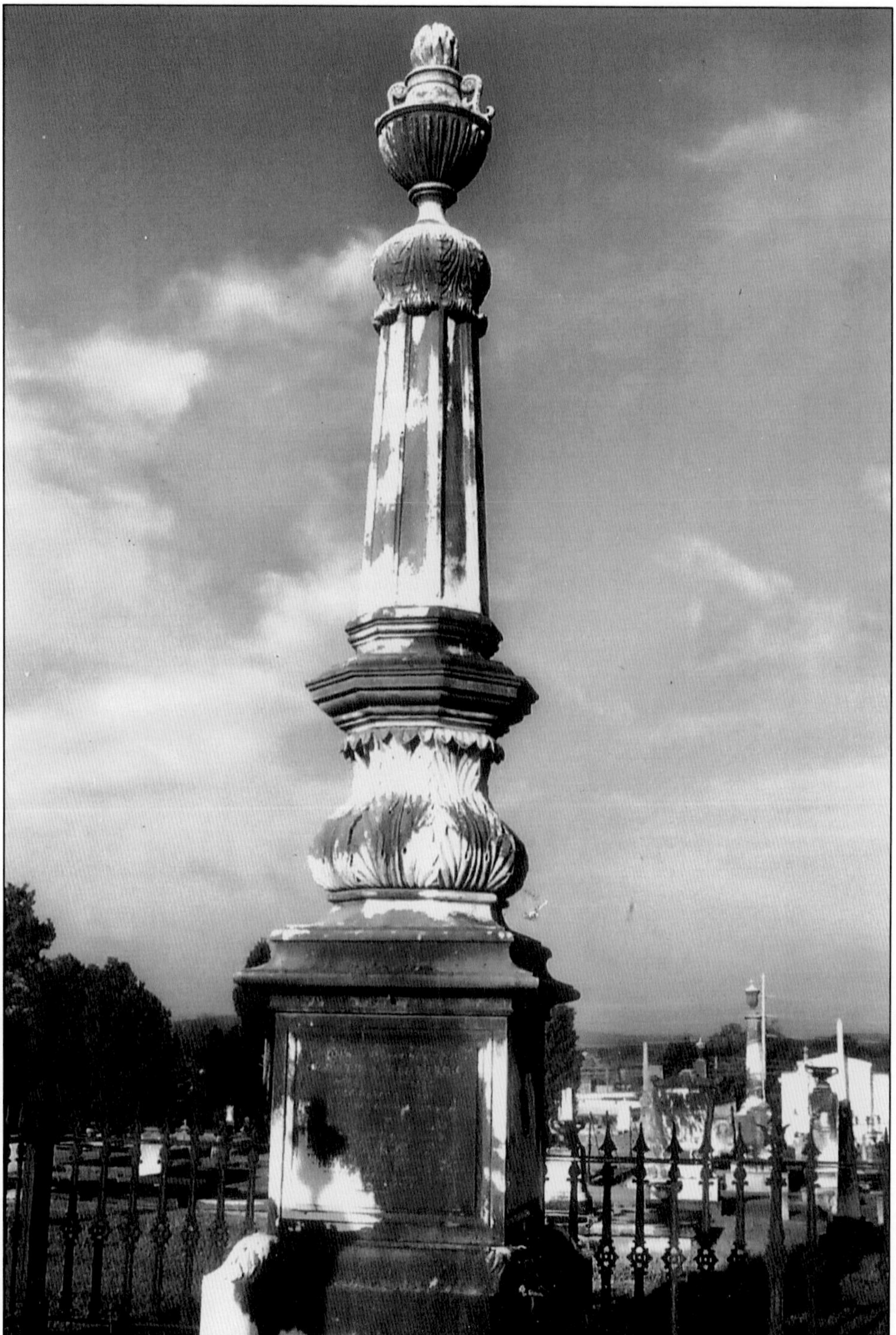

This is the largest monument in the cemetery; the inscription reads, "Here lieth the last of a family." Martin J. Kendrick was 22 when he died at the home of his uncle, William A. Redd, who administered the estate and commissioned this monument.

This beautiful Gothic-style monument stands in honor of Almira Williford, wife of James D. Williford and daughter of Martin and Matilda Brooks of Columbus. Almira died in Tallapoosa County, Alabama, in 1860. James D. Williford was a Columbus businessman, but when Almira died, he disappeared from the area after paying Henry McCauley to carve his wife's monument.

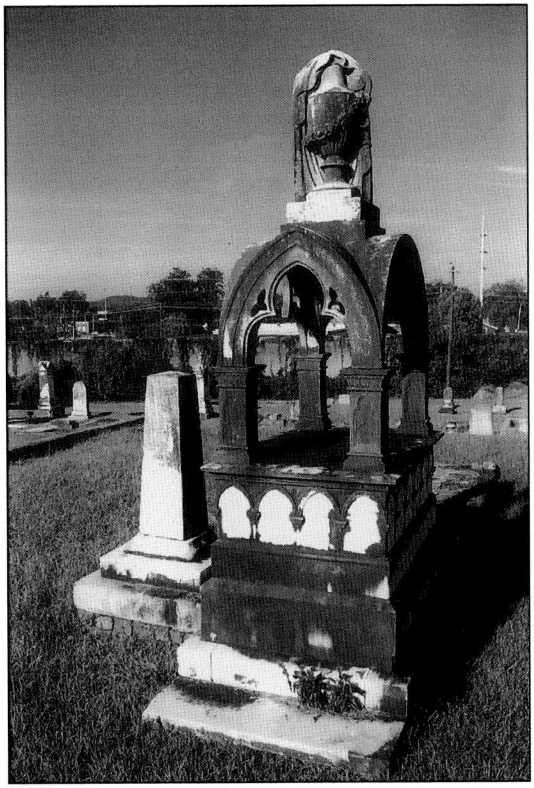

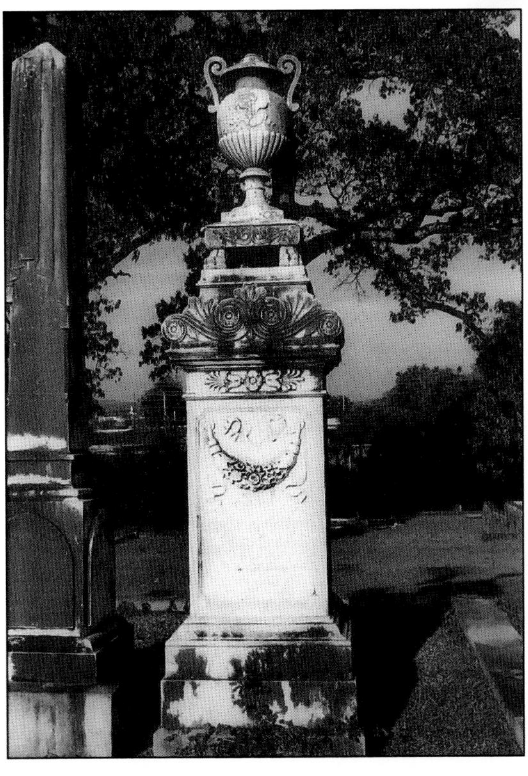

This impressive monument is in the Moffett family lot. Thomas Moffett, the first of seven children born to Henry Moffett and Dorinda Phillips Moffett, was 26 when he died in 1858 of typhoid fever. His father had drawn land in Muscogee County in the land lottery and made his name as a successful planter in Russell County, Alabama, and in Muscogee and Stewart Counties in Georgia. He served on the Russell County Board of Commissioners and in the Alabama legislature. In 1850, Thomas served as one of the directors of the Rock Island Paper Factory.

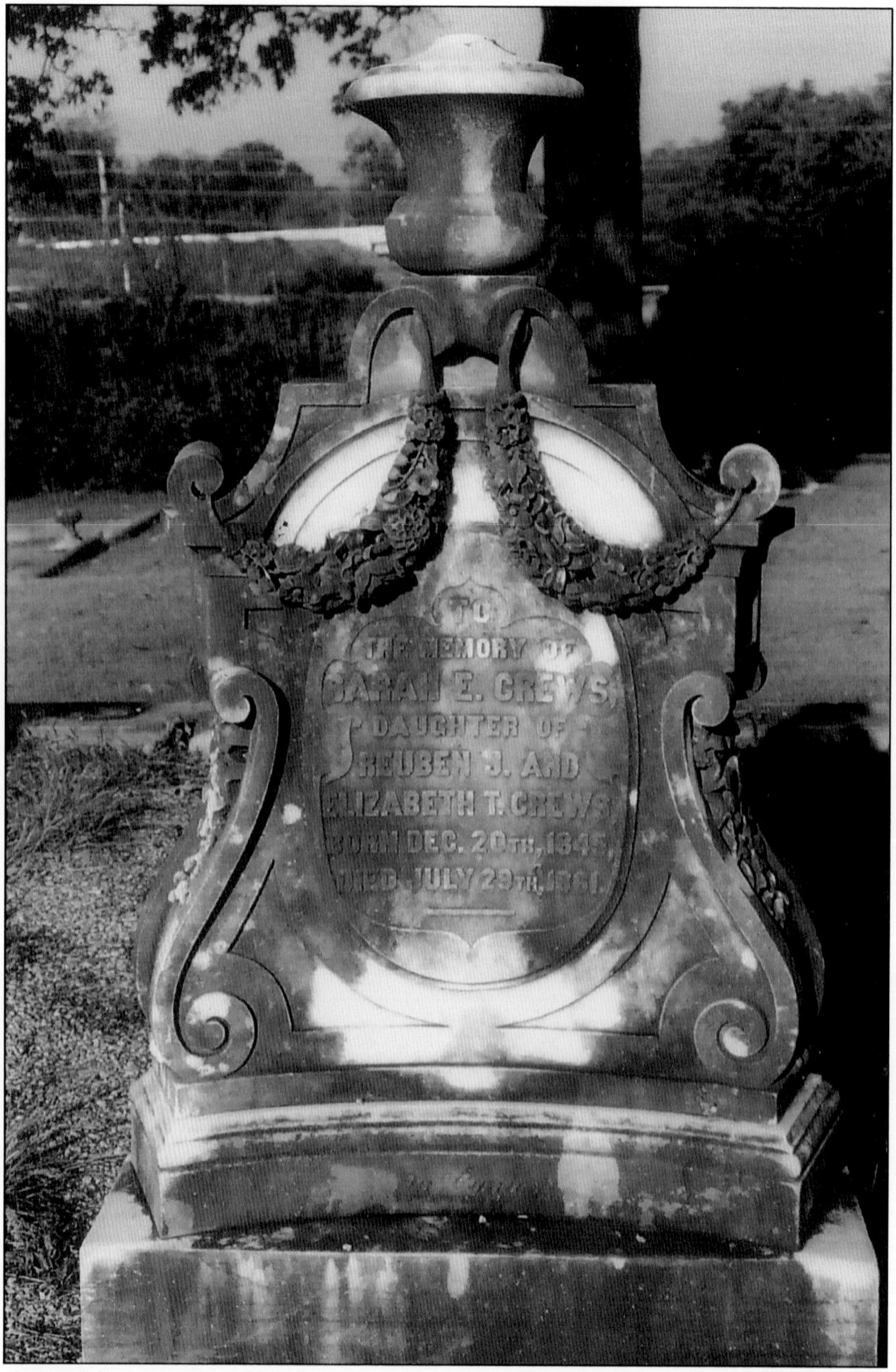

This beautifully carved monument also stands in the Moffett lot; it marks the burial place of Sarah E. Crews, who died at 16. She was the daughter of Reuben J. and Elizabeth T. Crews. Her father, who was in the Columbus area by 1832, began farming in Harris and Marion Counties, Georgia. The family lived near the present town of Ellerslie. Sculptor Henry McCauley carved this monument.

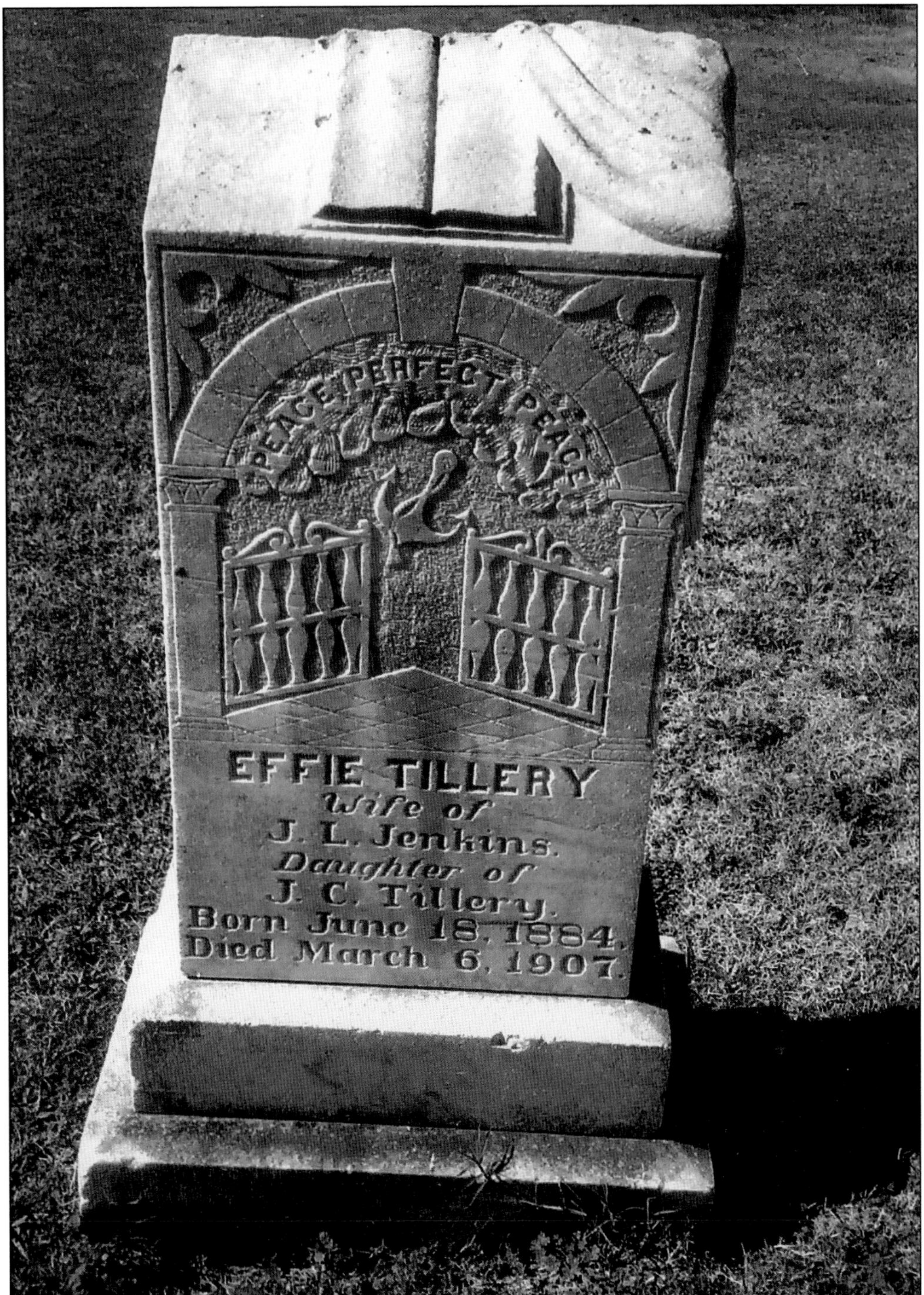

This carving symbolizes the gates of heaven opening up to receive the spirit of Effie Tillery, who died in 1907. After the turn of the century, techniques in monument carving became more mechanized and standardized, making markers like this all the more valuable for their individuality and craftsmanship.

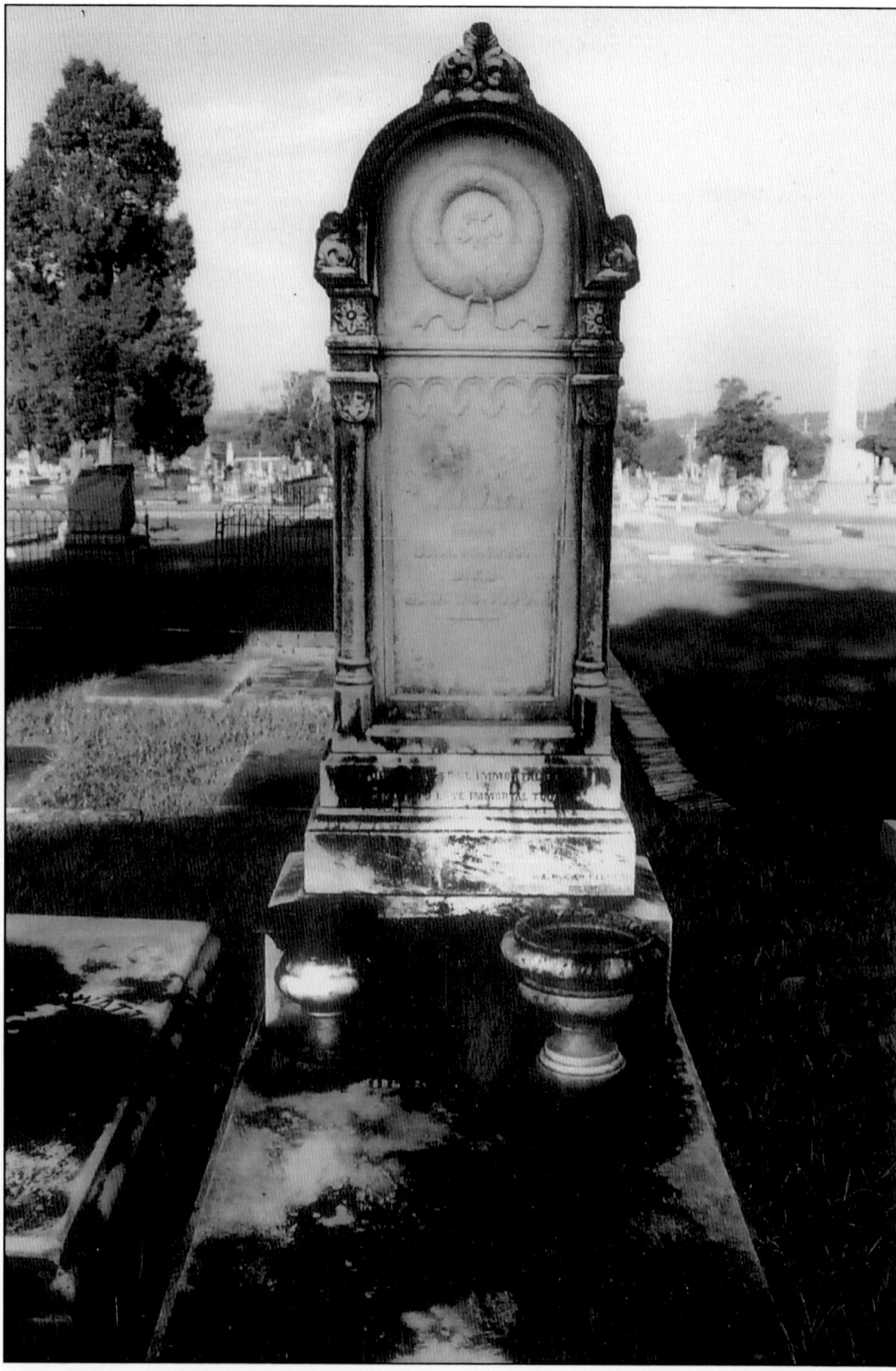

Sarah A. Garrett and William John Watt were married in Columbus on November 14, 1843. In the 1850s and 1860s they farmed in Harris and Stewart Counties. In the *1864 Census to Re-organize the Georgia Militia*, William Watt was the enrolling officer in Stewart County. After the Civil War he sold wholesale groceries, wagons, buggies, and harnesses in Columbus. Sarah died in 1879, and William erected this magnificent monument in her honor. Seen in the lower right are the signatures of carvers A.M. and J.H. Elledge.

Judge James Joseph Walton Biggers was a resident of Muscogee County as early as 1829. At 21 he moved to Harris County, where he became a planter with large land holdings near Fortson and Mulberry Grove. He later became judge of the Inferior Court. He was widely known and respected in the Chattahoochee Valley for his agricultural, civic, and religious contributions. (Courtesy of Mr. and Mrs. J.J.W. Biggers.)

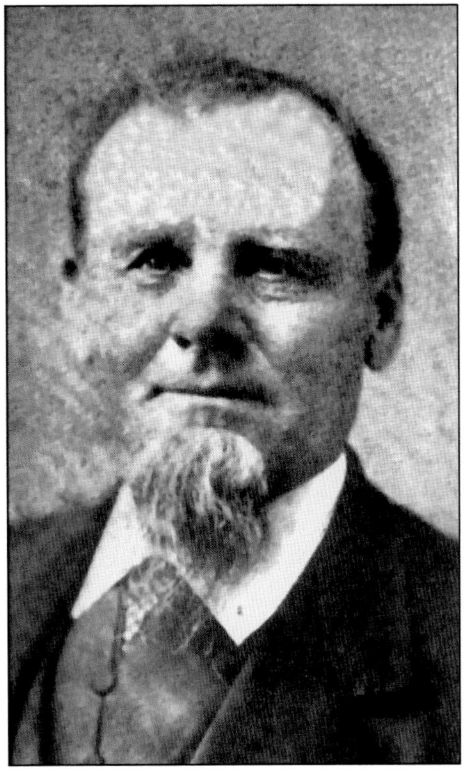

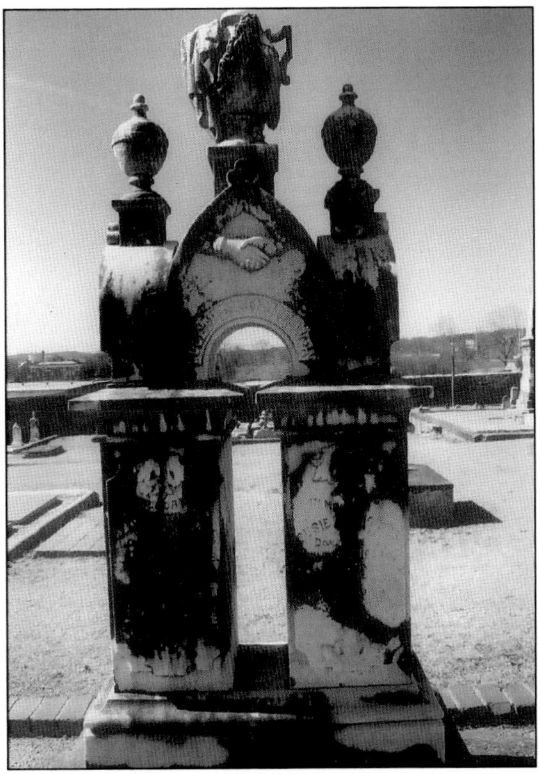

This monument in the Biggers family lot was erected for Judge Biggers's two daughters, Susie Lee, who died at 22, and Lolah Walton, who died at 14.

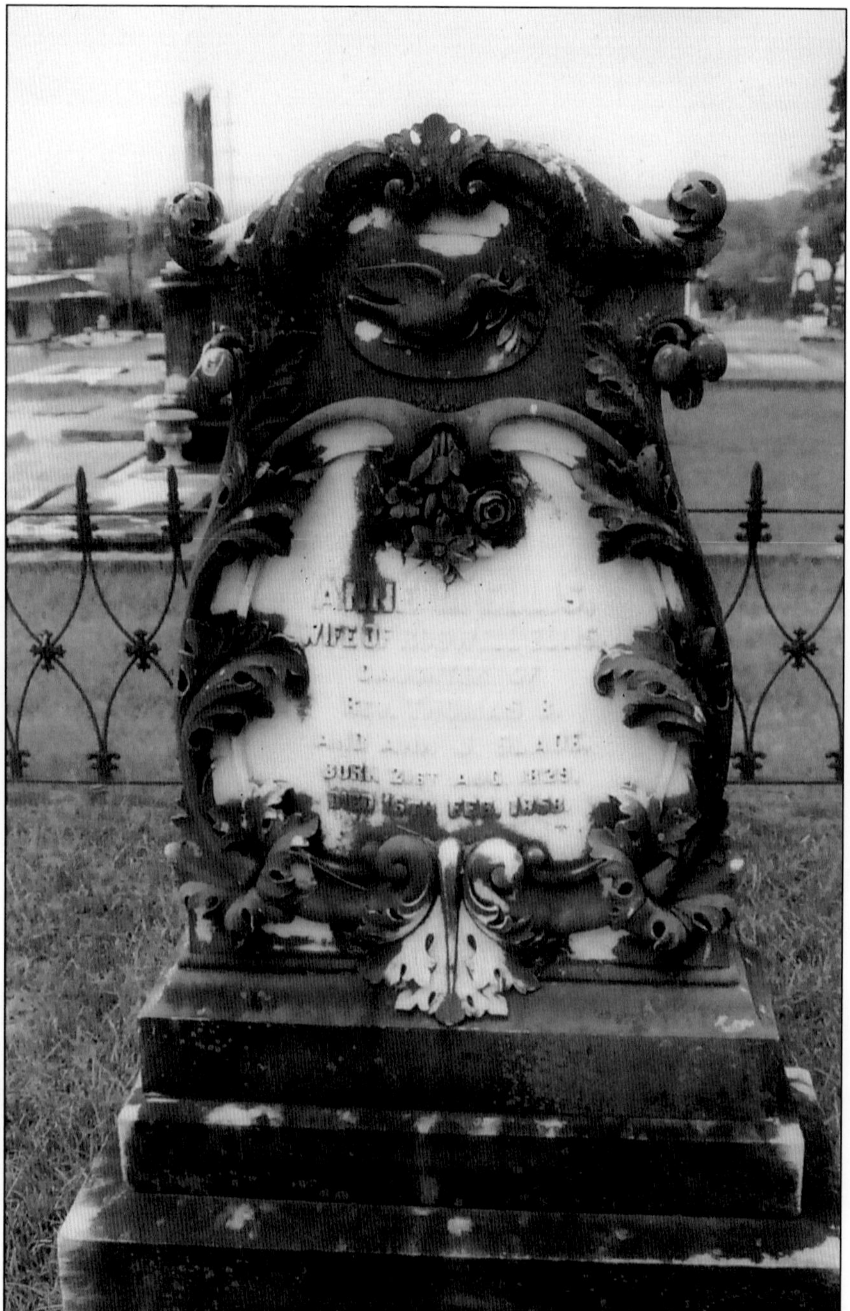

This beautiful monument marks the grave of Anne L. Ellis, age 29. Her husband Roswell Ellis commanded the Columbus Guards during the Civil War. Her father, the Reverend Thomas B. Slade, was known as a pioneer in female education in Georgia—he established the Slade Female Institute on Forsyth Street in Columbus in the 1840s. It became known as Sladeville Hall. He later moved his school to the El Dorado estate and changed its name to St. Elmo to reflect its name in the novel by Augusta Evans. The school operated for 50 years, serving "many fair daughters of Alabama, Florida and Georgia."

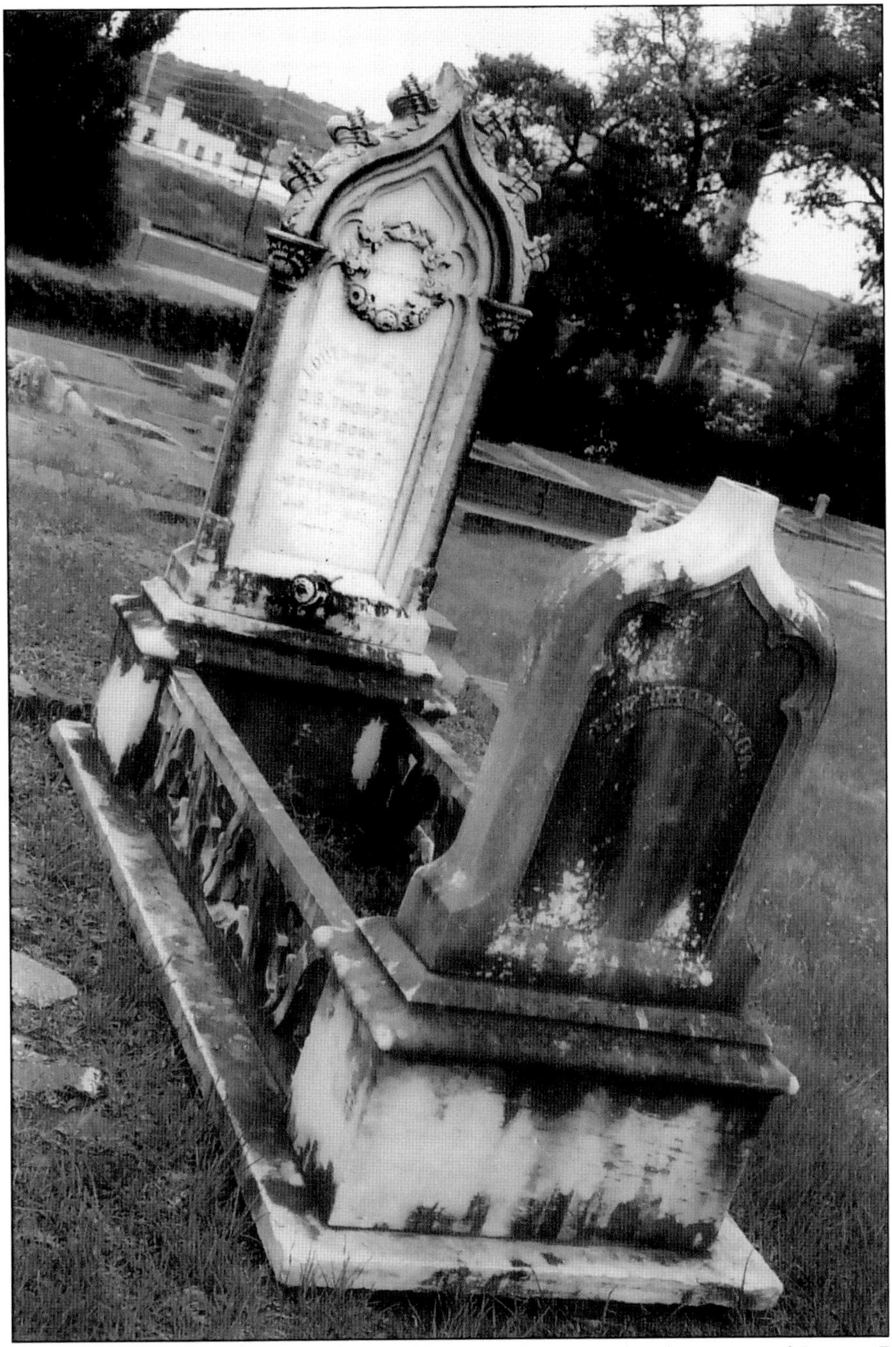

This elaborate monument, shaped in the form of a bed, marks the grave of Louisa Booth Thompson. Her husband was president of D.B. Thompson and Co. Tinware, operating at 143 Broad Street. They manufactured "wrought iron cooking stoves for hotels, boarding houses, steamboats, restaurants, and private families" ranging in price from \$50 to \$200. Thompson served as city alderman for several years, and in 1861 he briefly served as mayor of Columbus before leaving to join the service. He fought in defense of Savannah in the Civil War, then became one of the judges of the Muscogee County Inferior Court.

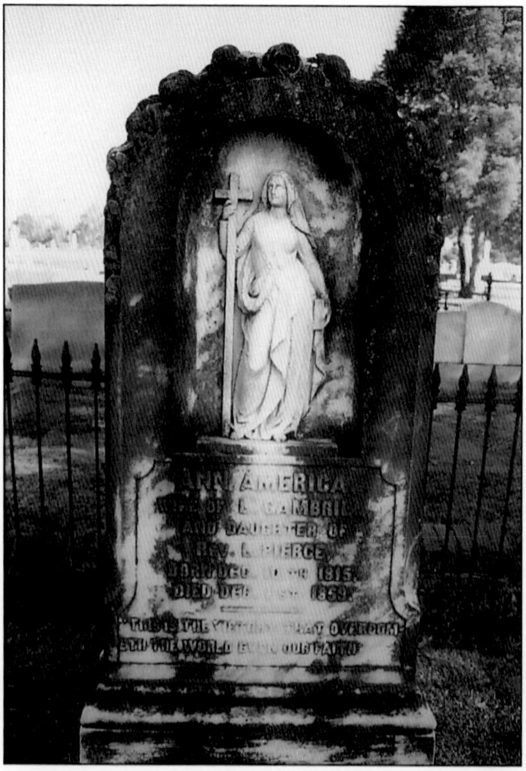

These two monuments carved by Henry McCauley honor two of the daughters of Rev. Lovick Pierce. They are intricately carved figures of women, so detailed that toenails and fingernails on the figures are visible. The figure on the stone of Ann America Pierce Gambrill, who died in 1859, signifies faith.

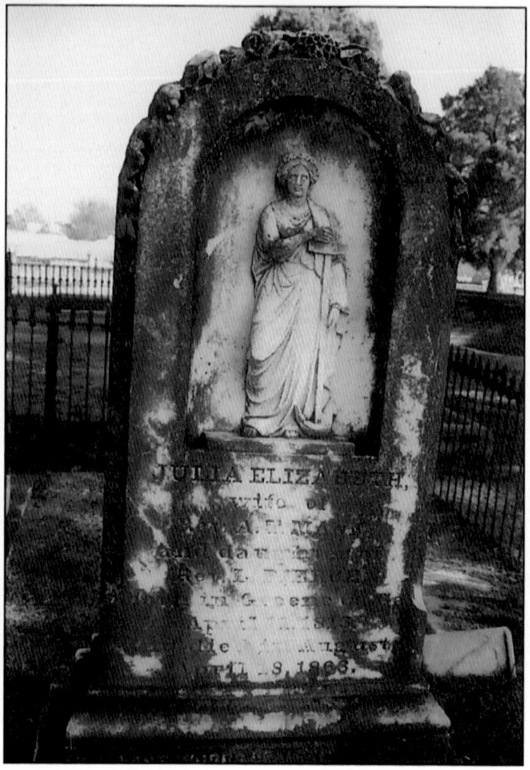

The figure on Julia Elizabeth Pierce Mann's stone carries an anchor signifying hope. Julia died in 1859 in Augusta, Georgia.

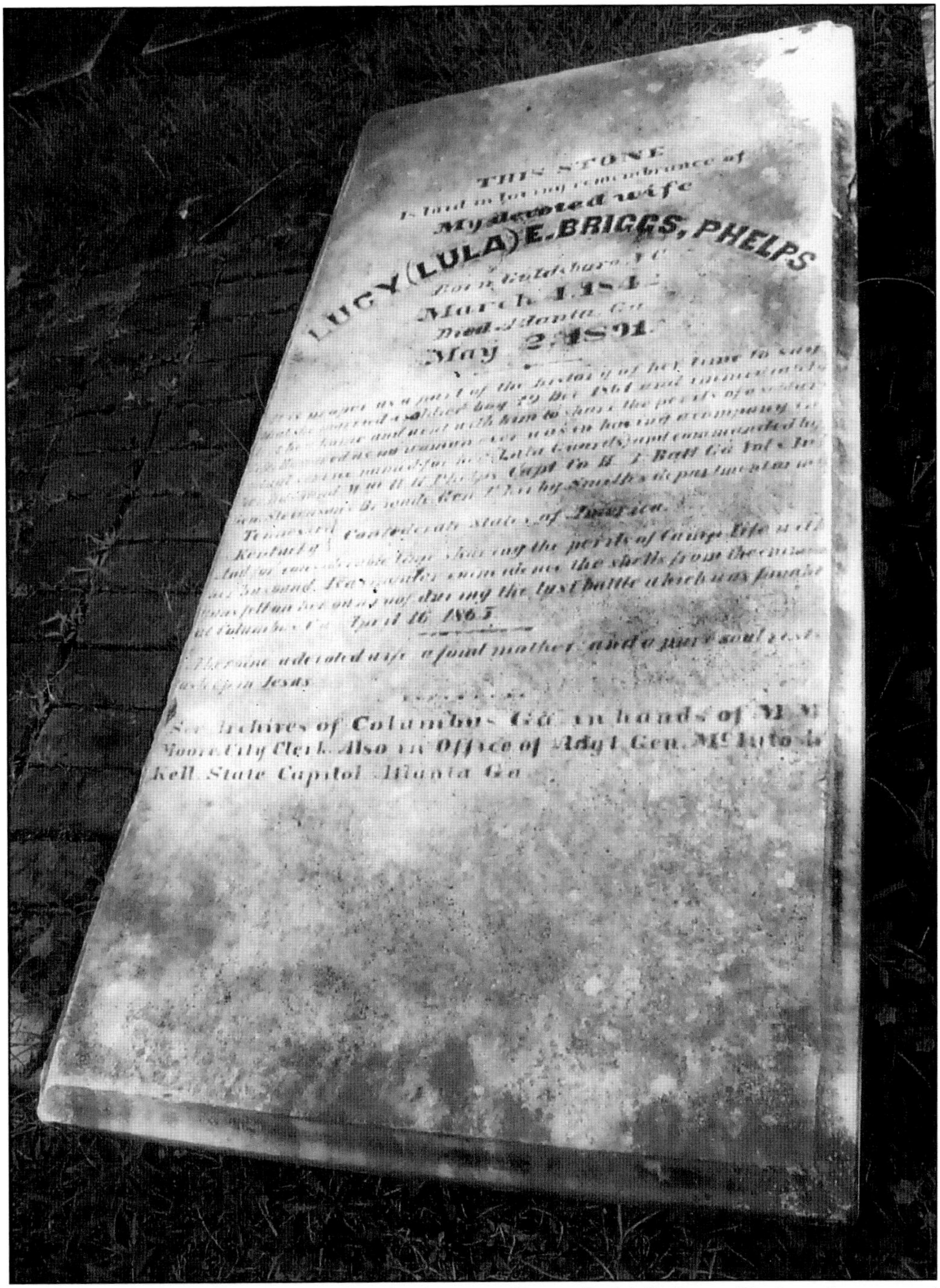

This one-of-a kind gravestone recites the history of Lucy (Lula) E. Briggs Phelps, who married a soldier in 1861 and followed him in the war. "Honored as no woman ever was in having a company in actual service named for her (Lula Guards) and commanded by her husband, William H.H. Phelps, Capt. Co. H 3 Batt., Ga. Vol. Inf. . . . She shared the perils of camp life with her husband, and later the shells from enemy guns fell on her own roof during the Battle of Columbus on April 16, 1865, the last skirmish east of the Mississippi River."

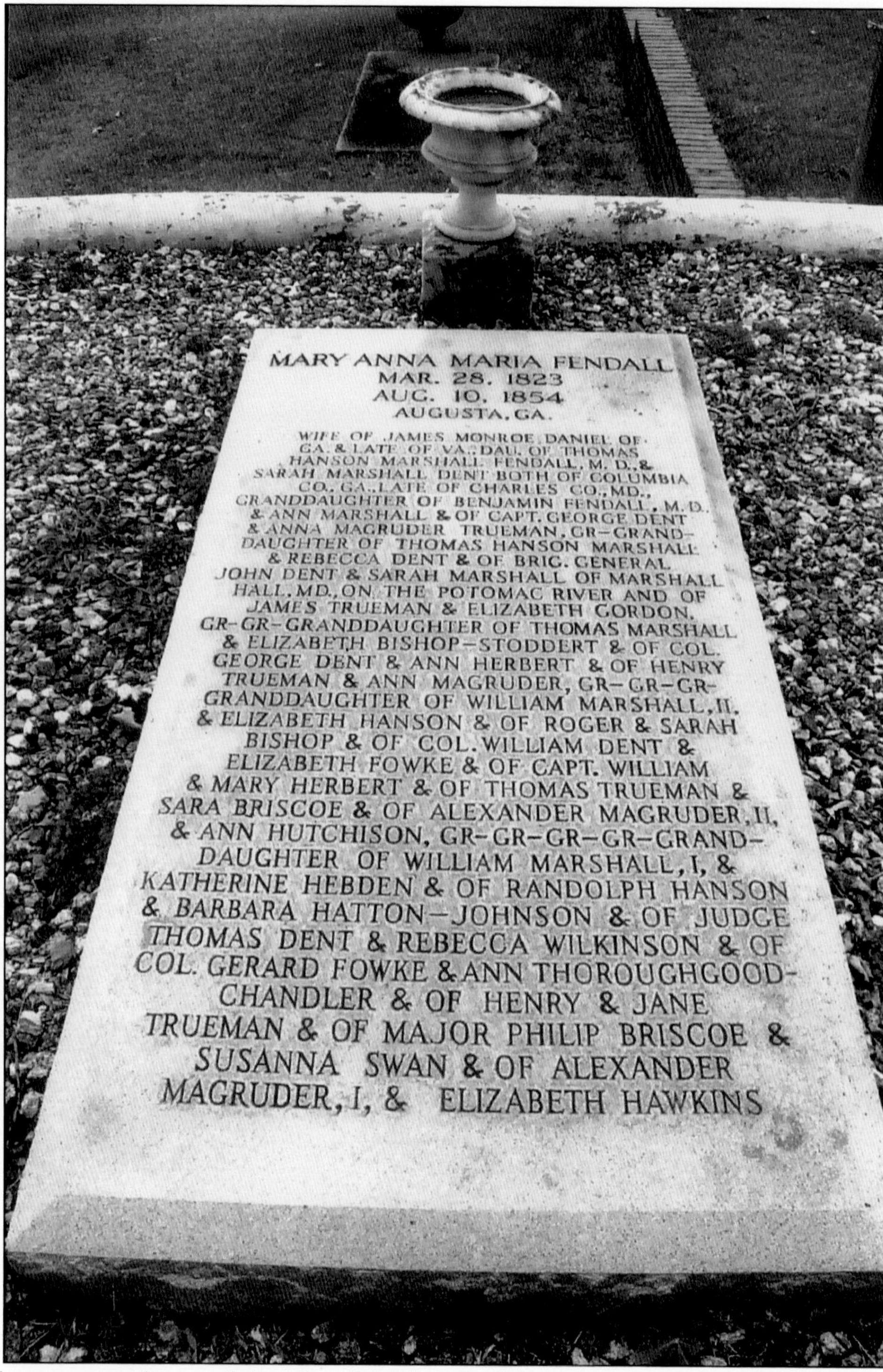

This unique tombstone of Mary Ann Fendall, wife of James Monroe Daniel, lists her ancestors through six generations. The grave markers of three other family members resting in a nearby lot also include a list of ancestors.

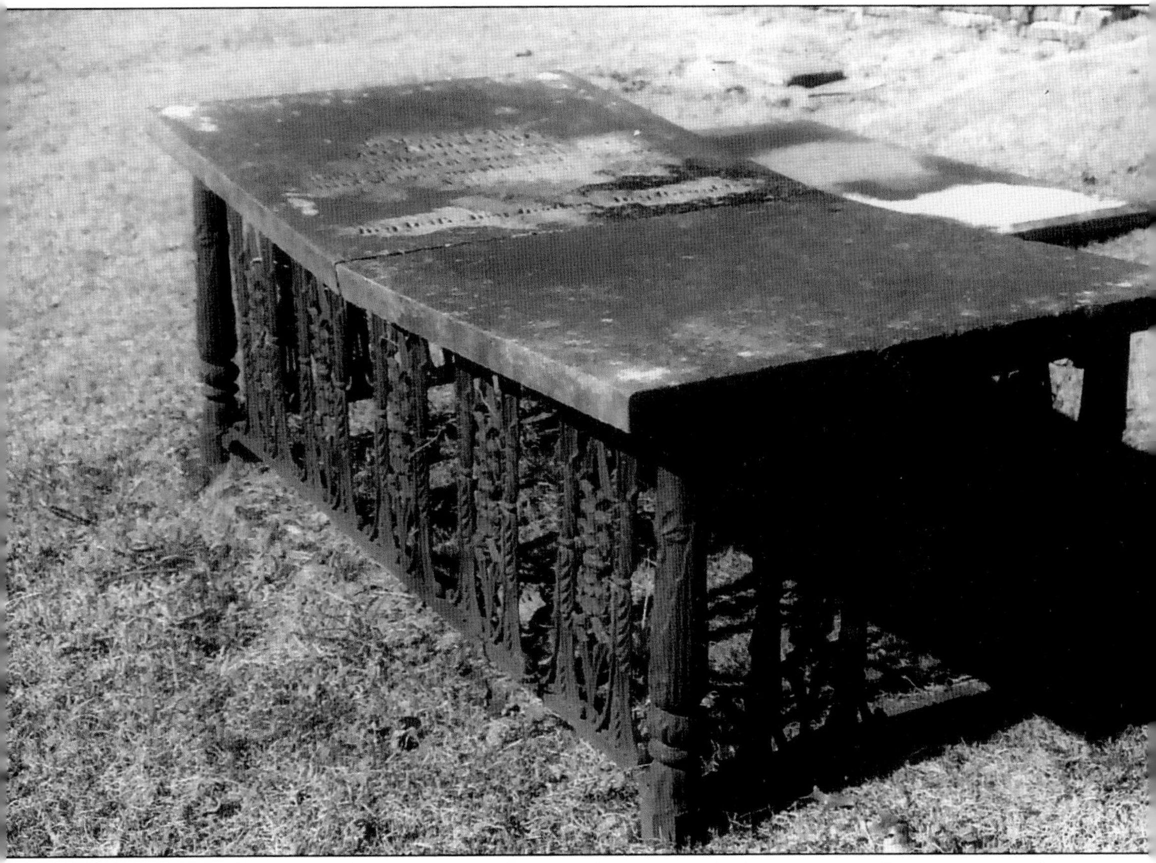

This unusual tabletop tomb, with a wrought iron foundation, belongs to Ann Louisa Levy, who was born in Bristol, Pennsylvania, in 1813 and died of consumption in Columbus on February 12, 1856. She was the wife of Charles P. Levy, who also died of consumption and was buried in August 1865 in an unmarked grave.

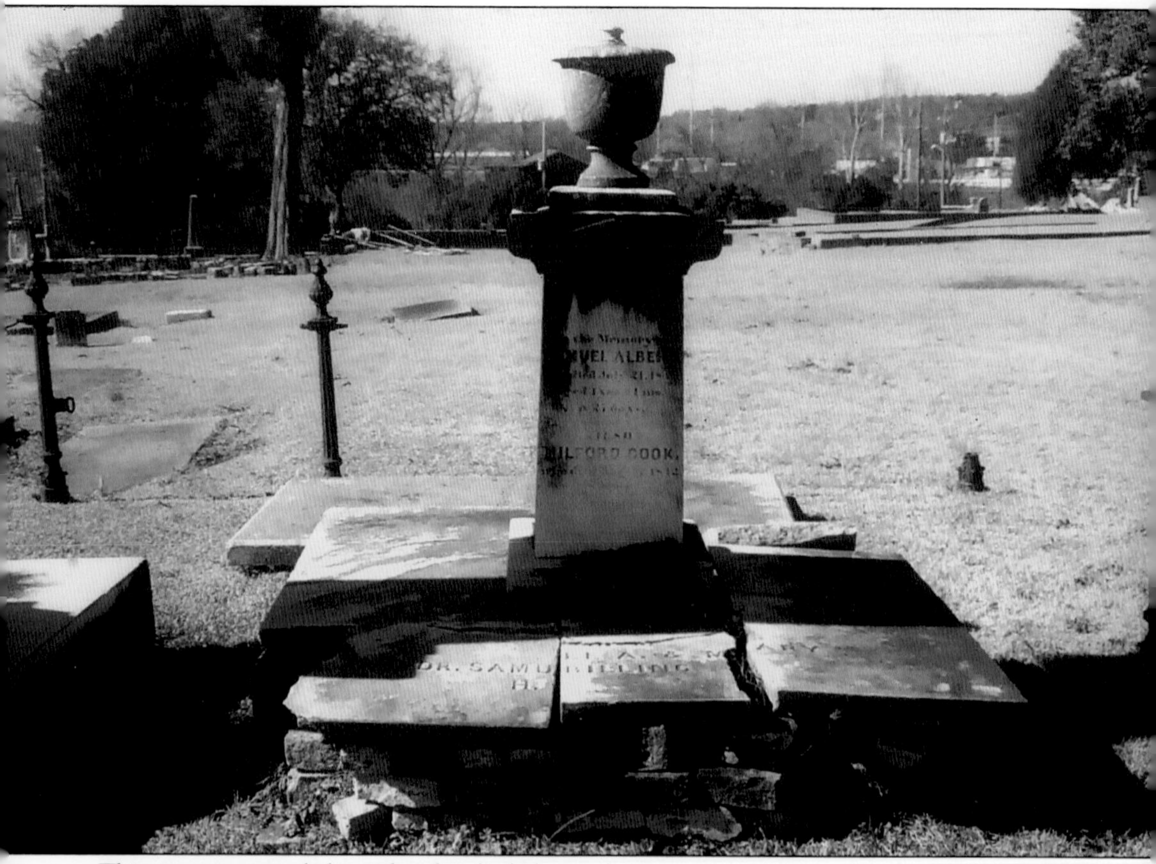

This monument is dedicated to five little boys who were the children of Dr. Samuel A. Billing and Mary H. Billing. Four of them were only one year of age when they died. As an early arrival in Columbus, Dr. Billing practiced as a physician and druggist in partnership with J.J. Boswell. He served on the city council in 1846 and later on the board of health and as city physician. This monument is signed by the stone carvers Madden and Adams and is typical of their work.

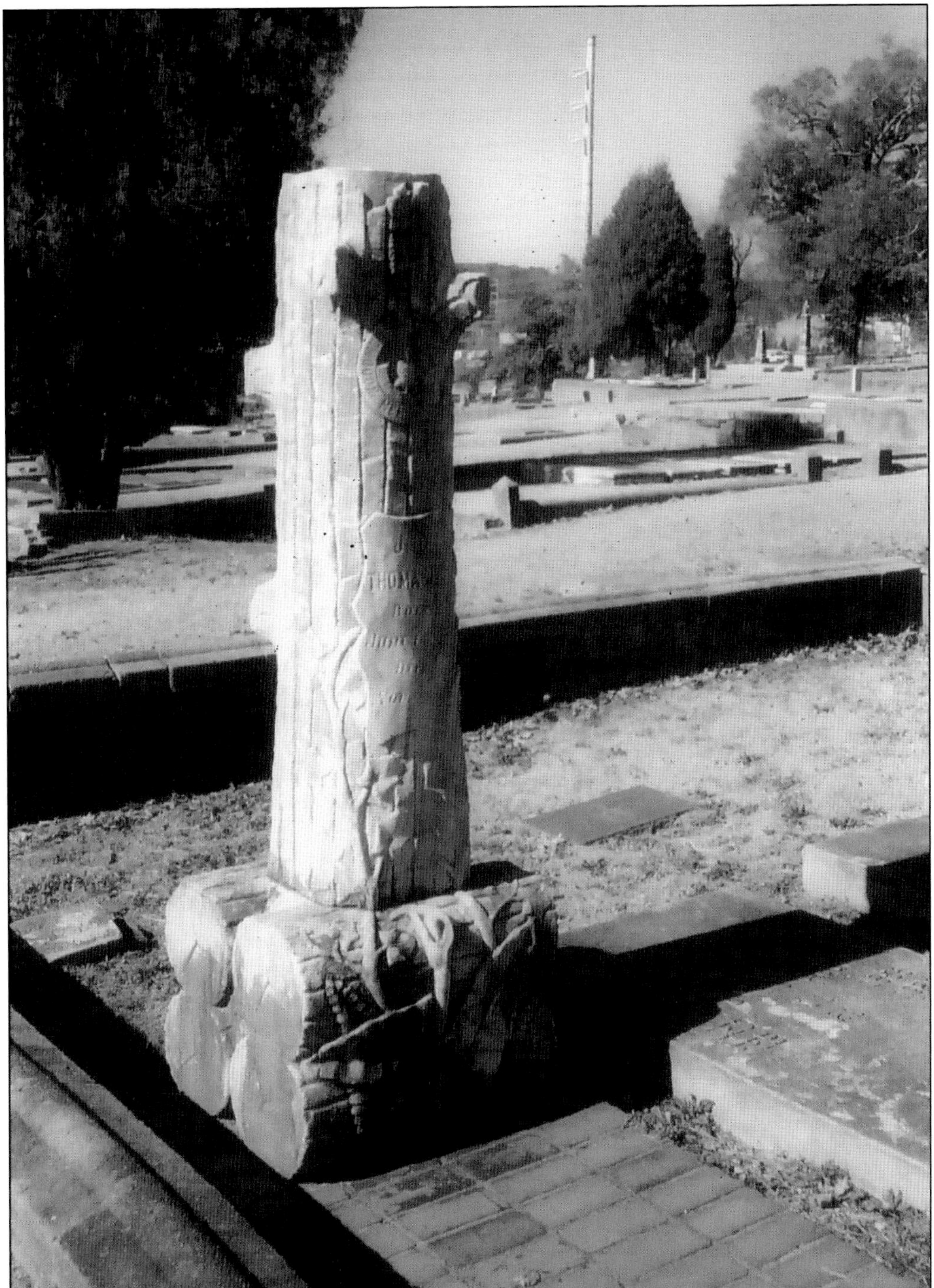

This tree stump marking the grave of Jefferson D. Thomason was furnished by Woodmen of the World, a fraternal society that provided insurance and cemetery markers for its members. Four stacked logs compose the base, which is topped by a tall, upright log. Vines entwine the logs and a calla lily peeks out from the base. Jefferson Thomason worked as an engineer for the Central Railroad. He lived in the Linwood subdivision for which the cemetery was named.

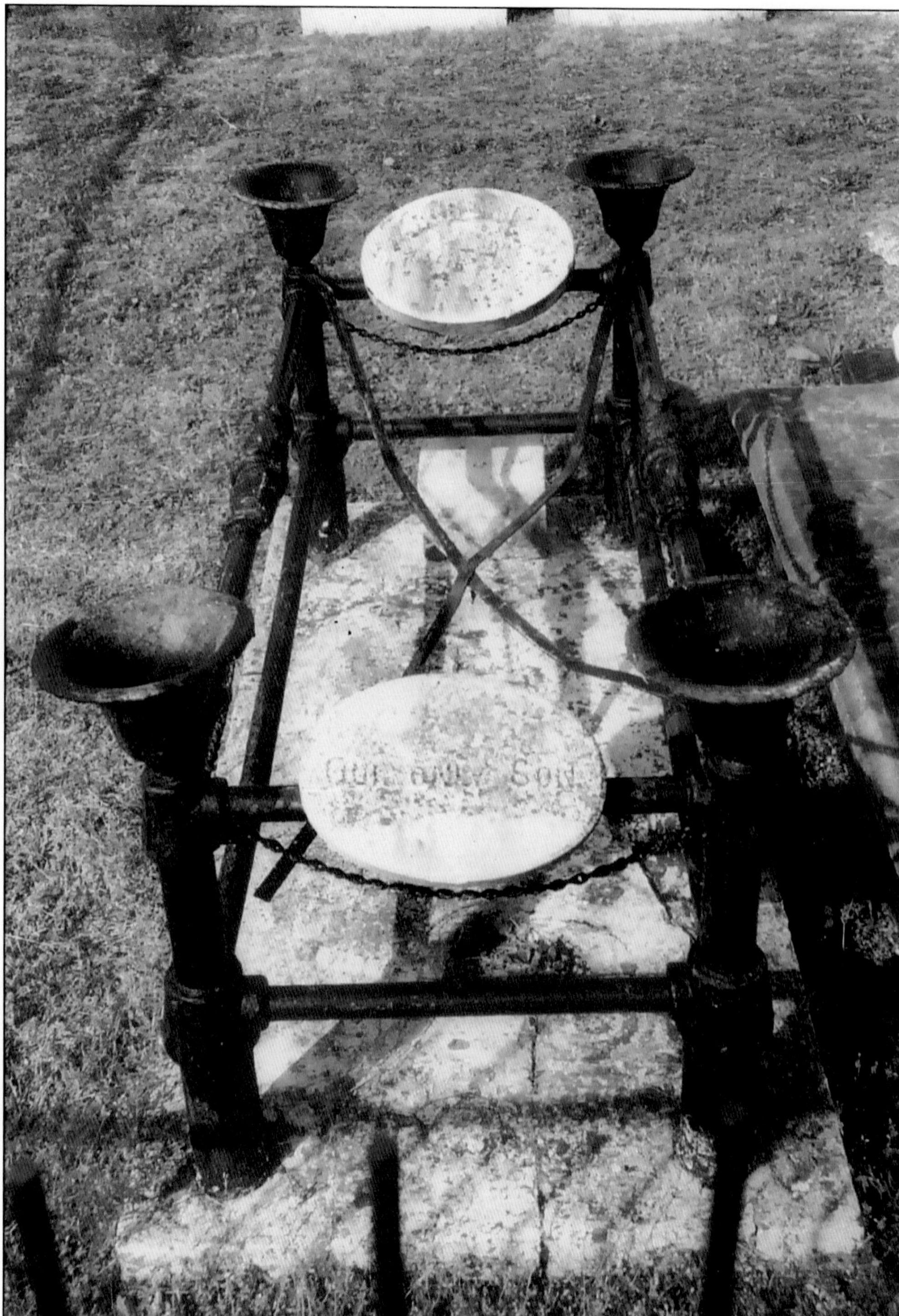

This unusual marker of black metal, shaped like a bed frame, is found in the Goulding lot. Each corner has a container that could be used to hold flowers. The only inscription says, "Robert—our only son."

Bibliography

Barfield, Louise Calhoun. *History of Harris County*. Columbus, GA: Columbus Office Supply Co., 1961, reprinted 1978.
Columbus Council Records
Chenoweth, Nouna Illges, et. al. *Our Heritage: Illges-Barnett and Related Families*. Birmingham: Oxmoor Press, 1974.
Cornell, Nancy J. *1864 Census for Re-Organizing the Georgia Militia*. Baltimore: Genealogical Publishing Co., 1999.
Dameron, J. David. *General Henry Lewis Benning: This Was a Man*. Athens, GA: Iberian Press, 2001.
Galer, Mary Jane. *Columbus, Georgia, Lists of People, 1828–1852*. Athens, GA: Iberian Press, 2000.
Hammett, Frances Pauline. *Comprehensive Topical Index, All Names and Places of History of Harris County, Georgia 1827–1861*. Columbus, GA: Cherith Creek Designs, 1991.
Harris, Roger. *Our Town, an Introduction to the History of Columbus, Georgia*. Columbus, GA: Communicorp, 1992.
Historic Columbus Foundation. *Heritage Park, A Celebration of the Industrial Heritage of Columbus, Georgia*. Columbus, GA: Columbus Productions, 1999.
Kyle, F. Clason. *Images: A Pictorial History of Columbus, Georgia*. Norfolk: The Donning Co., 1986.
Levere, William C. *The History of the Sigma Alpha Epsilon Fraternity, Vol. 1*. Chicago: Lakeside Press, 1911.
Lupold, John S. *Columbus, Georgia, 1828–1978*. Columbus, GA: Columbus Sesquicentennial Inc., 1978.
Martin, John H. *Columbus, Georgia, From its Selection as a "Trading Town" in 1827 to its Partial Destruction by Wilson's Raid in 1865*. Columbus, GA: Thos. Gilbert, 1875.
National Society of the Colonial Dames of America in the State of Georgia. *Early Georgia Portraits, 1715–1870*. Athens, GA: UGA Press, 1975.
Peddy, T. *Fort Mitchell, Alabama, 1825–1840*. Unpublished.
Pierce, Lovick Wilson and Esther Pierce Maxwell. *Two Brothers: Reddick and Lovick Pierce*. Atlanta: Cherokee Publishing Co., 1981
Telfair, Nancy. *A History of Columbus, Georgia, 1828–1928*. Columbus, GA: Historical Publishing Company, 1929.
Thomas, Kenneth H. *Columbus, Georgia, in Vintage Postcards*. Charleston, SC: Arcadia, 2001.
Worsley, Etta Blanchard. *Columbus on the Chattahoochee*. Columbus, GA: Columbus Office Supply, 1951.